JOHN PAUL II
and INTERRELIGIOUS DIALOGUE

John Paul II
and Interreligious Dialogue

BYRON L. SHERWIN
HAROLD KASIMOW
editors

Wipf & Stock
PUBLISHERS
Eugene, Oregon

Wipf and Stock Publishers
199 W 8th Ave, Suite 3
Eugene, OR 97401

John Paul II and Interreligious Dialogue
Edited by Sherwin, Byron L. and Kasimow, Harold
Copyright©1999 Orbis Books
ISBN: 1-59752-404-2
Publication date 9/30/2005
Previously published by Orbis Books, 1999

The editors are grateful to the following for permission to include copyrighted material in this volume:

To Dawa Tsering, the representative of His Holiness the Dalai Lama, for permission to publish Brother Wayne Teasdale's interview with His Holiness,

To Alfred A. Knopf, Inc., for permission to reprint excerpts from *Crossing the Threshold of Hope* by His Holiness John Paul II,

To The Liturgical Press of Collegeville, Minnesota, for permission to reprint "Pope John Paul II on Islam" by Mahmoud Ayoub from its © 1997 Michael Glazier book entitled *Open Catholicism: The Tradition at Its Best: Essays in Honor of Gerald S. Sloyan*.

In Memory

of

Joseph Cardinal Bernardin

To the Buddhist community, which reflects numerous Asian traditions as well as American, I wish respectfully to acknowledge your way of life, based upon compassion and loving kindness and upon a yearning for peace, prosperity and harmony for all beings. May all of us give witness to compassion and loving kindness in promoting the true good of humanity.

To the Islamic community: I share your belief that mankind owes its existence to the one, compassionate God who created heaven and earth. In a world in which God is denied or disobeyed, in a world that experiences so much suffering and so greatly needs God's mercy, let us then strive together to be courageous bearers of hope. . . .

To the Jewish community: I repeat the Second Vatican Council's conviction that the Church "cannot forget that she received the revelation of the Old Testament through the people with whom God in his mercy established the Ancient Covenant. Nor can she forget that she draws sustenance from the root of that good olive tree onto which has been grafted the wild olive branches of the Gentiles" (Romans 11:17–24; *Nostra Aetate,* para. 4). With you, I oppose every form of anti-Semitism. May we work for the day when all peoples and nations may enjoy security, harmony and peace.

—JOHN PAUL II
Los Angeles, September 1987

Contents

Part Three
JEWISH RESPONSES

Part Four
MUSLIM RESPONSES

Part Five
CATHOLIC REFLECTIONS

Foreword

CARDINAL EDWARD IDRIS CASSIDY

There are many aspects of Pope John Paul II's pontificate that will surely attract the attention of future historians. Already a number of biographies of the Pope have been published, all of which seek to find explanations for the various and at times radically innovative activities of the Pontiff by delving deeply into his early life and formation in his native Poland at a time of great national trial and tragedy.

In the period following the Second World War, an event of tremendous importance for the Catholic Church took place that, together with his early life experience, has played — and continues to do so — a fundamental role in John Paul's thinking and approach to the questions that he faces daily as Bishop of Rome and Head of the Catholic Church throughout the world. It was as the young Archbishop of Krakow that Karol Wojtyla took part in the Second Vatican Council. His contribution to the work of the Council is well known and appreciated by all those who have taken the trouble to inquire.

John Paul II remains today one of the very few bishops still active who were present at all the sessions of the Second Vatican Council. His pontificate is intimately related to the work and teaching of that great twentieth-century gathering of the bishops of the Catholic Church from all over the world.

It was during that Council that the bishops of the Catholic Church reflected on the relationship of the Church with other great religions, and opened the way for a new dialogue based on the desire for deeper understanding and respect. This new approach is outlined especially in the Second Vatican Council's *Declaration on the Relationship of the Church to Non-Christian Religions* (*Nostra Aetate*), but is reflected and has its foundation in two other Council documents: *The Declaration of Religious Freedom* (*Dignitatis Humanae*) and the very basic *Dogmatic Constitution on the Church* (*Lumen Gentium*).

The years since the Second Vatican Council have seen the Catholic

Church engaged most seriously in seeking to introduce the teaching of these documents into the daily life of its institutions and members. Pope Paul VI and Pope John Paul II have led the way in these efforts, both by their personal commitment to the cause and by the establishment of two dicasteries of the Roman Curia dedicated to this task: the Holy See's Commission for Religious Relations with the Jews and the Pontifical Council for Interreligious Dialogue. Episcopal conferences and bishops throughout the world have in turn created their own national and diocesan commissions, or similar organisms for the same purpose.

In the present volume, edited by Rabbi Dr. Byron L. Sherwin and Dr. Harold Kasimow, we see all this illustrated in the edited excerpts from the writings and speeches of John Paul II on Judaism, Islam, Buddhism, and interreligious dialogue. Certainly, no other Pope has ever contributed so much and so widely to a greater understanding among religions. Not only has he received with brotherly courtesy and deep respect leaders and representatives of the great religions who have come to Rome, but his pastoral visits to the Catholic Church throughout the world have provided a valuable opportunity for him to bring his message to the farthest ends of the earth. The unprecedented meeting in Assisi on October 27, 1986, of religious leaders of a great number of faiths, who came to pray for peace in the world and to give witness to their dedication to the cause of reconciliation among people of all religions, has been followed up by similar events being organized almost yearly and has borne fruit in many other initiatives promoting the cause of world peace and solidarity.

In his introduction to this book, Harold Kasimow quickly places his finger, as it were, on the fundamental principle of John Paul's thinking in this connection. For the Pope, every child born into this world is formed in the image of God, is loved by God, is respected by God. God desires that each and every one of God's children be brought to the joy of God's Kingdom. No Christian can say that he or she loves God but despises those whom God loves (see 1 John 4:20).

The great religions bring God and God's children closer together. For the Pope and for the Catholic Church, in its authentic teaching, God has intervened in history in a special way, by the birth of a Savior who comes to free men and women from their sins and to open for them the door to eternal life. This Savior, Jesus Christ, is the one mediator between God and the human race (1 Timothy 2:5).

Harold Kasimow reflects at some length on the difficulty that such an understanding may create for interreligious dialogue, but comes firmly to the conclusion that the Pope has deep respect and esteem for other faiths and that men and women of other faiths should be ready to enter into dialogue with him, for such dialogue, in Kasimow's words, "not only leads to understanding the other, but is a path that deepens our own self-understanding." There is a mystery in all this that we poor creatures cannot fully understand. For my part, I am perfectly happy to leave the final judgment to God, the all-merciful. Woe to me, however, if in the meantime I am lacking in respect and love for those created in the divine image.

In the present publication, Rabbi Sherwin and Dr. Kasimow have brought together leaders and scholars from Buddhism, Islam, and Judaism to enter into a "dialogue" with John Paul II. We are taken into a sort of roundtable discussion rich in valuable insights into these three faiths and their relations with the Church of the present Pope. We hear the authoritative voice of the Dalai Lama and other highly qualified exponents of each of these religions and at the end a Catholic response from the Secretary of the Pontifical Council for Interreligious Dialogue, Bishop Michael Fitzgerald. It is an experience that the reader will not easily forget.

These last thirty-odd years have taught us many things about interreligious dialogue. We have come above all, I think, to realize just how necessary such dialogue has become. Many prejudices, stereotypes, and myths have for centuries darkened our minds and prevented our relationships from developing. Misunderstanding has been much more common than understanding, calumny more frequent than truth, enmity more normal than friendship.

We are not yet, by far, out of the woods. Yet there has been real progress. There is a growing realization that deeper knowledge of *the other* and respect for *the other* are vital elements in the search for justice, peace, and the well-being of the human race, and indeed of all creation.

It is with special satisfaction that I refer to the new situation that has been created in Catholic-Jewish relations. Together in Prague in September 1990, Jews and Catholics were able to recognize with John Paul II that "a new spirit is in the making" between these two faith communities, "a spirit which emphasizes cooperation, mutual understanding and reconciliation; goodwill and common goals to replace the past spirit of suspicion, resentment and distrust" ("Statement by the International Catholic-Jewish Liaison Committee" [Prague, September 6, 1990], *Information Service of the Pontifical Council for Promoting Christian Unity* 75, no. 4 [1990]: 176). It is obvious that Christian-Jewish relations are particularly privileged by the fact that Christianity finds its roots in Judaism. Christians see in the Jewish people their "elder brothers" in faith; both

Jews and Christians look to the same Sacred Scriptures for guidance in their devotion and daily living. Each faith community has of course its own identity; there are important differences that must be respected; but together they have the possibility of bringing a brilliant light into a world that seems more and more determined to walk in darkness and in the shadow of death.

I join with the editors of this volume in recalling with affection Joseph Cardinal Bernardin, the late Archbishop of Chicago, who by word, deed, and unfailing dedication to the task contributed during his lifetime in an extraordinary way to the development — in his archdiocese, in the United States of America, and far beyond the borders of his native land — of relationships between the Catholic Church and peoples of other faiths. May his memory be a source of inspiration and encouragement to future generations.

Preface

One of the startling achievements of the papacy of John Paul II has been in the area of interreligious dialogue. More than any of his predecessors, John Paul II has consistently and boldly initiated dialogic relations with religions historically in tension with and/or theologically ignored by Roman Catholicism, such as Islam and Buddhism. In addition, he has dramatically sought to strengthen dialogue with religions with which the Church — particularly since Vatican II — has initiated dialogue, such as Judaism. The purpose of this volume is to examine the Pope's teachings on these three very diverse faiths — Judaism, Islam, and Buddhism — and to see how leading scholars and theologians of various perspectives within each of those faiths evaluate and understand the Pope's views of their faith-traditions and the relationship between Catholicism and those respective faiths that seem to flow from those views. The Pope appears convinced that interfaith dialogue can serve as a potent path to combined efforts on behalf of furthering the causes of peace, understanding, and human dignity. The goal of this book is to further the journey along this path.

We wish to express our deepest gratitude to the eminent scholars and religious leaders who have contributed to this book, especially His Holiness the Dalai Lama and His Eminence Edward Cardinal Cassidy. Our heartfelt gratitude goes to Dr. William Burrows, of Orbis Books, for supporting this endeavor and for seeing through to publication our earlier Orbis volume, *No Religion Is an Island: Abraham Joshua Heschel and Interreligious Dialogue*. We are both profoundly grateful to Pam Spitzner, who worked with great diligence, efficiency, and speed to ensure an accurate and timely typescript. The present volume is dedicated to the memory of His Eminence Joseph Cardinal Bernardin, seventh Archbishop of Chicago, who was instrumental in bringing together people of different faiths in interreligious dialogue so that they might be a blessing to one another.

BYRON L. SHERWIN
HAROLD KASIMOW

Introduction

John Paul II and Interreligious Dialogue

An Overview

HAROLD KASIMOW

As a Jew deeply committed to interfaith dialogue, I am moved by the passionate voice of Pope John Paul II, the world's most influential spiritual leader. Although I find a number of his ideas problematic, I am very impressed with his love for humanity, for each individual person, regardless of his or her faith commitment. What is most critical for him is the fact that every man and woman is created in the image and likeness of God. Every human being is a unique child of God. The Pope's tireless activity on behalf of all human beings, his deep spirituality, and his struggle for peace and justice have been greatly admired by people of different faiths.

I have been amazed by Pope John Paul II's strong commitment to interfaith dialogue. This brilliant intellectual and mystic believes that interfaith dialogue can help to repair and transform the world. The Pope is well aware of the violence and destruction being carried out today in the name of religion and is deeply preoccupied with the religious factor in the wars being waged on our planet. Speaking to the participants at the World Conference on Religion and Peace held at the Vatican in 1994, he stated:

> Today the religious leaders must clearly show that they are pledged to the promotion of peace precisely because of their religious be-

lief. Religion is not, and must not become, a pretext for conflict, particularly when religious, cultural and ethnic identity coincide. …Religion and peace go together: to wage war in the name of religion is a blatant contradiction.[1]

John Paul II seems to be convinced that interreligious dialogue is a path that can promote respect among members of different religions and help to bring peace and harmony to a world torn by conflict and war, poverty, and the destruction of the environment, a world that is captivated by materialism and secularism, in deep need of finding significant existence. In his message for the Twenty-Fifth Annual World Day of Prayer for Peace, he stated: "It can be said that a religious life, if it is lived authentically, cannot fail to bring forth fruits of peace and brotherhood, for it is in the nature of religion to foster an ever-increasing fraternal relationship among people."[2] The Pope is not speaking only about the three Abrahamic faiths, but clearly has in mind also Asian religions. However, he is especially grieved by the wars caused by the children of Abraham: "I consider dialogue between Jews, Christians, and Muslims to be a priority. In coming to know each other better, in growing to esteem one another, and in living out, with respect for consciences, the various aspects of their religion, they will be, in part of the world and elsewhere, 'artisans of peace.' "[3]

This essay will explore John Paul II's theology of world religions before examining his specific statements on Buddhism, Islam, and Judaism, the three non-Christian traditions to which the Pope has given special attention.

Christian Attitudes toward Other Faiths

Some background on how Christianity historically has viewed the non-Christian religions of the world will provide a context for understanding John Paul II's attitude toward other religious traditions. A number of eminent Christian scholars deeply committed to interfaith relations speak of three major Christian responses to a religiously plural world: the exclusivist view, the inclusivist view, and the pluralist view.[4] The predominant Christian response throughout the ages has been the exclusivist one, which claims that Christianity is the only true path to salvation. Exclusivists point to many biblical passages in support of their position. For example:

And He said to them, "Go out to the whole world, proclaim the good news to all creation. He who believes and is baptized will be saved. He who does not believe will be condemned." (Mark 16: 15–16)

I am the way, I am the truth, and I am the life. No one comes to the Father except by Me. (John 14:6)

There is no salvation in anyone else at all, for there is no other name under heaven granted to man by which we may receive salvation. (Acts 4:12)

Throughout its history, the Roman Catholic Church has supported a literal interpretation of these passages. The Fourth Lateran Council (1215) stated: "There is one universal church of believers, outside which there is no salvation at all for any."[5] Cyprian of Carthage may have been thinking only of Christians, and not members of other faiths, when he stated: "Outside the Church, there is no salvation." Yet this became the prevalent Catholic attitude toward non-Catholic traditions.

The inclusivist response has a much more positive view of other religions. According to this approach, members of other religious traditions may attain salvation due to the fact that the grace of Christ is present in these traditions. The inclusivist view, which has many variations, and had advocates in the early Church,[6] was developed in great detail by the eminent Jesuit theologian Karl Rahner (1904–84). Rahner, who was a very influential voice during the Second Vatican Council, claimed that the Christian tradition is "the absolute religion, intended for all men, which can't recognize any other religion beside itself as of equal right."[7] However, since God desires to save all human beings, "there are supernatural, grace-filled elements in non-Christian religions."[8] Rahner makes it clear that salvation is caused by the power and grace of Christ. In fact, Rahner considers a non-Christian to be an "anonymous Christian."[9] The inclusivist view of other faiths has become very attractive to many Catholics, as well as Protestants, although many do not view non-Christians as "anonymous Christians."

The central thrust of the pluralist view is clearly captured in the following statement by Brian Hebblethwaite:

Christians must cease to think of their faith as bearing witness to God's final and absolute self-revelation to man. Rather, they must learn to recognize their experiences of God in Christ to be but one of many different saving encounters with the divine which have been given to different historical and cultural segments of mankind.[10]

Paul Knitter, a prominent Catholic theologian, has presented the pluralist perspective in a most perceptive and persuasive way:

> Other religions *may be* just as effective and successful in bringing their followers to truth, and peace, and well-being with God as Christianity has been for Christians; . . . these other religions, again because they are so different from Christianity, may have just as important a message and vision for all peoples as Christianity does.
>
> Only if Christians are truly open to the possibility (which, I will argue below, is for Christians a probability bordering on a necessity) that there *are* many true, saving religions and that Christianity is one among the ways in which God has touched and transformed our world, only then can authentic dialogue take place.[11]

I am a Jewish pluralist. As such, I am committed to the Jewish path, not because it is superior, but because it is my path. I view the concept of the chosen people as God choosing the Jews to follow the path of the Torah, while at the same time choosing the Hindus to follow the Vedas, the Buddhists to follow the Dharma, the Muslims to follow the Qur'an, and Christians to follow Jesus of Nazareth. This seems to me to be in the spirit of my great teacher Abraham Joshua Heschel, who stated that "[i]n this aeon diversity of religions is the will of God."[12]

Many have serious doubts about the strength of the pluralists' commitment to their traditions, seeing that pluralists encourage not only dialogue, but deep involvement with other faiths. From my own experience with Buddhism, I feel that Buddhism has enriched my understanding and appreciation of the Jewish tradition. Although I can become very immersed in Buddhist meditation during the practice of zazen, this experience is radically different for me than a Yom Kippur service. At the deepest level, a distinction remains between my tradition, the tradition in which I was originally nourished, and other religious traditions. I love the parents of a number of my friends, but they are not my parents. All the traditions which I have studied produce saints, but all saints are not the same. As William Burrows states: "The uniqueness of Christ and Christian life lies in the distinct structure of existence. The Christian manner of being a saint . . . is unique."[13] Note that he does not say it is superior. Paul Knitter is a good example of a Roman Catholic pluralist who has a strong commitment to Christ and the Christian tradition and who at the same time holds that there can be many ways by which human beings can seek and attain truth and salvation.

Pope John Paul II's Theology of World Religions

I find Pope John Paul II's encyclical *Redemptoris Missio* (*RM*), dated December 7, 1990, and his book *Crossing the Threshold of Hope,* rich sources for his views on interfaith dialogue, his understanding of the world mission of the Church, and his attitude toward other faiths. *Redemptoris Missio* is considered to be "central to the teaching of John Paul II."[14] John Paul II, who was a university professor for a number of years in Poland, is a sophisticated theologian whose statements deserve very careful reading. Even so, they remain open to different interpretations. Yet, as we begin to study this text, it becomes clear that the Pope is an inclusivist. The following are some key passages from this important document:

> If we go back to the beginning of the Church, we find a clear af-
> firmation that Christ is the one Savior of all, the only one able to
> reveal God and lead to God. . . . [F]or all people — Jews and Gen-
> tiles alike — salvation can only come from Jesus Christ. . . . God's
> revelation becomes definitive and complete through his only-
> begotten Son. . . . In this definitive Word of his revelation, God has
> made himself known in the fullest possible way. He has revealed
> to mankind *who he is.* This definitive self-revelation of God is the
> fundamental reason why the Church is missionary by her very na-
> ture. She cannot do other than proclaim the Gospel, that is, the
> fullness of the truth which God has enabled us to know about
> himself.[15]

This position is repeated again in *Crossing the Threshold of Hope,* where we get a glimpse of the Pope's spontaneous view on this issue:

> Here, before all else, we need to explain the *Christian doctrine of
> salvation and of the mediation of salvation,* which always originates in
> God. "For there is one God. There is also one mediator between
> God and the human race, Christ Jesus, himself human" (1 Timo-
> thy 2:5). "There is no salvation through . . . any other name" (Acts
> 4:12).[16]

> In order to hope for salvation from God, man must stop beneath
> Christ's Cross. . . . Contained within the Cross and the Resurrec-

tion is the certainty that God saves man, that He saves him through Christ, through His Cross and His Resurrection.[17]

Everyone who looks for salvation, not only the Christian, must stop before the Cross of Christ.[18]

John Paul II, who was influential in the drafting of Vatican II's *Nostra Aetate* declaration, quotes from it to respond to the question of salvation:

However, the Church proclaims, and is bound to proclaim that *Christ is "the way and the truth and the life"* [John 14:6], in whom men must find the fullness of religious life and in whom God has reconciled everything to Himself.[19]

The Pope's position seems quite clear: salvation comes through Christ. Therefore, the Christian has a duty to make these truths known to every human being on earth, including Jews. The Pope sees this as a demand made by Christ himself when Christ stated: "Go, therefore, and make disciples of all nations" (Matthew 28:19). John Paul's comment is that "these words, uttered by the Redeemer of the world, have borne astonishing *fruit.*"[20] The Pope adds: "*The mission of evangelization is an essential part of the Church.* The Second Vatican Council made this point in a colorful way by affirming that 'the Church . . . by her nature is missionary.'"[21] Reading the above, we must agree with Tad Szulc, who contends that for John Paul II the "most powerful driving force is the sense of mission."[22] John Paul II, who is sincerely dedicated to interfaith relations as a means of promoting justice and peace and mutual understanding among religions, is at the same time the most devoted and influential Christian missionary of our century.

However, John Paul II is not an exclusivist. His ideas on other religions are far richer and more complex than what I have presented thus far. He often speaks of his deep esteem for members of other faiths. He tells us that when he observes the faith in the hearts of members of other religions, it reminds him of the words of Jesus, who said, "Not even in Israel have I found such faith" (Matthew 8:10).[23] Both in *Redemptoris Missio* and in *Crossing the Threshold of Hope,* John Paul II makes it clear that members of other faiths may, in fact, attain salvation. In *Redemptoris Missio* he states: "The universality of salvation means that it is granted not only to those who explicitly believe in Christ and have entered the Church. Since salvation is offered to all, it must be made concretely available to all."[24] The Pope continues that "salvation in Christ is accessible by virtue of a grace which, while having a mysterious relationship to the Church, does not make [members of other faiths] formally part of the Church, but enlightens them in a way which is accommodated to their spiritual and material situation. This grace comes from Christ; it is the result of his Sacrifice and is communicated by the Holy Spirit."[25] In *Crossing the Threshold of Hope,* John Paul II clarifies his position on salvation for members of other faiths. He states that

> the Church is guided by the faith that *God the Creator wants to save all humankind in Jesus Christ,* the only mediator between God and man, inasmuch as He is the Redeemer of all humankind. The Paschal Mystery is equally available to all, and, through it, the way to eternal salvation is also open to all.[26]

The Pope explains that people are saved not only in the Church but also through the Church; thus there are different forms of relation to the Church, but people are ultimately always saved by the grace of Christ. The Pope's position on this issue seems to be similar to that of Karl Rahner. To my knowledge, the Pope has never used the term "anonymous Christian" for members of other faiths.

John Paul II ardently desires the universal unity of all Christians and hopes for the conversion of all human beings on the planet. For all their beauty and spirituality, non-Christian religions, because they do not accept Christ, are not equal to Christianity.

Pope John Paul II on Dialogue and Proclamation

A close reading of *Redemptoris Missio* reveals a certain tension between the Pope's repeated stress on interreligious dialogue and on proclamation as two component elements of mission. The Pope states: "Interreligious dialogue is part of the Church's evangelizing mission. . . . The Church sees no conflict between proclaiming Christ and engaging in interreligious dialogue."[27] To many people mission and dialogue seem in tension because the aim of mission is not just to enrich the other person, to make him or her a more spiritual member of his or her community. The aim of mission is to convert the person to Christ. The view of Abraham Joshua Heschel, the most influential Jew in shaping the final statement on Jews by the Second Vatican Council, will help us understand a Jewish reaction to the Pope's position.[28] Heschel told Carl Stern that "[w]hen a statement came out of the Ecumenical

Council expressing the hope that the Jews would eventually join the Church, I came out with a very strong rebuke. I said, 'I'd rather go to Auschwitz than give up my religion.' "[29] It was actually Heschel who persuaded Paul VI to cross out a paragraph in which there was a reference to converting the Jews.[30] For Heschel, the final declaration *Nostra Aetate,* adopted in October 1965 by the Second Vatican Council, was "of great historic importance" because of "the omission of any reference to conversion of the Jews."[31] Heschel helps us understand that linking mission with interreligious dialogue is a very serious obstacle for genuine conversation between Christians and Jews.

Mission is also problematic for other non-Christian faiths. Dr. Havanpola Ratanasara, president of the College of Buddhist Studies in Los Angeles, in welcoming the Pope to his city, said, "We Buddhists . . . are always yearning for peace, prosperity, and harmony for all beings, and our goal in life is the improvement of life for all beings, rather than their religious conversion."[32] Today, the idea of conversion is becoming a problem even for people like Ratanasara, who belongs to a missionary religion. It is a problem because the missionary believes that he or she has a deeper grasp of the truth that is valid for every human being. This feeling may lead the missionary to a sense of spiritual superiority rather than humility. It is difficult to deny that that is a real danger to the spiritual life of the missionary. Real listening to the member of another religious community may be very difficult under such circumstances.

In his book *Jesus and the Other Names: Christian Mission and Global Responsibility,* Paul Knitter makes some very insightful remarks regarding John Paul II's statement that "dialogue should be conducted and implemented with the conviction that the Church is the ordinary means of salvation and that she alone possesses the fullness of the means of salvation." Knitter's comment is that "when one already has the fullness of truth, there can't be too much still to learn."[33] Augustine Kanjamala, an Indian Divine Word Missionary priest, criticizes John Paul II for the exact same reason as does Knitter. Speaking of the Pope's encyclical *Redemptoris Missio,* Kanjamala states: "Belief that 'fullness of revelation' (56) and 'fullness of the means of salvation' (55) are present only in the Church conveys the idea that the Church has nothing seriously new to learn. Genuine dialogue — which is of primary importance in the Indian context — seems impossible with such a mindset."[34]

The question remains: Should non-Christians enter into dialogue with the Roman Catholic Church in view of the fact that the Church clearly hopes to convert them? I realize that many people involved in interfaith relations believe that nothing significant will emerge when one encounters a person whose primary aim is conversion. Mahmoud Ayoub, who is one of the most spiritual Muslim scholars and one who is deeply involved in interfaith dialogue, states: "On the eve of the twenty-first century, after the development and dissemination of the scientific study of religion and the steady advance of global communication, meaningful dialogue is only possible on the basis of religious and cultural pluralism."[35] I have pondered this issue for quite some time and have had great difficulty in reaching a conclusion. However, after a real engagement with the thought of John Paul II, I am leaning in the direction of giving an affirmative response to my question. That is, I think that one should enter into dialogue with inclusivists like John Paul II for a number of reasons.

First, I have no doubt that the Pope has deep respect and esteem for other faiths. I am also very moved by his stress on our common humanity and the deep faith that unites members of different religious traditions. He has stated: "Respect and esteem 'for the other' and for what he has in the depths of his heart is essential to dialogue."[36] Second, dialogue, in a sense, is even more urgent with exclusivists and inclusivists than with pluralists. The Pope has stated many times in different contexts that dialogue not only leads to understanding the other, but is a path that deepens our own self-understanding. I am convinced that meetings in such a spirit between members of different faiths can lead to affection and compassion for each other and can help to move those involved in the direction of harmony and peace.

Knitter argues that the primary mission of the Church should be to promote the Kingdom of God rather than to proclaim Jesus. For Knitter, the Kingdom of God, which aims to unite all people, is more important than the Church.[37] The Pope, on the other hand, who does not really believe that the Kingdom can be separated from the Church, seems to subordinate the Kingdom to the Church, just as he subordinates dialogue to proclamation.[38] Yet, throughout his extensive travels, John Paul II has raised his powerful voice against coercion in proselytizing and has made many moving and beautiful statements about non-Christian religions. Speaking to the religious leaders of Sri Lanka, he declared:

Especially since the Second Vatican Council, the Catholic Church has been fully committed to *pursuing the path of dialogue and cooperating with members of other religions.* Interreligious dialogue is a precious means by which the followers of various religions discover shared points of contact in the spiritual life, while acknowledging the differences which exist among them. The Church respects the freedom of individuals to seek the truth and to embrace it according to the dictates of conscience. In this light she firmly rejects proselytism and the use of unethical means to gain conversions.[39]

John Paul II has devoted his life to furthering the Kingdom, and to this aim we should add our strength.

The Buddhist Tradition

The following quotations from *Crossing the Threshold of Hope* capture the Pope's main assumptions about Buddhism:

The "enlightenment" experienced by Buddha comes down to the conviction that the world is bad, that it is the source of evil and of suffering for man.[40]

Buddhism is in large measure an *"atheistic" system*. We do not free ourselves from evil through the good which comes from God; we liberate ourselves only through detachment from the world, which is bad. The fullness of such a detachment is not union with God, but what is called nirvana, a state of perfect indifference with regard to the world. *To save oneself* means, above all, to free oneself from evil by becoming *indifferent to the world, which is the source of evil*. This is the culmination of the spiritual process.[41]

Because I believe that John Paul wishes to see an honest and open encounter between Roman Catholicism and the religions of the world, I am surprised by his portrayal of Buddhism. It seems to me to be in the spirit of nineteenth- and early twentieth-century writings on Buddhism by Christian missionaries. Buddhists throughout the world have been deeply offended by his negative description of their tradition, and in January 1995, when John Paul went to Sri Lanka, the Catholic bishops made a public apology, insisting that the Pope had not meant to hurt the feelings of Buddhists.[42]

As a person who has been involved in dialogue with Buddhists, I do not think that the idea that Buddhism is atheistic, that it is not preoccupied with the idea of a supreme being, is upsetting to all Buddhists. On the contrary, many Buddhists argue that the *idea* of God is an attachment from which we must free ourselves. They argue that the

Buddha did not believe in a theistic concept of God. It is a false idea that has brought serious problems for humanity. Gunapala Dharmasiri, a contemporary Buddhist monk from Sri Lanka, states:

> What is meant here is that the implied world view of the Christian concept of God was morally disastrous. It was factually wrong and therefore morally misleading. Firstly, it preached a narrow and alienated view of man. Man was said to be essentially superior to all other creatures because he was created in the image of God. Thereby, man becomes logically qualitatively different from other creatures. This idea inflated and strengthened man's ego, thus alienating man from the rest of creation.[43]

What is truly problematic for Buddhists are the Pope's claims that according to Buddhism "the world is bad, that it is the source of evil and suffering for man," and that nirvana is "a state of perfect indifference with regard to the world." According to Buddhism, the world in itself is not bad. The source of our suffering is our own desires, our thirst, greed, and clinging to a permanent self, which is an illusion. When we free ourselves from the false notion of a permanent self, then this earth can become for us a paradise. It appears to me that John Paul, like many other Western students of Buddhism, gets stuck on the first of the Four Noble Truths. It does teach that life is suffering. Therefore, John Paul concludes that Buddhism is pessimistic. However, he does not pay sufficient attention to the fact that the Noble Truths go on to tell us that we can overcome suffering by extinguishing the greed which causes the suffering in the first place. Nirvana is not, as the Pope claims, "a state of perfect indifference with regard to the world." Rather, it is seeing the world with new, awakened eyes. Through the process of meditation, we can totally transform the way we see the world. After attaining nirvana, the Buddha did not leave the world, but devoted the next forty-five years to teaching humanity how to attain joy by becoming more fully present to the world. Millions of Buddhists would bear witness that the Buddha's compassionate heart helped them to attain joy in this very life.

I cannot agree with John Paul II and other Western scholars who claim that Buddhism is preoccupied only with personal salvation and not with the transformation of society. My understanding is that the aim of Buddhism is not only to perfect character but also to beautify the entire universe. As the British scholar of Buddhism Trevor Ling has stated:

For Buddhism is not, as so many Westerners have imagined, a private cult of escape from the real world. The word "imagined" is used deliberately because such a view of Buddhism can proceed only from the exercise of the imagination, not from knowledge of the Buddha's teaching, or of the nature of the Buddhist community, the *Sangha,* or from Buddhist history. To speak of Buddhism as something concerned with the private salvation of the individual soul is to ignore entirely the basic Buddhist repudiation of the notion of the individual soul. The teaching of the Buddha was not concerned with the private destiny of the individual, but with something much wider, the whole realm of sentient being, the whole of consciousness. This inevitably entailed a concern with social and political matters, and these receive a large share of attention in the teaching of the Buddha as it is represented in the Pali texts.[44]

A moving statement by a young Western Buddhist priest, written shortly before she died, speaks directly to this controversial issue:

I'd be embarrassed to tell anyone, it sounds so wishy-washy, but now I have maybe 50 or 60 years (who knows?) of time, of a life, open, blank, ready to offer. I want to live it for other people. What else is there to do with it? Not that I expect to change the world or even a blade of grass, but it's as if to give myself is all I can do, as the flowers have no choice but to blossom. . . . So I must go deeper and deeper and work hard, no longer for me but for everyone I can help. . . . Thus, I should also work politically, work to make people's surroundings that much more tolerable, work for a society that fosters more spiritual, more human, values. A society for people, not profits.[45]

Does she seem like a person who negates the world? I do not think so. I do not believe that John Paul II intended to anger the Buddhist world. Buddhism is an extremely complex and diverse religious tradition, and it seems that the Pope's knowledge of Buddhism is based predominantly on Christian interpretations rather than on Buddhist sources.

John Paul II is the most influential supporter of interfaith dialogue so desperately needed in today's world, and thus I can only hope that he will carefully reconsider his view of Buddhism, a tradition which so many Roman Catholics and other non-Buddhists have found to be spiritually enriching to their lives.

The Muslim Tradition

Before I examine John Paul's view of Islam and Muhammad, it will be helpful to briefly explore the most prevalent Christian attitude toward Islam, one that has been espoused since the beginning of Islam. Of all the major religious traditions with which Christianity came into contact, it is Islam that came under the most intense attack. Isma'il Raji al Faruqi helps us to understand why Islam was so maligned:

> It is the only religion that contended and fought with most of the world religions on their own homeground, whether in the field of ideas or on the battlefields of history. . . . Moreover, Islam is the only religion that in its interreligious and international conflict with Judaism, Christianity, Hinduism, and Buddhism, succeeded significantly and in major scale in all the fights it undertook. . . . No wonder, then, that it is the religion with the greatest number of enemies and, hence, the religion most misunderstood.[46]

The most severe attack was reserved for the prophet of Islam, who was called both "an impostor" and "a lecher," with some of the most negative statements about him coming from Thomas Aquinas, Dante, and Martin Luther. W. C. Smith, the eminent theologian and historian of religion, appears to have been the first Christian to raise the question whether it is possible for a committed Christian to see the Qur'an as the word of God. Hans Küng, who was once admired by John Paul II, appears to be the first Catholic scholar to accept Muhammad as a prophet of God.

There are many theological reasons why Islam is so problematic to Christianity as well as to Judaism. Muslims claim that the Qur'an is the final word of God. Although Moses and Jesus are true prophets, the Jews and Christians are claimed to have distorted the authentic revelations received by their prophets. Therefore, the Qur'an remains the only reliable sacred text, and Muhammad is the greatest and final prophet of God. For many Muslims throughout history, and continuing in our time, Islam remains the only path that leads to salvation. In the words of Sayyid Abul A'la Mawdudi, "This must also be clearly understood that now, through Muhammad (peace be upon him) alone can we know the straight path of Islam. The Qur'an and the life-example of Muhammad (peace be upon him) are the only reliable sources that are available to mankind to learn God's Will in its totality."[47]

The divinity of Jesus is the greatest problem with Christianity from the Muslim perspective. Whereas most Jewish scholars have concluded that Christianity is not idolatry, Islam believes that it is. For Muslims, attributing divinity to any human being is idolatrous and is the only unforgivable sin.

In *Crossing the Threshold of Hope*, John Paul II devotes only four pages to Islam in a chapter titled "Muhammad?" He begins by citing *Nostra Aetate*. This document speaks of the high regard which the Catholic Church has for Muslims because they are monotheists who worship one God. Writing twenty-five years after *Nostra Aetate*, John Paul expresses his admiration for Muslim "fidelity to prayer." He states:

> The image of believers in Allah who, without caring about time or place, fall to their knees and immerse themselves in prayer remains a model for all *those who invoke* the true God, in particular for those Christians who, having deserted their magnificent cathedrals, pray only a little or not at all.[48]

John Paul II also speaks of the great hospitality with which he has been welcomed while visiting Muslim countries. These are his only positive comments about Islam. As in *Nostra Aetate*, nothing is said about Muhammad. The negative remarks are also brief. From these remarks, it appears that John Paul II has read the Qur'an, which makes his comments even more problematic for Muslims. The following seems to be his major negative statement about the Muslim tradition:

> Whoever knows the Old and New Testaments, and then reads the Koran, clearly sees the *process by which it completely reduces Divine Revelation*. It is impossible not to note the movement away from what God said about Himself, first in the Old Testament through the Prophets, and then finally in the New Testament through His Son. In Islam all the richness of God's self-revelation, which constitutes the heritage of the Old and New Testaments, has definitely been set aside.
>
> Some of the most beautiful names in the human language are given to the God of the Koran, but He is ultimately a God outside of the world, a God who is *only Majesty, never Emmanuel*, God-with-us. *Islam is not a religion of redemption*. There is no room for the Cross and the Resurrection.[49]

Because of John Paul's desire to encourage genuine dialogue with Islam, I find his remarks all the more surprising. His statement that the Qur'an "*completely reduces Divine Revelation*" is somewhat ambiguous.

What he seems to be saying is that there is such a radical difference between the Bible and the Qur'an that the Qur'an cannot possibly be divine revelation. That nothing is said about Muhammad in a chapter titled "Muhammad?" leads me to conclude that John Paul II does not view Muhammad as an authentic prophet.

John Paul's statement that the God of the Qur'an "is ultimately a God outside of the world, a God who is *only Majesty, never Emmanuel,* God-with-us" is a very pervasive Christian view of Islam. It is also a view held by many Christians of the Jewish tradition. In my article "Prayer and Intention: A Comparative Study of Judaism and Islam," I have tried to show that this is not, in fact, a view that is accepted by Jews and Muslims.[50]

Islam remains one of the most misunderstood religious traditions of the world. It will take many face-to-face meetings with Muslims for Christians, as well as for Jews, to gain a deeper understanding and appreciation of this faith.

The Jewish Tradition

John Paul's attitude toward the Jewish tradition is radically different from his view of Buddhism and Islam. In all his meetings and writings on Jews and Judaism, he expresses deep veneration and love for the Jewish people. The Pope's special love for the Jewish people has a theological as well as personal basis.

For the Pope, as well as for the Jews, the Hebrew Bible is *Torah min ha-shamayim* (Torah from heaven) which came into being by way of revelation. The Jews are precious because they continue to show the world "the beauty and profound truth of belief in the one God and Lord."[51] The God of the Jewish people is the God of the Catholic Church. The Pope seems to be in full agreement with Heschel, who, writing on the affinity of Jews and Christians, states:

> Above all, while dogmas and forms of worship are divergent, God is the same. What unites us? A commitment to the Hebrew Bible as Holy Scripture. Faith in the Creator, the God of Abraham, commitment to many of His commandments, to justice and mercy, a sense of contrition, sensitivity to the sanctity of life and to the involvement of God in history, the conviction that without the holy the good will be defeated, prayer that history may not end before the end of days, and so much more.[52]

In his meeting with Jewish leaders in Brasilia on October 15, 1991, the Pope stated:

> Adoring the one true God, in fact, we discover our common spiritual root, which is the consciousness of the brotherhood of all people. This awareness is truly the closest bond which unites Christians and the Jewish people. This common root also makes us love this people because, as the Bible says, "The Lord has loved Israel forever" (1 Kings 10:9), he has made a Covenant with it which has never been broken, placing in it the Messianic hope of the whole human race.[53]

John Paul consistently speaks of the Jews as "the people of God of the Old Testament" and "our elder brothers in the faith." He often speaks of the "spiritual link" between the Church and the Jews. He calls this "link" a sacred one, because it comes from the "mysterious will of God."[54] In a number of his speeches and in his book *Crossing the Threshold of Hope,* John Paul II speaks of Franz Rosenzweig and Martin Buber, two important Jewish thinkers of the twentieth century, with gratitude for building bridges of understanding between Jews and Christians. In fact, throughout his writings, John Paul II speaks of his own enrichment from the Jewish tradition, and he particularly admires the French Jewish thinker Emmanuel Levinas. Tad Szulc notes that John Paul has "tendered the hand of friendship of his church to Jews in a manner no other pope had ever done."[55]

A brief look at some of John Paul's early experiences and influences will help us understand the reasons for his special attachment to Judaism. Karol Wojtyla was born on May 18, 1920, in Wadowice, Poland, in a house owned by a Jewish family. The Jews of this town, about the size of Grinnell, Iowa, constituted about 25 percent of the population. Another Jewish family, the Beers, also rented an apartment in the same house as the Wojtylas. The daughter of the Beer family was interviewed fifty years later and spoke of her departure from Poland to Israel:

> I knew I was very popular with Polish boys and girls, but there was anti-Semitism, too. There was only one family who never showed any racial hostility toward us, and that was Lolek and his dad. . . . Then we decided to leave Poland for Palestine because we felt disaster faced the Jews. . . . I went to say goodbye to Lolek and his father. Mr. Wojtyla was upset about our departure, and when he asked me why, I told him. Again and again he said to me, "Not

all Poles are anti-Semitic. You know I am not!" I spoke to him frankly and said that very few Poles were like him. He was very upset. But Lolek was even more upset than his father. He did not say a word, but his face went very red. I said farewell to him as kindly as I could, but he was so moved that he could not find a single word in reply. So I just shook the father's hand and left.[56]

Other Jews of this town who knew the Pope as a young man also tell how he protected Jews from anti-Semites. During World War II, John Paul was a member of an underground theater group which had as one of its purposes to work against the Nazis.[57] In reading the history of Jewish life in Poland, we hear a great deal about Polish anti-Semitism, but we must keep in mind that in no other country, not even in Spain, did the Jews live in such relative peace and security for so long a time as they did in Poland. In his appraisal of East European Jewish history, Heschel stated: "I feel justified in saying that it was the golden period in Jewish history, in the history of the Jewish soul."[58]

Some of the most prominent Christian Poles, who were friends of the Jews, were very influential on John Paul. These included King Kazimierz the Great, who encouraged Jews to settle in Poland, and the poet and playwright Cyprian Norwid. Norwid wrote a poem titled "Polish Jews" in which he argued that Poland had the "priceless heritage" of two different, but great cultures: Polish and Jewish. On many occasions John Paul II has spoken about this special bond between the Polish and the Jewish people. In his address to the Jewish community of Poland on June 9, 1991, the Pope said:

> I heartily echo the words that I found in the pastoral letter of the Polish bishops dated 30 November 1990: "The same land was a common homeland for Poles and Jews for ages; the mutual loss of life, a sea of terrible suffering and of the wrongs endured should not divide, but unite us. The places of execution, and in many cases, the common graves call for this unity."[59]

Karol Wojtyla of Krakow, the first Polish Pope and first non-Italian Pope in 456 years, often speaks out against anti-Semitism, which he sees as "a sin against God and humanity."[60] He speaks of Auschwitz as "one of the darkest and most tragic moments in history"[61] and also as "the greatest tragedy of our century: the greatest trauma."[62]

In his paper on John Paul II on Islam, Professor Ayoub raises the question of why the Pope specifically targets Muslims for conversion, but not Jews. Ayoub suggests one reason is that

> Jewish-Christian dialogue has made far better progress towards achieving a common language among equal participants than has Muslim-Christian dialogue. Another reason is that most of world Jewry has for centuries shared with the West a common history and culture. Islam, on the other hand, has for long been "the mysterious other" and the Muslim world an arch rival to Western Christendom.[63]

I would add two other reasons. The first is the special affinity between Judaism and Christianity. They are the only two traditions that have a sacred text in common: the Hebrew Bible. The second is the fact that Pope John Paul II lived through the Holocaust in Poland. This may also help explain why he has never, to my knowledge, spoken of mission to the Jews.

Abraham Joshua Heschel was thrilled when Angelo Giuseppe Roncalli became Pope John XXIII. After he convened the Second Vatican Council, Heschel exclaimed: "Yes, I witnessed a miracle: there came Pope John."[64] On one occasion, when John XXIII passed by the Synagogue of Rome, he stopped his car to bless the Jews who were coming *out* of the synagogue. On April 13, 1986, John Paul II went *inside* the synagogue and blessed the Jews.

Conclusion

Cardinal Francis Arinze observed that to many people it may appear that there is a "tension between the missionary thrust of Christianity and the call to respect the religious views of others."[65] Such a tension is also present in the Pope's attitude toward other faiths. Although the Pope is an inclusivist, at times he makes pronouncements that seem to be in the spirit of pluralism. For example, on a number of occasions he has stated that dialogue is the will of God.[66] I do not view this tension as a real conflict. A distinction must be made between the Pope's encyclical *Redemptoris Missio* and his book *Crossing the Threshold of Hope,* on the one hand, and his numerous addresses given during meetings with members of other faiths. It is in these face-to-face meetings that the Pope makes very positive statements about other traditions and even quotes from their sacred texts. For example, in his address to the people of Sri Lanka, he declared:

I express my highest regard for the *followers of Buddhism,* the majority religion in Sri Lanka, with its *Brahamaviharas,* the four great values of *Metta, Karuna, Mudita and Upekka:* loving kindness, compassion, sympathy and equanimity; with its ten transcendental virtues and the joys of the *Sangha* expressed so beautifully in the *Theragathas.* I ardently hope that my visit will serve to strengthen the goodwill between us, and that it will reassure everyone of the Catholic Church's desire for interreligious dialogue and cooperation in building a more just and fraternal world. To everyone I extend the hand of friendship, recalling the splendid words of the *Dhammapada:* "Better than a thousand useless words, is one single word that gives peace. . . . "[67]

Pointing to the affinity between Islam and Christianity in an address to Muslims of the Philippines, the Pope stated:

Dear Muslims, my brothers: I would like to add that we Christians, just like you, seek the basis and model of mercy in God himself, the God to whom your Book gives the very beautiful name of *al-Rahman,* while the Bible calls him *al-Rahum,* the Merciful One.[68]

And, in a rare reference to the Qur'an, the Pope stated:

As I have often said in other meetings with Muslims, your God and ours is one and the same, and we are brothers and sisters in the faith of Abraham. . . . All true holiness comes from God, who is called "The Holy One" in the sacred books of the Jews, Christians, and Muslims. Your holy Koran calls God "Al Quddus," as in the verse: "He is God besides whom there is no other, the Sovereign, the Holy, the (source of) Peace" (Koran 59, 23).[69]

These statements made to Buddhists and Muslims in person are clearly very different in spirit from those made when the Pope is speaking about the doctrines of those traditions. Both in *Redemptoris Missio* and *Crossing the Threshold of Hope,* John Paul II is dealing with the creeds and doctrines of other faiths, many of which he finds problematic — and says so. However, when he is in meetings with people, he sees them as being created in the image of God; thus, his concern and compassion for the sublime dignity of each person come to the fore. During such moments when he sees the faith in the hearts of human beings, he transcends any labels, such as exclusivism, inclusivism, or pluralism.

Notes

1. Pope John Paul II, "To the Participants in the Sixth Assembly of the World Conference on Religion and Peace (WCRP) at the Synod Hall," Rome, November 3, 1994, in *Interreligious Dialogue: The Official Teaching of the Catholic Church (1963–1995),* ed. Francesco Gioia (Boston: Pauline Books, 1997), 530. The Pope, who has acknowledged that "Catholics have not always been peacemakers," realizes the great need in these difficult times to bring together the world's spiritual leaders to work for peace. The Pope invited religious leaders from many faiths for a Day of Prayer for Peace held on October 27, 1986, in Assisi. For a brief summary of this groundbreaking event, see Thomas Michel and Michael Fitzgerald, eds., *Recognize the Spiritual Bonds Which Unite Us: Sixteen Years of Christian-Muslim Dialogue* (Vatican City: Pontifical Council for Interreligious Dialogue, 1994), 93–95. For the Pope's speech concluding this event, see Gioia, ed., *Interreligious Dialogue,* 347–52.

2. Pope John Paul II, "Message for the Twenty-Fifth Annual World Day of Prayer for Peace," January 1, 1992, in *Spiritual Pilgrimage: Texts on Jews and Judaism 1979–1995: Pope John Paul II,* ed. Eugene J. Fisher and Leon Klenicki (New York: Crossroad, 1995), 161.

3. Pope John Paul II, "Address to the Diplomatic Corps Accredited to the Holy See," January 11, 1992, in Fisher and Klenicki, eds., *Spiritual Pilgrimage,* 162.

4. Alan Race, editor of the journal *World Faiths Encounter,* develops this model in great detail. See his book *Christians and Religious Pluralism: Patterns in the Christian Theology of Religions* (Maryknoll, N.Y.: Orbis Books, 1982). See also Diana L. Eck, *Encountering God: A Spiritual Journey from Bozeman to Banaras* (Boston: Beacon Press, 1993), especially chapter 7. And see also Paul Knitter, *Jesus and the Other Names: Christian Mission and Global Responsibility* (Maryknoll, N.Y.: Orbis Books, 1996).

5. In John H. Leith, ed., *Creeds of the Churches: A Reader in Christian Doctrine from the Bible to the Present* (Garden City, N.Y.: Doubleday, 1963), 58.

6. Race, *Christians,* 42–43.

7. Karl Rahner, "Christianity and the Non-Christian Religions," in *Christianity and Other Religions: Selected Readings,* ed. John Hick and Brian Hebblethwaite (Philadelphia: Fortress Press, 1981), 56.

8. Ibid., 61.

9. Ibid., 75.

10. Brian Hebblethwaite, introduction to Hick and Hebblethwaite, eds., *Christianity and Other Religions,* 8.

11. Paul F. Knitter, *One Earth Many Religions: Multifaith Dialogue and Global Responsibility* (Maryknoll, N.Y.: Orbis Books, 1995), 30.

12. Abraham Joshua Heschel, "No Religion Is an Island," in *No Religion Is an Island: Abraham Joshua Heschel and Interreligious Dialogue,* ed. Harold Kasimow and Byron L. Sherwin (Maryknoll, N.Y.: Orbis Books, 1991), 14.

13. Quoted in Knitter, *Jesus,* 106.

14. Marcello Zago, "Commentary on *Redemptoris Missio,*" in *Redemption and Dialogue: Reading* Redemptoris Missio *and* Dialogue and Proclamation, ed. William R. Burrows (Maryknoll, N.Y.: Orbis Books, 1993), 56.

15. *RM* 5; reprinted in Burrows, ed., *Redemption,* 7–8.

16. Pope John Paul II, *Crossing the Threshold of Hope* (New York: Alfred A. Knopf, 1994), 136; italics here and in other quotations from the book are in the original.

17. Ibid., 68.

18. Ibid., 73.

19. Ibid., 80–81.

20. Ibid., 109.

21. Ibid., 115.

22. Tad Szulc, *Pope John Paul II: The Biography* (New York: Scribner, 1995), 319.

23. Pope John Paul II, "To Representatives of the Shinto Religion," Rome, February 28, 1979, in Gioia, ed., *Interreligious Dialogue,* 216.

24. *RM* 10; reprinted in Burrows, ed., *Redemption,* 10.

25. Ibid.

26. John Paul II, *Crossing,* 81.

27. *RM* 55; reprinted in Burrows, ed., *Redemption,* 35.

28. Heschel's impact on the Second Vatican Council is described in Marc H. Tanenbaum, "Jewish-Christian Relations: Heschel and Vatican II" (lecture delivered at the Jewish Theological Seminary of America, February 21, 1983).

29. "Carl Stern's Interview with Dr. Heschel," in Abraham Joshua Heschel, *Moral Grandeur and Spiritual Audacity,* ed. Susannah Heschel (New York: Farrar, Straus and Giroux, 1996), 405.

30. Ibid.

31. Quoted in "Session VIII: Discussion," in *Vatican II: An Interfaith Appraisal: International Theological Conference, University of Notre Dame: March 20–26, 1966,* ed. John H. Miller (Notre Dame, Ind.: University of Notre Dame Press, 1966), 373.

32. Pope John Paul II and Dr. Havanpola Ratanasara, "An Interreligious Exchange," *Origins* 17 (1987): 302.

33. Knitter, *Jesus,* 142.

34. Augustine Kanjamala, "*Redemptoris Missio* and Mission in India," in Burrows, ed., *Redemption,* 203.

35. Mahmoud Ayoub, "Pope John Paul II on Islam," in *Open Catholicism: The Tradition at Its Best: Essays in Honor of Gerard S. Sloyan,* ed. David Efraymson and John Raines (Collegeville, Minn.: Liturgical Press, 1997), 201.

36. John Paul II, "To Representatives of the Shinto Religion," 218.

37. Knitter, *Jesus,* especially chapters 6 and 7.

38. *RM* 44; reprinted in Burrows, ed., *Redemption,* 28.

39. Pope John Paul II, "To the Religious Leaders of Sri Lanka," Colombo, January 21, 1995, in Gioia, ed., *Interreligious Dialogue*, 539–40; italics in the original.

40. John Paul II, *Crossing*, 85.

41. Ibid., 86.

42. Szulc, *Pope John Paul II*, 467.

43. Gunapala Dharmasiri, *A Buddhist Critique of the Christian Concept of God* (Antioch, Calif.: Golden Leaves Publishing Co., 1988), 260. Venerable Madawela Punnaji, a Sri Lankan Buddhist monk, in his article "Why Buddhists Should Not Quarrel with the Pope," states: "Although some writers have branded Buddhism as atheistic, it is clearly not. Buddhists do have the concept of 'deva'" (*Dialogue* 22, n.s. [1995]: 15). The journal *Dialogue* is published in Sri Lanka. The entire issue, titled *Pope and Buddhism*, is devoted to Buddhist and Christian responses to the Pope's *Crossing the Threshold of Hope*. I especially recommend the article "The Christian and Buddhist Responses to the Pope's Chapter on Buddhism: An Analytic Report," by Aloysius Pieris, S.J.

44. Trevor Ling, *The Buddha: Buddhist Civilization in India and Ceylon* (New York: Scribner, 1973), 122.

45. Maura O'Halloran, *Pure Heart, Enlightened Mind: The Zen Journal and Letters of Maura "Soshin" O'Halloran* (Boston: Charles E. Tuttle, 1994), 233.

46. Isma'il Raji al Faruqi, "Islam," in *The Great Asian Religions*, comp. Wing-tsit Chan et al. (London: Macmillan, 1969), 307.

47. Sayyid Abul A'la Mawdudi, *Towards Understanding Islam* (Gary, Ind.: International Islamic Federation of Student Organizations, 1970), 78–79.

48. John Paul II, *Crossing*, 93.

49. Ibid., 92.

50. Harold Kasimow, "Prayer and Intention: A Comparative Study of Judaism and Islam," in *Essays in Islamic and Comparative Studies: Papers Presented to the Islamic Studies Group of the American Academy of Religion*, ed. Isma'il Raji al Faruqi (Washington, D.C.: International Institute of Islamic Thought, 1982), 9–16.

51. Quoted in Fisher and Klenicki, eds., *Spiritual Pilgrimage*, 159.

52. Heschel, "No Religion Is an Island," 9.

53. Quoted in Fisher and Klenicki, eds., *Spiritual Pilgrimage*, 159.

54. Ibid., 55–56.

55. Szulc, *Pope John Paul II*, 21.

56. Quoted in ibid., 70.

57. Ibid., 34.

58. Abraham Joshua Heschel, *The Earth Is the Lord's* (New York: Harper and Row, 1966), 10.

59. Quoted in Fisher and Klenicki, eds., *Spiritual Pilgrimage*, 151.

60. Ibid., 140.

61. Ibid., 209.

62. Ibid., 201.

63. Ayoub, "Pope John Paul II on Islam," 198.

64. Quoted in "Session VIII: Discussion," 373.

65. Francis Arinze, "The Urgency of Dialogue with Non-Christians," *Origins* 14 (1985): 647.

66. See his speech "To the Leaders of Christian Religions and Other Religions of Bangladesh," Dacca, November 19, 1986, in Gioia, ed., *Interreligious Dialogue*, 356–58.

67. Pope John Paul II, "To the People of Sri Lanka," Colombo, January 20, 1995, in Gioia, ed., *Interreligious Dialogue,* 533–34; emphasis in the original.

68. Pope John Paul II, "To Representatives of Muslims of the Philippines," Davao, February 20, 1981, in Gioia, ed., *Interreligious Dialogue*, 237.

69. Pope John Paul II, "To the Participants in the Symposium on 'Holiness in Christianity and in Islam,'" Rome, May 9, 1985, in Gioia, ed., *Interreligious Dialogue,* 283.

Part One

IN HIS OWN WORDS

1

John Paul II on
Interreligious Dialogue

From *Crossing the Threshold of Hope*

You speak of many religions. Instead I will attempt to show the *common fundamental element* and the *common root* of these religions.

The [Second Vatican] Council defined the relationship of the Church to non-Christian religions in a specific document that begins with the words *"Nostra aetate" ("In our time")* [henceforth: *NA* — Ed.]. It is a concise and yet very rich document that authentically hands on the Tradition, faithful to the thought of the earliest Fathers of the Church.

From the beginning, Christian Revelation has viewed the spiritual history of man as including, in some way, all religions, thereby demonstrating *the unity of humankind with regard to the eternal and ultimate destiny of man.* The Council document speaks of this unity and links it with the current trend to bring humanity closer together through the resources available to our civilization. The Church sees the promotion of this unity as one of its duties: *"There is only one community and it consists of all peoples.* They have only one origin, since God inhabited the entire earth with the whole human race. And they have one ultimate destiny, God, whose providence, goodness, and plan for salvation extend to all.... Men *turn to various religions to solve mysteries of the human condition*, which today, as in earlier times, burden people's hearts: the nature of man; the meaning and purpose of life; good and evil; the origin and purpose of suffering; the way to true happiness; death; judgment and retribution after death; and finally, the ultimate ineffable mystery which is the origin and destiny of our existence. From ancient times up to

today all the various peoples have shared and continue to share an awareness of that enigmatic power that is present throughout the course of
things and throughout the events of human life, and, in which, at times,
even the Supreme Divinity or the Father is recognizable. This awareness
and recognition imbue life with an intimate religious sense. Religions
that are tied up with cultural progress strive to solve these issues with
more refined concepts and a more precise language" (NA 1–2).

Here the Council document brings us to the Far East — first of all
to Asia, a continent where the Church's missionary activity, carried out
since the times of the apostles, has borne, we must recognize, very mod-
est fruit. It is well known that only a small percentage of the population
on what is the largest continent believes in Christ.

This does not mean that the Church's missionary effort has lapsed —
quite the opposite: that effort has been and still remains intense. And
yet the tradition of very ancient cultures, antedating Christianity, remains
very strong in the East. Even if faith in Christ reaches hearts and minds,
the negative connotations associated with the image of life in Western
society (the so-called Christian society) present a considerable obstacle
to the acceptance of the Gospel. Mahatma Gandhi, Indian and Hindu,
pointed this out many times, in his deeply evangelical manner. He was
disillusioned with the ways in which Christianity was expressed in the
political and social life of nations. Could a man who fought for the liberation of his great nation from colonial dependence accept Christianity
in the same form as it had been imposed on his country by those same
colonial powers?

The Second Vatican Council realized this difficulty. This is why the
document on the relations between the Church and Hinduism and other
religions of the Far East is so important. We read: "In Hinduism men
explore the divine mystery and express it through an endless bounty of
myths and through penetrating philosophical insight. They seek freedom from the anguish of our human condition, either by way of the
ascetic life, profound meditation, or by taking refuge in God with love
and trust. The various schools of Buddhism recognize the radical inadequacy of this malleable world and teach a way by which men, with
devout and trusting hearts, can become capable either of reaching a state
of perfect liberation, or of attainment, by their own efforts or through
higher help, supreme illumination" (NA 2).

Further along, the Council remarks that "The Catholic Church rejects
nothing that is true and holy in these religions. The Church has a high regard for their conduct and way of life, for those precepts and doctrines
which, although differing on many points from that which the Church

believes and propounds, often *reflect a ray of that truth which enlightens all men*. However, the Church proclaims, and is bound to proclaim that *Christ is 'the way and the truth and the life'* (John 14:6), in whom men must find the fullness of religious life and in whom God has reconciled everything to Himself" (*NA* 2).

The words of the Council recall the conviction, long rooted in the Tradition, of the existence of the so-called *semina Verbi* (seeds of the Word), present in all religions. In the light of this conviction, the Church seeks to identify the *semina Verbi* present in the great traditions of the Far East, in order to trace a common path against the backdrop of the needs of the contemporary world. We can affirm that here the position of the Council is inspired by a *truly universal concern*. The Church is guided by the faith that *God the Creator wants to save all humankind in Jesus Christ*, the only mediator between God and man, inasmuch as He is the Redeemer of all humankind. The Paschal Mystery is equally available to all, and, through it, the way to eternal salvation is also open to all.

In another passage the Council says that the Holy Spirit works effectively even outside the visible structure of the Church (cf. *Lumen Gentium* 13), making use of these very *semina Verbi*, that constitute a kind of *common soteriological root present in all religions*.

I have been convinced of this on numerous occasions, both while *visiting the countries of the Far East* and while meeting representatives of those religions, especially during the historic *meeting at Assisi*, where we found ourselves gathered together praying for peace.

Thus, instead of marveling at the fact that providence allows such a great variety of religions, we should be amazed at the number of common elements found within them.

At this point it would be helpful to recall all the *primitive religions,* the *animistic religions* which stress ancestor worship. It seems that those who practice them are particularly close to Christianity, and among them, the Church's missionaries also find it easier to speak a common language. Is there, perhaps, in this veneration of ancestors a kind of preparation for the Christian faith in the Communion of Saints, in which all believers — whether living or dead — form a single community, a single body? And faith in the Communion of Saints is, ultimately, faith in Christ, who alone is the source of life and of holiness for all. There is nothing strange, then, that the African and Asian animists would become believers in Christ more easily than followers of the great *religions of the Far East*.

As the Council also noted, these last religions possess the *characteristics of a system*. They are *systems of worship* and also *ethical systems,* with a strong emphasis on good and evil. Certainly among these belong Chinese Confucianism and Taoism: Tao means eternal truth — something similar to the "Word" — which is reflected in the action of man by means of truth and moral good. The religions of the Far East have contributed greatly to the history of morality and culture, forming a national identity in the Chinese, Indians, Japanese, and Tibetans, and also in the peoples of Southeast Asia and the archipelagoes of the Pacific Ocean.

Some of these peoples come from age-old cultures. The indigenous peoples of Australia boast a history tens of thousands of years old, and their ethnic and religious tradition is older than that of Abraham and Moses.

Christ came into the world for all these peoples. He redeemed them all and has His own ways of reaching each of them in the present eschatological phase of salvation history. In fact, in those regions, many accept Him and many more have an implicit faith in Him (cf. Hebrews 11:6).

From *The Catechism of the Catholic Church*
(Approved by John Paul II, June 25, 1992, paras. 842–48, 856)

The Church's bond with non-Christian religions is in the first place the common origin and end of the human race: "All nations form but one community. This is so because all stem from the one stock which God created to people the entire earth, and also because all share a common destiny, namely God. His providence, evident goodness, and saving designs extend to all against the day when the elect are gathered together in the holy city" (*NA* 1).

The Catholic Church recognizes in other religions that search, among shadows and images, for the God who is unknown yet near since he gives life and breath to all things, and wants all men to be saved. Thus, the Church considers all goodness and truth found in these religions as "a preparation for the Gospel, and given by him who enlightens all men that they may at length have life."

In their religious behavior, however, men also display the limits and errors that disfigure the image of God in them: "Very often, deceived by the Evil One, men have become vain in their reasoning, and have exchanged the truth of God for a lie, and served the creature rather than the Creator. Or else, living and dying in this world without God, they are exposed to ultimate despair."

To reunite all his children, scattered and led astray by sin, the Father willed to call the whole of humanity together into his Son's Church. The Church is the place where humanity must rediscover its unity and salvation. The Church is "the world reconciled." She is that bark which "in the full sail of the Lord's cross, by the breath of the Holy Spirit, navigates safely in this world." According to another image dear to the Church Fathers, she is prefigured by Noah's ark, which alone saves from the flood.

How are we to understand this affirmation, often repeated by the Church Fathers? Reformulated positively, it means that all salvation comes from Christ the Head through the Church which is his Body: "Basing itself on Scripture and Tradition, the Council teaches that the Church, a pilgrim now on earth, is necessary for salvation: that one Christ is the mediator and the way of salvation; he is present to us in his body which is the Church. He himself explicitly asserted the necessity of faith and Baptism, and thereby affirmed at the same time the necessity of the Church, which men enter through Baptism as through a door. Hence they could not be saved who, knowing that the Catholic Church was founded as necessary by God through Christ, would refuse either to enter it, or to remain in it."

This affirmation is not aimed at those who, through no fault of their own, do not know Christ and his Church: "Those who, through no fault of their own, do not know the Gospel of Christ or his Church, but who nevertheless seek God with a sincere heart, and, moved by grace, try in their actions to do his will as they know it through the dictates of their conscience — those too may achieve eternal salvation."

"Although in ways known to himself God can lead those who, through no fault of their own, are ignorant of the Gospel, to that faith without which it is impossible to please him (cf. Hebrews 11:6), the Church still has the obligation and also the sacred right to evangelize all men. . . . "

The missionary task implies a *respectful dialogue* with those who do not yet accept the Gospel. Believers can profit from this dialogue by learning to appreciate better "those elements of truth and grace which are found among peoples, and which are, as it were, a secret presence of God." They proclaim the Good News to those who do not know it, in order to consolidate, complete, and raise up the truth and the goodness that God has distributed among men and nations, and to purify them from error and evil "for the glory of God, the confusion of the demon, and the happiness of man."

"All men are bound to seek the truth, especially in what concerns God and his Church, and to embrace it and hold on to it as they come to know it." This duty derives from "the very dignity of the human person." It does not contradict a "sincere respect" for different religions which frequently "reflect a ray of that truth which enlightens all men," nor the requirement of charity, which urges Christians "to treat with love, prudence, and patience those who are in error or ignorance with regard to the faith."

Message for the World Day of Peace
(Rome, December 8, 1982)

I consider it useful to recall at this point the *qualities of true dialogue.* They apply in the first place to dialogue between individuals. But I am thinking also and especially of dialogue between social groups, between political forces in a nation, between States within the international community. They also apply to dialogue between the vast human groupings which are distinguished from one another and which face one another on the levels of race, culture, ideology or religion. The students of warfare recognize that most conflicts find their roots here, at the same time as being connected with the great present-day antagonisms of East-West on the one hand, and North-South on the other.

Dialogue is a central and essential element of ethical thinking among people, whoever they may be. Under the aspect of an exchange, of communication between human beings that language makes possible, it is in fact a common quest.

Basically, it presupposes the *search for what is true, good and just* for every person, for every group and every society, in the grouping in which one is a member of or in the grouping which presents itself as the opposing one.

It therefore demands first of all *openness and welcome:* that each party should explain its thoughts, but should also listen to the explanation of the situation such as the other party describes it and sincerely feels it, with the real problems which are property to the party, its rights, the injustices of which it is aware, the reasonable solutions which it suggests. How could peace become established while one party has not even taken the trouble to consider the conditions of the other party's existence!

To engage in dialogue thus presupposes that each party should accept the *difference* and the *specific nature* of the other party. It also presupposes that each party should become aware of what separates it from the other, and that it should assume it, with a risk of tension that comes from it, without renouncing through cowardice or constraint what it knows to be true and just, for this would result in a shaky compromise. On the other hand, one should not attempt to reduce the other party to a mere object, but should consider the party to be an intelligent, free and responsible subject.

Dialogue is at the same time the search for what is and what *remains common to people*, even in the midst of tensions, oppositions and conflicts. In this sense, it is to make the other party a neighbor. It is to accept its contribution, to share with it responsibility before truth and justice. It is to suggest and to study all the possible formulas for honest reconciliation, while being able to link to the just defense of the interests and honor of the party which one represents the no less just understanding and respect for the reasons of the other party, as well as the demands of the general good which are common to both.

Furthermore, is it not more and more obvious that all the peoples of the earth find themselves in a situation of mutual interdependence on the economic, political and cultural levels? Anyone who attempts to free himself from this solidarity would soon suffer from it himself.

Finally, true dialogue is the search for what is good *by peaceful means.* It is the persistent determination to have recourse to all the possible formulas of negotiation, mediation and arbitration, to act in such a way that the factors which bring people together will be victorious over the factors of division and hate. It is a recognition of the inalienable dignity of human beings. It rests upon respect for human life. It is a wager upon the social nature of people, upon their calling to go forward together, with continuity, by a meeting of minds, wills and hearts toward the goal that the Creator has fixed for them. This goal is to make the world a place for everybody to live in and worthy of everybody.

The political virtue of such a dialogue could not fail to bear fruit for peace. My esteemed predecessor Paul VI devoted to dialogue a large part of his first encyclical, *Ecclesiam Suam*. He wrote: "Openness to dialogue which is disinterested, objective and frank, is in itself a declaration in favor of free and honest peace. It excludes pretense, rivalry, deceit and betrayal." This virtue of dialogue demands of the political leaders of today much clear-sightedness, honesty and courage, not only with regard to other peoples, but with regard to the public opinion of their own people. It presupposes often a true conversion. But there is no other possibility in the face of the threat of war. Once again, it is not an illusion. It would be easy to quote our contemporaries who have gained honor by practicing it thus.

From the Encyclical *Redemptoris Missio*
(December 7, 1990)

Interreligious dialogue is a part of the Church's evangelizing mission. Understood as a method and means of mutual knowledge and enrichment, dialogue is not in opposition to the mission *ad gentes;* indeed, it has special links with that mission and is one of its expressions. This mission, in fact, is addressed to those who do not know Christ and his Gospel, and who belong for the most part to other religions. In Christ, God calls all peoples to himself and he wishes to share with them the fullness of his revelation and love. He does not fail to make himself present in many ways, not only to individuals but also to entire peoples through their spiritual riches, of which their religions are the main and essential expression, even when they contain "gaps, insufficiencies and errors." All of this has been given ample emphasis by the Council and the subsequent Magisterium, without detracting in any way from the fact that *salvation comes from Christ and that dialogue does not dispense from evangelization.*

In the light of the economy of salvation, the Church sees no conflict between proclaiming Christ and engaging in interreligious dialogue. Instead, she feels the need to link the two in the context of her mission *ad gentes.* These two elements must maintain both their intimate connection and their distinctiveness; therefore, they should not be confused, manipulated or regarded as identical, as though they were interchangeable.

I recently wrote to the bishops of Asia: "Although the Church gladly acknowledges whatever is true and holy in the religious traditions of Buddhism, Hinduism and Islam as a reflection of that truth which enlightens all men, this does not lessen her duty and resolve to proclaim without fail Jesus Christ who is 'the way, and the truth and the life. . . . ' The fact that the followers of other religions can receive God's grace and be saved by Christ apart from the ordinary means which he has established does not thereby cancel the call to faith and baptism which God wills for all people." Indeed Christ himself "while expressly insisting on the need of faith and baptism, at the same time confirmed *the need for the Church*, into which people enter through Baptism as through a door." Dialogue should be conducted and implemented with the conviction that *the Church is the ordinary means of salvation* and that *she alone* possesses the fullness of the means of salvation.

Dialogue does not originate from tactical concerns or self-interest, but is an activity with its own guiding principles, requirements and dignity. It is demanded by deep respect for everything that has been brought about in human beings by the Spirit who blows where he wills. Through dialogue, the Church seeks to uncover the "seeds of the Word," a "ray of that truth which enlightens all men" (*NA* 2); these are found in individuals and in the religious traditions of mankind. Dialogue is based on hope and love, and will bear fruit in the Spirit. Other religions constitute a positive challenge for the Church; they stimulate her both to discover and acknowledge the signs of Christ's presence and the working of the Spirit, as well as to examine more deeply her own identity and to bear witness to the fullness of Revelation which she has received for the good of all.

This gives rise to the spirit which must enliven dialogue in the context of mission. Those engaged in this dialogue must be consistent with their own religious traditions and convictions, and be open to understanding those of the other party without pretense or close-mindedness, but with truth, humility and frankness, knowing that dialogue can enrich each side. There must be no abandonment of principles nor false irenicism, but instead a witness given and received for mutual advancement on the road of religious inquiry and experience, and at the same time for the elimination of prejudice, intolerance and misunderstandings. Dialogue leads to inner purification and conversion which, if pursued with docility to the Holy Spirit, will be spiritually fruitful.

A vast field lies open to dialogue, which can assume many forms and expressions: exchanges between experts in religious traditions or official representatives of those traditions; cooperation for integral development and safeguarding religious values; a sharing of respective spiritual experiences; the so-called "dialogue of life," through which believers of different religions bear witness before each other in daily life to their own human and spiritual values and help each other to live according to those values, in order to build a more just and fraternal society.

Each member of the faithful and all Christian communities are called to practice dialogue, although not always to the same degree or in the same way. The contribution of the laity is indispensable in this area, for they "can favor the relations which ought to be established with the followers of various religions through their example in the situations in which they live and in their activities." Some of them also will be able to make a contribution through research and study.

I am well aware that many missionaries and Christian communities find, in the difficult and often misunderstood path of dialogue, their only way of bearing sincere witness to Christ and offering generous service to others. I wish to encourage them to persevere with faith and love, even in places where their efforts are not well received. Dialogue is a path toward the Kingdom and will certainly bear fruits, even if the times and seasons are known only to the Father (cf. Acts 1:7).

To the Secretariat for Non-Christians
(Rome, April 27, 1979)

The late Paul VI, who founded this Secretariat, and so much of whose love, interest and inspiration was lavished on non-Christians, is no longer visibly among us, and I am convinced that some of you wondered whether the new Pope would devote similar care and attention to the world of the non-Christian religions.

In my encyclical *Redemptor Hominis* I endeavored to answer any such question. In it I made reference to Paul VI's first encyclical, *Ecclesiam Suam*, and to the Second Vatican Council, and then I wrote: "The Ecumenical Council gave a fundamental impulse to forming the Church's self-awareness by so adequately and competently presenting to us a view of the terrestrial globe as a map of various religions. . . . The Council document on non-Christian religions, in particular, is filled with deep esteem for the great spiritual values, indeed for the primacy of the spiritual, which in the life of mankind finds expression in religion and then in morality, with direct effects on the whole of culture." The non-Christian world is indeed constantly before the eyes of the Church and of the Pope. We are truly committed to serve it generously.

It is also good to recall that it will shortly be the fifteenth anniversary of Paul VI's solemn announcement in St. Peter's basilica on Pentecost Sunday 1964 of the setting up of this Secretariat. With God's blessing, the seed sown on that day has now grown to be a clear, definite sign which, through a network of local organizations, is operative practically throughout the world, wherever the Church is. The Secretariat is the symbol and expression of the Church's will to enter into communication with every person, and in particular with the multitudes of those who seek in the non-Christian religious traditions meaning and guidance for their lives. A Christian finds it of the highest interest to observe truly religious people, to read and listen to the testimonies of their wisdom, and to have direct proof of their faith to the point of recalling at times the words of Jesus: "Not even in Israel have I found such faith" (Matthew 8:10). At the same time the Christian has the tremendous responsibility and the immense joy of speaking to these people with simplicity and openness (the *parrhesia* of the apostles!) of "the mighty works of God" (Acts 2:11), of what God himself has done for the happiness and salvation of all at a particular time and in a particular man, whom he raised up to be our brother and Lord, Jesus Christ, "descended from David according to the flesh . . . Son of God in power according to the Spirit of holiness" (Romans 1:4). . . .

It is my hope and desire that commitment to the dialogue of salvation should be strengthened throughout the Church, including countries where there is a Christian majority. Education for dialogue with followers of other creeds should form part of the training of Christians, especially young Christians.

In his apostolic exhortation *Evangelii Nuntiandi*, Paul VI wrote that the encounter with the non-Christian religions "certainly raises complex and delicate questions that must be studied in the light of Christian tradition and the Church's Magisterium, in order to offer to the missionaries of today and tomorrow" — and I would like to add: and to all Christians — "new horizons in their contacts with non-Christian religions." You are aware that your work is a delicate one. It must be pursued with generosity and joy, and without fear, but also with the luminous conviction that dialogue is, in the words of Paul VI, "a method of accomplishing the apostolic mission; it is an example of the art of spiritual communication."

To the Plenary Session of the Secretariat for Non-Christians
(Rome, March 3, 1984)

No one can fail to see the importance and the need which interreligious dialogue assumes for all religions and all believers, called today more than ever to collaborate so that every person can reach his transcendent goal and realize his authentic growth and to help cultures preserve their own religious and spiritual values in the presence of rapid social changes.

Dialogue is fundamental for the Church, which is called to collaborate in God's plan with its methods of presence, respect, and love toward all persons. Because of this, since my first encyclical, then in the various meetings with different personalities, and above all on the occasion of my journeys, I myself have always emphasized the importance, the reasons and the goals of this dialogue. For the Church, dialogue is based on the very life of God, one and triune. God is Father of all humanity; Christ has joined every person to himself; the Spirit works in each individual. Therefore, dialogue is also based on love for the human person as such, who is the primary and fundamental way of the Church, and on the bond existing between culture and the religions which people profess.

This friendly relationship between believers of various religions is born of respect and love for one another; it presumes the exercise of fundamental freedoms to practice one's own faith completely and to compare it with that of others.

During these years the exercise of dialogue has demonstrated new paths and needs. First of all, the local Churches have established sincere and constructive relationships with the believers of other religions present within their same culture. This Secretariat itself has been a stimulus for such development; it must continue to specify and examine an appropriate apostolate for relations with non-Christians, promoting the exchange of ideas and reflection. As far as the local Churches are concerned, they must commit themselves in this direction, helping all the faithful to respect and to esteem the values, traditions and convictions of other believers. At the same time they must promote a solid and suitable religious education of the Christians themselves, so that they know how to give a convinced witness of the great gift of faith.

No local Church is exempt from this duty, which is made urgent by continuous changes. Because of migration, travel, social communication and personal choices, believers of different religions and cults easily meet each other and often live together. Therefore, an apostolate which promotes respect, acceptance, and witness is necessary so that spiritual values inspire our societies, which are tempted to selfishness, atheism and materialism.

In order to promote this apostolate, it is more important than ever to constitute a special commission within the heart of every Episcopal conference.

Experience also demonstrates that dialogue is carried out in many forms. There is the *doctrinal field*, which is very important for a profound understanding, and also the field of *daily relationship* among believers, who are called to mutual respect and common awareness. The dialogue of life, in fact, favors peaceful coexistence and *working together* for a more just society, so that a person might grow in being and not in having. The family deserves particular attention in this area. These frequent domestic relationships enable one to know people in their history and their values and to compare them with the Gospel. In consistency with one's own faith, it is also possible to enrich one another through comparing *spiritual experiences* and sharing forms of prayer as ways of meeting with God.

All Christians are called to dialogue. Some have an expertise which is very useful, while others make a notable contribution through their special gifts. I am thinking particularly of *intermonastic dialogue* and of other movements, groups and institutions. Adequate preparation and a constant deepening of one's own ecclesial identity is necessary for all.

Dialogue with non-Christians can also be a way of realizing unity among Christian churches which are moved by the same love of Christ. Mutual collaboration in this area is evident through the participation in this Plenary Assembly by the director of the corresponding sub-unit of the World Council of Churches. But dialogue is not an easy thing. Religion itself can be made an instrument and become the excuse for polarization and division. In the current world situation, to engage in dialogue means learning to forgive, since all the religious communities can point to possible wrongs suffered through the centuries. It means trying to understand the hearts of others, which is particularly difficult when there is lack of agreement. It means, first of all, putting oneself at the service of all humanity and of the one God. One must not stop at easy or apparent results. This commitment is born from theological virtues and grows with them. . . .

Dialogue finds its place within the Church's salvific mission; for this reason, it is a dialogue of salvation: "Closely united with men in their life and work, Christ's disciples hope to render to others true witness of Christ and to work for their salvation, even where they are not able to proclaim Christ fully."

In this ecclesial activity, it is also necessary to avoid exclusivism and dichotomies. Authentic dialogue becomes witness, and true evangelization is accomplished by respecting and listening to one another. Even though "there is a time for everything," prudence and discernment will teach us what is appropriate in each particular situation: collaboration, witness, listening, or exchange of values. Saints like Francis of Assisi and great missionaries like Matteo Ricci and Charles de Foucauld are examples of this. When we live fully in Christ we will become ever more suitable instruments of his cooperation and we will follow his method, expressing the love of him who gave himself for us.

In this Jubilee year we cannot forget the role of dialogue for reconciliation among peoples and with God; this is an essential condition for the peaceful coexistence and unity willed by God and re-established by Christ. . . .

To the Plenary Session of the Pontifical Council
for Interreligious Dialogue
(Rome, November 13, 1992)

Interreligious dialogue at its deepest level is always a *dialogue of salvation*, because it seeks to discover, clarify and understand better the signs of the age-long dialogue which God maintains with mankind. From the Christian's point of view, it presupposes the desire to make Jesus Christ better known, recognized and loved, but it requires that this proclamation should be carried out in the Gospel spirit of understanding and peace. These ideas are amply discussed in the document *Dialogue and Proclamation*, issued by your Council in collaboration with the Congregation for the Evangelization of Peoples. I avail myself of the occasion of your Plenary Assembly to recommend this document to all the pastors of the Church. It addresses a question which has practical implications for the Catholic community in every part of the world, namely, the relationship between the Church's mission to preach salvation in Jesus Christ the Son of God, and her mission to enter a dialogue with all men and women of goodwill, with profound respect for their outlook and experience. Both aspects of the one mission are legitimate and necessary. They are intimately related but not interchangeable. *Dialogue and Proclamation* indicates how unilateral emphases should be avoided lest the Christian message itself be distorted.

Since your last Plenary Assembly, another document has been issued which touches upon the subject of interreligious dialogue.

I refer to the encyclical *Redemptoris Missio*, on the permanent validity of the Church's missionary mandate. While affirming in this encyclical that proclaiming the Gospel is the permanent priority of mission, I also stated that "interreligious dialogue is part of the Church's evangelizing mission," and that "each member of the faithful and all Christian communities are called to practice dialogue, although not always to the same degree or in the same way." It should be evident to all that interreligious dialogue has taken on a new and immediate urgency in the present historical circumstances. We can only be deeply disturbed and saddened by the resurgence of prejudices and aggressive attitudes which are sometimes preached in the name of God but which have no basis in belief in the almighty and merciful Creator. *Believers*, while remaining faithful to their own religious convictions and without falling into false irenicism, *can and should engage in a truthful, humble and frank dialogue with the followers of other religious traditions, in order to eliminate intolerance and misunderstanding.* Genuine dialogue leads to inner purification and conversion, and only such a spiritual renewal will save the world from further widespread sufferings.

I am happy to hear that you have been examining the reactions to these documents, both within the Church and among the followers of other religions. In reaffirming the validity of these teachings of the Magisterium, I encourage you to reflect on how to spread the message which is contained in them, a *message of love and respect for our brothers and sisters of other traditions.* . . .

Contact with the religions of Asia, especially Hinduism and Buddhism, which are noted for their contemplative spirit, their methods of meditation and asceticism, can contribute greatly to the inculturation of the Gospel on that continent. A wise exchange between Catholics and the followers of other traditions can help in discerning points of contact in the spiritual life and in the expression of religious beliefs, without ignoring the differences. Such a discernment is all the more urgent where people have lost their roots in their own tradition and are looking to other sources for spiritual support and enrichment. The growth of so-called new or alternative religious movements is evidence of how widespread this trend is becoming. There is a challenge here to the Christian communities of Asia. I am happy that the Pontifical Councils for Interreligious Dialogue, for Promoting Christian Unity, for Dialogue with Non-Believers and for Culture are continuing to study this phenomenon together in order to provide pastoral guidance.

This leads to a further point: the importance of theological reflection on the doctrinal foundations of the Church's efforts to promote interreligious dialogue. Catholic universities and faculties, seminaries and houses of formation, should be equipped to train leaders in the field of collaboration with other believers. . . .

Your Council can play an active part in encouraging Catholics to join with others in earnest prayer for peace, while at the same time recalling valid guidelines so that this joint prayer does not lead to religious indifferentism or a clouding of revealed truth. The truth is that "interreligious contacts, together with ecumenical dialogue, are now seen to be obligatory paths, in order to ensure that the many painful wounds inflicted over the course of centuries will not be repeated, and indeed that any such wounds still remaining will soon be healed."

Finally, I express my gratitude to you all for your Council's generous sharing in my apostolic service to the Church throughout the world. Your work contributes to the fulfillment of what I have always considered a very important part of my ministry: the fostering of more friendly relations with the followers of other religious traditions. May the Lord, through the gift of the Holy Spirit and the intercession of Mary, reward you with light, strength and joy.

To Representatives of the Various Religions of the World at the Conclusion of the World Day of Prayer for Peace
(Assisi, October 27, 1986)

In concluding this World Day of Prayer for Peace, to which you have come from many parts of the world, kindly accepting my invitation, I would like now to express my feelings, as a brother and friend, but also as a believer in Jesus Christ, and, in the Catholic Church, the first witness of faith in him.

In relation to the last prayer, the Christian one, in the series we have all heard, I profess here anew my conviction, shared by all Christians, that in Jesus Christ, as Savior of all, true peace is to be found, "peace to those who are far off and peace to those who are near" (Ephesians 2:17). His birth was greeted by the angels' song: "Glory to God in the highest and peace among men with whom he is pleased" (Luke 2:14). He preached love among all, even among foes, proclaimed blessed those who work for peace (cf. Matthew 5:9) and through his death and Resurrection he brought about reconciliation between heaven and earth (cf. Colossians 1:20). To use an expression of the Apostle Paul: "He is our peace" (Ephesians 2:14).

It is my faith conviction which has made me turn to you, representatives of the Christian churches and ecclesial communities and world religions, in deep love and respect. With the other Christians we share many convictions and, particularly, in what concerns peace. With the world religions we share a common respect for and obedience to conscience, which teaches all of us to seek the truth, to love and serve all individuals and peoples, and therefore to make peace among individuals and among nations.

Yes, we all hold that conscience and obedience to the voice of conscience is an essential element on the road toward a better and peaceful world. Could it be otherwise, since all men and women in this world have a common nature, a common origin and a common destiny? If there are many and important differences among us, there is also a common ground, whence to operate together in the solution of this dramatic challenge of our age: true peace or catastrophic war?

Yes, there is the dimension of prayer, which in the very real diversity of religions tries to express communication with a Power above all our human forces. Peace depends basically on this Power, which we call God, and as Christians believe has revealed himself in Christ. This is the meaning of this World Day of Prayer.

For the first time in history, we have come together from everywhere, Christian churches and ecclesial communities, and world religions, in this sacred place dedicated to St. Francis, to witness before the world, each according to his own conviction, to the transcendent quality of peace. The form and content of our prayers are very different, as we have seen, and there can be no question of reducing them to a kind of common denominator.

Yet, in this very difference we have perhaps discovered anew that, regarding the problem of peace and its relation to religious commitment, there is something which binds us together.

The challenge of peace, as it is currently posed to every human conscience, is the problem of a reasonable quality of life for all, the problem of survival for humanity, the problem of life and death. In the face of such a problem, two things seem to have supreme importance and both of them are common to us all.

The first is the inner imperative of the moral conscience, which enjoins us to respect, protect and promote human life, from the womb to the deathbed, for individuals and peoples, but especially for the weak, the destitute, the derelict: the imperative to overcome selfishness, greed and the spirit of vengeance.

The second common thing is the conviction that peace goes much beyond human efforts, particularly in the present plight of the world, and therefore its source and realization is to be sought in that reality beyond all of us.

This is why each of us prays for peace. Even if we think, as we do, that the relation between that reality and the gift of peace is a different one, according to our respective religious convictions, we all affirm that such a relation exists. This is what we express by praying for it.

I humbly repeat here my own conviction: peace bears the name of Jesus Christ.

But, at the same time and in the same breath, I am ready to acknowledge that Catholics have not always been faithful to this affirmation of faith. We have not always been "peacemakers."

For ourselves, therefore, but also perhaps, in a sense, for all, this encounter at Assisi is an act of *penance*. We have prayed, each in his own way; we have fasted; we have marched together.

In this way we have tried to open our hearts to the divine reality beyond us and to our fellow men and women.

Yes, while we have *fasted*, we have kept in mind the sufferings which senseless wars have brought about and are still bringing about for humanity. Thereby we have tried to be spiritually close to the millions who are the victims of hunger throughout the world.

While we *have walked in silence*, we have reflected on the path our human family treads: either in hostility, if we fail to accept one another in love; or as a common journey to our lofty destiny, if we realize that other people are our brothers and sisters. The very fact that we have come to Assisi from various quarters of the world is in itself a sign of this common path which humanity is called to tread. Either we learn to walk together in peace and harmony, or we drift apart and ruin ourselves and others. We hope that this pilgrimage to Assisi has taught us anew to be aware of the common origin and common destiny of humanity. Let us see in it an anticipation of what God would like the developing history of humanity to be: a fraternal journey in which we accompany one another toward the transcendent goal which he sets for us.

Prayer, fasting, pilgrimage. This day at Assisi has helped us to become more aware of our religious commitments. But it has also made the world, looking at us through the media, more aware of the responsibility of each religion regarding problems of war and peace. Perhaps more than ever before in history, the intrinsic link between an authentic religious attitude and the great good of peace has become evident to all.

What a tremendous weight for human shoulders to carry! But at the same time, what a marvelous, exhilarating call to follow.

Although prayer is in itself action, this does not excuse us from working for peace. Here we are acting as the heralds of the moral awareness of humanity as such, humanity that wants peace, needs peace. . . .

To Followers of Various Religions in the United States
(Los Angeles, September 16, 1987)

It is my conviction that we must make use of every opportunity to show love and respect for one another in the spirit of *Nostra Aetate* which, as the theme of our meeting affirms, is indeed alive twenty-two years after its promulgation among the documents of the Second Vatican Council. This Declaration on the Relation of the Catholic Church to Non-Christian Religions speaks of "that which people have in common and of those things which tend to promote fellowship among them" (*NA* 1). This continues to be the basis of our efforts to develop a fruitful relationship among all the great religions of the world.

As I stated earlier this year, the Catholic Church remains firmly committed to the proclamation of the Gospel and to dialogue with people of other religions: proclamation of the Gospel, because as *Nostra Aetate* points out, the Church "must ever proclaim Christ, the way, the truth, and the life" (John 14:6) in whom people find the fullness of religious life, and in whom God has "reconciled all things to himself" (cf. 2 Corinthians 5:18–19; *NA* 2); dialogue and collaboration with the followers of other religions, because of the spiritual and moral goods that we share (cf. *NA* 2). That dialogue "is a complex of human activities, all founded upon respect and esteem for people of different religions. It includes daily living together in peace and mutual help, with each bearing witness to the values learned through the experience of faith. It means a readiness to cooperate with others for the betterment of humanity, and a commitment to search together for true peace. It means the encounter of theologians and other religious specialists to explore, with their counterparts from other religions, areas of convergence and divergence. Where circumstances permit, it means a sharing of spiritual experiences and insights. This sharing can take the form of coming together as brothers and sisters to pray to God in ways which safeguard the uniqueness of each religious tradition."

Throughout my Pontificate it has been my constant concern to fulfill this twofold task of proclamation and dialogue. On my pastoral visits around the world I have sought to encourage and strengthen the faith of Catholic people and other Christians as well. At the same time, I have been pleased to meet leaders of all religions in the hope of promoting greater interreligious understanding and cooperation for the good of the human family. I was very gratified at the openness and goodwill with which the World Day of Prayer for Peace in Assisi last October was received, not only by the various Christian churches and ecclesial communities, but by other religions of the world as well. I was also pleased that another World Day of Prayer subsequently took place in Japan at Mount Hiei.

What I said in Assisi also applies to our meeting today: "The fact that we have come here does not imply any intention of seeking a religious consensus among ourselves or negotiating our faith convictions. Neither does it mean that religions can be reconciled at the level of a common commitment in an earthly project which would surpass them all. Nor is it a concession to relativism in religious beliefs, because every human being must sincerely follow his or her upright conscience with the intention of seeking and obeying the truth. Our meeting attests only — and this is its real significance for the people of our time — that in the great battle for peace, humanity, in its very diversity, must draw from its deepest and most vivifying sources where its conscience is formed and upon which is founded the moral action of all people."

It is in that spirit that I wish, through you, to greet each of your communities before saying something further about the concern for peace that we all share.

To the Buddhist community, which reflects numerous Asian traditions as well as American, I wish respectfully to acknowledge your way of life, based upon compassion and loving kindness and upon a yearning for peace, prosperity and harmony for all beings. May all of us give witness to compassion and loving kindness in promoting the true good of humanity.

To the Islamic community: I share your belief that mankind owes its existence to the one, compassionate God who created heaven and earth. In a world in which God is denied or disobeyed, in a world that experiences so much suffering and so greatly needs God's mercy, let us then strive together to be courageous bearers of hope.

To the Hindu community: I hold in esteem your concern for inner peace and for the peace of the world, based not on purely mechanistic or materialistic political considerations, but on self-purification, unselfishness, love and sympathy for all. May the minds of all people be imbued with such love and understanding.

To the Jewish community: I repeat the Second Vatican Council's conviction that the Church "cannot forget that she received the revelation of the Old Testament through the people with whom God in his mercy established the Ancient Covenant. Nor can she forget that she draws sustenance from the root of that good olive tree onto which has been grafted the wild olive branches of the Gentiles" (cf. Romans 11:17–24; NA 4). With you, I oppose every form of anti-Semitism. May we work for the day when all peoples and nations may enjoy security, harmony and peace.

Dear brothers and sisters of these religions and of every religion: so many people today experience inner emptiness even amid material prosperity because they overlook the great questions of life: "What is man? What is the meaning and purpose of life? What is goodness and what is sin? What is the path to true happiness? What is death, judgment and retribution after death? What, finally, is that ultimate, ineffable mystery which embraces our existence, from which we take our origin and toward which we move?" (NA 1).

These profoundly spiritual questions, which are shared to some degree by all religions, also draw us together in a common concern for man's earthly welfare, especially world peace. As I said at Assisi, with the "world religions we share a common respect for and obedience to conscience, which teaches all of us to seek the truth, to love and serve all individuals and peoples, and therefore to make peace among individuals and among nations. . . . "

Message to the Peoples of Asia
(Manila, February 21, 1981)

Coming to the peoples of Asia — just as all those before me who, in different periods of history, proclaimed here Jesus Christ — I encounter today, in the same way, the local heritage and the ancient cultures that contain praiseworthy elements of spiritual growth, indicating the paths of life and conduct that are often so near to those found in the Gospel of Christ. Different religions have tried to respond to man's search for the ultimate explanation of creation and the meaning of man's journey through life. Hinduism uses philosophy to answer man, and Hindus practice asceticism and meditation in their ascent toward God. Buddhism teaches that by devout confidence man ascends to freedom and enlightenment. Other religions follow similar routes. Muslims adore the one God and associate themselves with Abraham, revering Christ and honoring Mary, professing esteem for moral living, prayer and fasting. The Catholic Church accepts the truth and goodness found in these religions, and she sees reflections there of the truth of Christ, whom she proclaims as "the way and the truth and the life" (John 14:6). She wishes to do everything possible to cooperate with other believers in preserving all that is good in their religions and cultures, stressing the things that are held in common, and helping all people to live as brothers and sisters.

The Church of Jesus Christ in this age experiences a profound need to enter *into contact and dialogue with all these religions.* She pays homage to the many moral virtues contained in these religions, as well as to the potential for spiritual living which so deeply marks the traditions and the cultures of whole societies. What seems to bring together and unite, in a particular way, Christians and the believers of other religions is an acknowledgement of the *need for prayer* as an expression of man's spirituality directed toward the Absolute. Even when, for some, he is the Great Unknown, he nevertheless remains always in reality the same living God. We trust that wherever the human spirit opens itself in prayer to this Unknown God, an echo will be heard of the same Spirit who, knowing the limits and weakness of the human person, himself prays in us and on our behalf, "expressing our plea in a way that could never be put into words" (Romans 8:26). The intercession of the Spirit of God who prays in us and for us is the fruit of the mystery of the redemption of Christ, in which the all-embracing love of the Father has been shown to the world.

All Christians must therefore be committed to dialogue with the believers of all religions, so that mutual understanding and collaboration may grow; so that moral values may be strengthened; so that God may be praised in all creation. Ways must be developed to make this dialogue become a reality everywhere, but especially in Asia, the continent that is the cradle of ancient cultures and religions. Likewise the Catholics and the Christians of other churches must join together in the search for full unity, in order that Christ may become ever more manifest in the love of his followers. The divisions that still exist between those who profess the name of Jesus Christ must be felt as an incentive to fervent prayer and to conversion of heart, so that a more perfect witness to the Gospel may be given. Christians will, moreover, join hands with all men and women of goodwill who share a belief in the inestimable dignity of each human person. They will work together in order to bring about a more just and peaceful society in which the poor will be the first to be served. Asia is the continent where the spiritual is held in high esteem and where the religious sense is deep and innate: the preservation of this precious heritage must be the common task of all.

In recalling the great spiritual and religious traditions of Asia, and in urging fraternal collaboration among all its inhabitants, I would also address the problems that still face the many nations of Asia and the continent as a whole. Economic difficulties and the persisting need for more rapid and wholesome development have rightly preoccupied your leaders and your peoples. Poverty still weighs heavily on large groups and classes in many countries. Not only are there wide contrasts in the social and economic situation of different nations, but also within individual countries great numbers of people still lack the basic minimum that is necessary for human beings to live in dignity and to take part in the advancement of their own community. Hunger is still a tragic reality for many parents and children, as is the lack of decent housing, health care and educational facilities. Great efforts have been made, various models have been applied, new ideologies have been adopted, but the results have not always been satisfactory. In some areas, economic progress has not been accompanied by an improvement in the quality of life; sometimes, in fact, it has unfortunately obscured important and essential values.

I cannot finish without sending a heartfelt greeting to my brothers and sisters in the Christian faith, to *all those with whom I confess the name of Jesus Christ* and, in particular, to those whom I love as the members of the Church that I have been called to guide and serve. To all the Catholic bishops, priests, religious and lay men and women I say: the Lord be with you! *Pax Domini sit semper vobiscum!* From her very beginning, the Church has been present in Asia, and you are the successors of the early Christians who spread the Gospel message of love and service throughout Asia. In many parts of this continent you are small in number, but in every country the Church has taken root. In the members of his Church — in you — Christ is Asian.

Christ and his Church cannot be alien to any people, nation or culture. Christ's message belongs to everyone and is addressed to everyone. The Church's mission is to proclaim Jesus Christ, born of the Virgin Mary, as the eternal Son of God and Savior of the world; to bear witness to his sacrificial love; to render service in his name. Like Christ, her teacher, the Church desires the well-being of all humanity. Wherever she is, the Church must sink her roots deeply into the spiritual and cultural soil of the country, assimilate all genuine values, enriching them also with the insights that she received from Jesus Christ, who is "the way and the truth and the life" (John 14:6) for all humanity. The Church's members will be at one and the same time good Christians and good citizens, making their contribution to building the society of which they are full members. They will want to be, in every society, the best sons and daughters of their homeland, working unselfishly in collaboration with others for the true good of the country.

The Church does not claim any privileges; she wants only to be free and unimpaired in pursuing her own mission. The principle of freedom of conscience and of religion is enshrined in the laws and customs of most of the nations. May it effectively guarantee to all the sons and daughters of the Catholic Church the free and public profession of their faith and their religious convictions. This also entails for the Church the possibility of freely establishing educational and charitable programs and institutions; moreover, these activities will benefit the interests of society as a whole. Christians see it indeed as their task to contribute to safeguarding sound morality in personal, family and social life. They see it as their duty to serve God in their brothers and sisters.

As true sons and daughters of their nation, true children of Asia, Christians give an eloquent testimony to the fact that the Gospel of Christ and the teaching of the Church flourish in the hearts and consciences of the people of every nation under the sun.

Many men and women have testified to this *truth by laying down their lives for the sake of Christ* in different places on the Asian continent. They did this in the same way as others before them did, during the first centuries of Christianity in Rome, or in the course of two millennia in different places around the world. My present pilgrimage in Asia is intimately bound to the Christian witness of faith given by the Japanese martyrs. The Church honors them with the conviction that the sacrifice of their lives will help to obtain salvation and peace, faith and love for all the people of this continent.

My final word is a *prayer for Asia*. Upon the heads of State and the governments of Asia, I invoke wisdom and strength, that they may lead their nations toward full human well-being and progress. Upon the leaders of the religions in Asia, I invoke assistance from on high, that they may always encourage believers in their quest for the Absolute. I pray that the parents and children of Asia will grow in love for each other and in service to their fellow citizens. And I commend to the almighty and merciful God the dignity and destiny of every man, woman and child on this continent — the dignity and destiny of all Asia!

Letter to the Bishops of Asia
(Rome, June 23, 1990)

The question of human rights prompts us to note the signs of *religious intolerance* manifested in some Asian countries. Under the pressure of particular groups, for example, certain governments in nations where there are many followers of Islam have assumed postures which seem not in keeping with that tolerance which is a part of the venerable Islamic tradition. Attempts are sometimes made to change legislation, introducing policies which effectively deny the rights of religious minorities. The intransigent attitudes of some, which leave no room for other religions, recognize as authentically Asian only that which can be expressed within their own religious categories. The regrettable phenomenon of intolerance is not, however, restricted to any single religious tradition.

On the eve of the third Christian millennium, an ever greater commitment to evangelization is imperative for all the local Churches in Asia which, though small, have shown themselves to be dynamic and strong in their witness to the Gospel. Their special challenge is to proclaim the Good News where different religions and cultures meet, at the crossroads of social, political and economic forces in today's world. In the light of this fundamental duty, your meeting is an opportunity to seek new ways of strengthening awareness in the local Churches of the need for first evangelization. Although the Church gladly acknowledges whatever is true and holy in the religious traditions of Buddhism, Hinduism and Islam as a reflection of that truth which enlightened all men, this does not lessen her duty and resolve to proclaim without fail Jesus Christ who is "the way, and the truth, and life" (John 14:6; *NA* 2). We should not forget Pope Paul VI's teaching on the matter: "Neither respect and esteem for these religions nor the complexity of the questions raised is an invitation to the Church to withhold from these non-Christians the proclamation of Jesus Christ." The fact that the followers of other religions can receive God's grace and be saved by Christ apart from the ordinary means which he has established does not thereby cancel the call to faith and baptism which God wills for all people. It is a contradiction of the Gospel and of the Church's very nature to assert, as some do, that the Church is only one way of salvation among many, and that her mission toward the followers of other religions should be nothing more than to help them to be better followers of those religions.

2

John Paul II on Buddhism

From *Crossing the Threshold of Hope*

Among the religions mentioned in the Council document *Nostra Aetate,* it is necessary to pay special attention to *Buddhism,* which from a certain point of view, like Christianity, is a religion of salvation. Nevertheless, it needs to be said right away that the doctrines of salvation in Buddhism and Christianity are opposed.

The *Dalai Lama,* spiritual leader of the Tibetans, is a well-known figure in the West. I have met him a few times. He brings Buddhism to people of the Christian West, stirring up interest both in Buddhist spirituality and in its methods of praying. I also had the chance to meet the Buddhist "patriarch" in Bangkok, Thailand, and among the monks that surrounded him there were several, for example, who came from the United States. Today we are seeing a certain *diffusion of Buddhism in the West.*

The *Buddhist doctrine of salvation* constitutes the central point, or rather the only point, of this system. Nevertheless, both the Buddhist tradition and the methods deriving from it have an almost exclusively *negative soteriology.*

The "enlightenment" experienced by Buddha comes down to the conviction that the world is bad, that it is the source of evil and of suffering for man. To liberate oneself from this evil, one must free oneself from this world, necessitating a break with the ties that join us to external reality — ties existing in our human nature, in our psyche, in our bodies. The more we are liberated from these ties, the more we become indifferent to what is in the world, and the more we are freed from suffering, from the evil that has its source in the world.

Do we draw near to God in this way? This is not mentioned in the "enlightenment" conveyed by Buddha. Buddhism is in large measure an *"atheistic" system*. We do not free ourselves from evil through the good which comes from God; we liberate ourselves only through detachment from the world, which is bad. The fullness of such a detachment is not union with God, but what is called nirvana, a state of perfect indifference with regard to the world. *To save oneself* means, above all, to free oneself from evil by becoming *indifferent to the world, which is the source of evil*. This is the culmination of the spiritual process.

At various times, attempts to link this method with the Christian mystics have been made — whether it is with those from northern Europe (Eckhart, Tauler, Suso, Ruysbroeck) or the later Spanish mystics (Saint Teresa of Avila, Saint John of the Cross). But when Saint John of the Cross, in the *Ascent of Mount Carmel* and in the *Dark Night of the Soul*, speaks of the need for purification, for detachment from the world of the senses, he does not conceive of that detachment as an end in itself. "To arrive at what now you do not enjoy, you must go where you do not enjoy. To reach what you do not know, you must go where you do not know. To come into possession of what you do not have, you must go where now you have nothing." In Eastern Asia these classic texts of Saint John of the Cross have been, at times, interpreted as a confirmation of Eastern ascetic methods. But this Doctor of the Church does not merely propose detachment from the world. He proposes detachment from the world in order to unite oneself to that which is outside of the world — by this I do not mean nirvana, but a personal God. Union with Him comes about not only through purification, but through love.

Carmelite mysticism begins at the point where the reflections of Buddha end, together with his instructions for the spiritual life. In the active and passive purification of the human soul, in those specific nights of the senses and the spirit, Saint John of the Cross sees, above all, the preparation necessary for the human soul to be permeated with the living flame of love. And this is also the title of his major work — *The Living Flame of Love.*

Therefore, despite similar aspects, there is a fundamental difference. *Christian mysticism* from every period — beginning with the era of the Fathers of the Eastern and Western Church, to the great theologians of Scholasticism (such as Saint Thomas Aquinas), to the northern European mystics, to the Carmelite mystics — is not born of a purely negative "enlightenment." It is not born of an awareness of the evil which exists in man's attachment to the world through the senses, the intellect, and the spirit. Instead, Christian mysticism is born of the *Revelation of the living God*. This God opens Himself to union with man, arousing in him the capacity to be united with Him, especially by means of the theological virtues — faith, hope, and, above all, love.

Christian mysticism in every age up to our own — including the mysticism of marvelous men of action like Vincent de Paul, John Bosco, Maximilian Kolbe — has built up and continues to build up Christianity in its most essential element. It also builds up civilization, particularly "Western civilization," which is marked by a *positive approach to the world*, and which developed thanks to the achievements of science and technology, two branches of knowledge rooted both in the ancient Greek philosophical tradition and in Judeo-Christian Revelation. The truth about God the Creator of the world and about Christ the Redeemer is a powerful force which inspires a positive attitude toward creation and provides a constant impetus to strive for its transformation and perfection.

The Second Vatican Council has amply confirmed this truth. To indulge in a negative attitude toward the world, in the conviction that it is only a source of suffering for man and that he therefore must break away from it, is negative not only because it is unilateral but also because it is fundamentally contrary to the development of both man himself and the world, which the Creator has given and entrusted to man as his task.

We read in *Gaudium et Spes:* "Therefore, the *world* which [the Council] has in mind is the world *of men, of the entire human family* considered in the context of all realities; the world which is the theater of human history and which bears the marks of humanity's struggles, its defeats, and its victories; the world which the Christians believe has been created and is sustained by the Creator's love, a world enslaved by sin but liberated by the crucified and resurrected Christ in order to defeat evil, and destined, *according to the divine plan, to be transformed and to reach its fulfillment.*"

These words indicate how between Christianity and the religions of the Far East, in particular Buddhism, there is an essentially different way of perceiving the world. For Christians, the world is God's creation, redeemed by Christ. It is in the world that man meets God. Therefore he does not need to attain such an absolute detachment in order to find himself in the mystery of his deepest self. For Christianity, it does not make sense to speak of the world as a "radical" evil, since at the beginning of the world we find God the Creator who loves His creation, a God who "gave his only Son, so that everyone who believes in him might not perish but might have eternal life" (John 3:16).

For this reason it is not inappropriate *to caution* those Christians who enthusiastically *welcome certain ideas originating in the religious traditions of the Far East* — for example, techniques and methods of meditation and ascetical practice. In some quarters these have become fashionable, and are accepted rather uncritically. First one should know one's own spiritual heritage well and consider whether it is right to set it aside lightly. Here we need to recall, if only in passing, the brief but important document of the Congregation for the Doctrine of the Faith "on certain aspects of Christian meditation." Here we find a clear answer to the question "whether and how [Christian prayer] can be enriched by methods of meditation originating in different religions and cultures."

A separate issue is the *return of ancient gnostic ideas under the guise of the so-called New Age.* We cannot delude ourselves that this will lead toward a renewal of religion. It is only a new way of practicing gnosticism — that attitude of the spirit that, in the name of a profound knowledge of God, results in distorting His Word and replacing it with purely human words. Gnosticism never completely abandoned the realm of Christianity. Instead, it has always existed side by side with Christianity, sometimes taking the shape of a philosophical movement, but more often assuming the characteristics of a religion or para-religion in distinct, if not declared, conflict with all that is essentially Christian.

To a Group of Japanese Buddhists and Shintoists
(Rome, February 20, 1980)

The Catholic Church expresses her esteem for your religions and for your high spiritual values, such as purity, detachment of heart, love for the beauty of nature, and benevolence and compassion for everything that lives.

It gives me great joy to know that you have come here to carry forward your dialogue and collaboration with the Holy See's Secretariat for Non-Christians. The themes you are discussing together, each from the standpoint of his own religion, are the relationship between man and nature and the relationship between religion and culture. I am deeply convinced that these are themes of great importance for the future of our world. Indeed, this conviction of mine is reflected in my first encyclical Redemptor Hominis. Be assured, then, that I shall follow this dialogue and subsequent ones with interest and appreciation.

On this earth we are pilgrims to the Absolute and Eternal, who alone can save and satisfy the heart of the human person. Let us seek his will together for the good of all humanity. . . .

To the Leaders of the Various Religions of Korea
(Seoul, May 6, 1984)

The Catholic Church is endeavoring to engage in friendly dialogue with all the great religions that have guided mankind throughout history. This we shall continue to do, so that our mutual understanding and collaboration may increase, and so that the spiritual and moral values we uphold may continue to offer wisdom and inner strength to the men and women of our time.

Religions today have a more vital role than ever to play in a society in rapid evolution such as Korea. In a sense, just as the individual must find his true "self" by transcending himself and strive to achieve harmony with the universe and with others, so too must a society, a culture, the community of human beings, seek to foster the spiritual values that are its soul. This imperative is all the more urgent, the deeper the changes that affect life today.

In this regard, the world looks to Korea with particular interest. For the Korean people throughout history have sought, in the great ethical and religious visions of Buddhism and Confucianism, the path to the renewal of self and to the consolidation of the whole people in virtue and in nobility of purpose. The profound reverence for life and nature, the quest for truth and harmony, self-abnegation and compassion, the ceaseless striving to transcend — these are among the noble hallmarks of your spiritual tradition that have led, and will continue to lead, the nation and the people through turbulent times to the haven of peace.

Our diversity in religious and ethical beliefs calls upon all of us to foster genuine fraternal dialogue and to give special consideration to what human beings have in common and to what promotes fellowship among them (cf. *NA* 1). Such concerted effort will certainly create a climate of peace in which justice and compassion can flourish.

We Catholics have just celebrated the Jubilee Year of the Redemption. In that period of grace we have endeavored to live the gift of reconciliation granted us in Christ and have made efforts to reconcile ourselves with God and with our fellow man. Would it not be a good thing indeed, if also between believers of different traditions and between religions themselves a similar meeting of minds and hearts could be realized by our common goodwill and our duty to serve the human family's wellbeing?

When the Catholic Church proclaims Jesus Christ and enters into dialogue with believers of other religions, she does so in order to bear witness to his love for all people of all times — a love that was manifested on the cross for the reconciliation and salvation of the world. It is in this spirit that the Church seeks to promote deeper fellowship with all peoples and religions.

May I address a particular greeting to the members of the Buddhist tradition as they prepare to celebrate the festivity of the Coming of the Lord Buddha? May your rejoicing be complete and your joy fulfilled. . . .

3

John Paul II on Islam

From *Crossing the Threshold of Hope*

In the declaration *Nostra Aetate* we read: "The Church also has a high regard for the Muslims, who worship one God, living and subsistent, merciful and omnipotent, the Creator of heaven and earth" (*NA* 3). As a result of their monotheism, believers in Allah are particularly close to us. . . .

Whoever knows the Old and New Testaments, and then reads the Koran, clearly sees the *process by which it completely reduces Divine Revelation*. It is impossible not to note the movement away from what God said about Himself, first in the Old Testament through the Prophets, and then finally in the New Testament through His Son. In Islam all the richness of God's self-revelation, which constitutes the heritage of the Old and New Testaments, has definitely been set aside.

Some of the most beautiful names in the human language are given to the God of the Koran, but He is ultimately a God outside of the world, a God who is *only Majesty, never Emmanuel*, God-with-us. *Islam is not a religion of redemption.* There is no room for the Cross and the Resurrection. Jesus is mentioned, but only as a prophet who prepares for the last prophet, Muhammad. There is also mention of Mary, His Virgin Mother, but the tragedy of redemption is completely absent. For this reason not only the theology but also the anthropology of Islam is very distant from Christianity.

Nevertheless, *the religiosity of Muslims deserves respect.* It is impossible not to admire, for example, their *fidelity to prayer.* The image of believers in Allah who, without caring about time or place, fall to their knees and immerse themselves in prayer remains a model for all *those who invoke the* true God, in particular for those Christians who, having deserted their magnificent cathedrals, pray only a little or not at all.

The Council has also called for the Church to have a *dialogue* with followers of the "Prophet," and the Church has proceeded to do so. We read in *Nostra Aetate:* "Even if over the course of centuries Christians and Muslims have had more than a few dissensions and quarrels, this sacred Council now urges all to forget the past and to work toward mutual understanding as well as toward the preservation and promotion of social justice, moral welfare, peace, and freedom for the benefit of all mankind" (*NA* 3). . . .

Nevertheless, concrete difficulties are not lacking. In countries where *fundamentalist movements* come to power, human rights and the principle of religious freedom are unfortunately interpreted in a very one-sided way — religious freedom comes to mean freedom to impose on all citizens the "true religion." In these countries the situation of Christians is sometimes terribly disturbing. Fundamentalist attitudes of this nature make reciprocal contacts very difficult. All the same, the Church remains always open to dialogue and cooperation.

To the People of Pakistan
(Davao, February 20, 1981)

It is especially gratifying to witness *how the bonds which unite all those who believe in God have been strengthened in recent years.* I am thinking in a particular way of the bonds of dialogue and trust which have been forged between the Catholic Church and Islam. By means of dialogue we have come to see more clearly the many values, practices and teachings which both our religious traditions embrace: for example, our belief in the one almighty and merciful God, the Creator of heaven and earth, and the importance which we give to prayer, almsgiving and fasting. I pray that this mutual understanding and respect between Christians and Muslims, and indeed between all religions, will continue and grow deeper, and that we will find still better ways of cooperation and collaboration for the good of all.

To the Participants in the Symposium on "Holiness in Christianity and in Islam"
(Rome, May 9, 1985)

As I have often said in other meetings with Muslims, your God and ours is one and the same, and we are brothers and sisters in the faith of

Abraham. Thus it is natural that we have much to discuss concerning true holiness in obedience and worship to God.

All true holiness comes from God, who is called "The Holy One" in the sacred books of the Jews, Christians, and Muslims. Your holy Koran calls God "Al-Quddus," as in the verse: "He is God, besides whom there is no other, the Sovereign, the Holy, the (source of) Peace" (Koran 59, 23). The prophet Hosea links God's holiness with his forgiving love for mankind, a love which surpasses our ability to comprehend: "I am God, not man; I am the Holy One in your midst and have no wish to destroy" (Hosea 11:9). In the Sermon on the Mount, Jesus teaches his disciples that holiness consists in assuming, in our human way, the qualities of God's own holiness which he has revealed to mankind: "Be holy, even as your heavenly Father is holy" (Matthew 5:48).

Thus, the Koran calls you to uprightness (*al-salah*), to conscientious devotion (*al-taqwa*), to goodness (*al-husn*), and to virtue (*al-birr*), which is described as believing in God, giving one's wealth to the needy, freeing captives, being constant in prayer, keeping one's word, and being patient in times of suffering, hardship and violence (Koran 2, 177). Similarly, St. Paul stresses the love we must show toward all, and the duty to lead a blameless life in the sight of God: "May the Lord be generous in increasing your love and make you love one another and the whole human race as much as we love you. And may he so confirm your hearts in holiness that you may be blameless in the sight of our God and Father when our Lord Jesus Christ comes with all his saints" (1 Thessalonians 3:12–13).

In today's world, it is more important than ever that men and women of faith, assisted by God's grace, should strive for true holiness. Self-centered tendencies, such as greed, the lust for power and prestige, competition, revenge, the lack of forgiveness, and the quest for earthly pleasures — all these threaten to turn mankind from the path to goodness and holiness which God has intended for all of us. The countless numbers of good people around the world — Christians, Muslims, and others — who quietly lead lives of authentic obedience, praise, and thanksgiving to God and selfless service of their neighbor, offer humanity a genuine alternative, "God's way," to a world which otherwise would be destroyed in self-seeking, hatred, and struggle.

May the God of holiness bless your efforts throughout these days!

To the Young Muslims of Morocco
(Casablanca, August 19, 1985)

I often meet young people, usually Catholics. It is the first time that I find myself with young Muslims.

Christians and Muslims have many things in common, as believers and as human beings. We live in the same world, marked by many signs of hope, but also by multiple signs of anguish. For us, Abraham is a model of faith in God, of submission to his will and of confidence in his goodness. We believe in the same God, the one God, the living God, the God who created the world and brings his creatures to their perfection.

It is therefore toward this God that my thought goes and that my heart rises. It is of God himself that, above all, I wish to speak with you; of him, because it is in him that we believe, you Muslims and we Catholics. I wish also to speak with you about human values, which have their basis in God, these values which concern the blossoming of our person, as also that of our families and our societies, as well as that of the international community. The mystery of God — is it not the highest reality from which depends the very meaning which man gives to his life? And is it not the first problem that presents itself to a young person, when he reflects upon the mystery of his own existence and on the values which he intends to choose in order to build his growing personality? . . .

In a world which desires unity and peace, but which experiences a thousand tensions and conflicts, should not believers favor friendship between the men and the peoples who form one single community on earth? We know that they have one and the same origin and one and the same final end: the God who made them and who waits for them, because he will gather them together.

For its part, the Catholic Church, twenty years ago at the time of the Second Vatican Council, undertook in the person of its bishops, that is, of its religious leaders, to seek collaboration among believers. It published a *document on dialogue between the religions, Nostra Aetate*. It affirms that all men, especially those of living faith, should respect each other, should rise above all discrimination, should live in harmony and serve the universal brotherhood (cf. *NA* 5). The Church shows particular attention to the believing Muslims, given their faith in the one God, their sense of prayer, and their esteem for the moral life (cf. *NA* 3). It desires that Christians and Muslims together "promote harmony for all men, social justice, moral values, peace and liberty" (*NA* 3).

Dialogue between Christians and Muslims is today more necessary than ever. It flows from our fidelity to God and supposes that we know how to recognize God by faith, and to witness to him by word and deed in a world ever more secularized and at times even atheistic.

The young can build a better future if they first put their faith in God and if they pledge themselves to build this new world in accord with God's plan, with wisdom and trust.

Today we should witness to the spiritual values of which the world has need. The first is *our faith in God.*

God is the source of all joy. We should also witness to our worship of God, by our adoration, our prayer of praise and supplication. Man cannot live without prayer, any more than he can live without breathing. We should witness to *our humble search for his will;* it is he who should inspire our pledge for a more just and more united world. God's ways are not always our ways. They transcend our actions, which are always incomplete, and the intentions of our heart, which are always imperfect. God can never be used for our purposes, for he is above all.

This witness of faith, which is vital for us and which can never tolerate either infidelity to God or indifference to the truth, is made with respect for the other religious traditions. Everyone hopes to be respected for what he is in fact, and for what he conscientiously believes. We desire that all may reach the fullness of the divine truth, but no one can do that except through the free adherence of conscience, protected from exterior compulsions which would be unworthy of the free homage of reason and of heart which is characteristic of human dignity. There is the true meaning of religious liberty, which at the same time respects God and man. God awaits the sincere veneration of such worshippers in spirit and in truth.

We are convinced that "we cannot truly pray to God the Father of all mankind, if we treat any people in other than brotherly fashion, for all mankind is created in God's image" (*NA* 5).

Therefore, we must also *respect, love and help every human being,* because he is a creature of God. In a certain sense, each person is God's image and representative, because he is the road leading to God, and because he does not fully fulfill himself unless he knows God, unless he accepts him with all his heart, and unless he obeys him to the extent of the ways of perfection.

Furthermore, this obedience to God and this love for man should lead us *to respect man's rights.* These rights are the expression of God's will and the demands of human nature such as it was created by God.

Therefore, respect and dialogue require reciprocity in all spheres, especially in that which concerns basic freedoms, more particularly religious freedom. They favor peace and agreement between the peoples. They help to resolve together the problems of today's men and women, especially those of the young. . . .

Man is a *spiritual being*. We believers know that we do not live in a closed world. We believe in God. We are worshippers of God. We are seekers of God.

The Catholic Church regards with respect and *recognizes the equality of your religious progress*, the richness of your spiritual tradition. We Christians, also, are proud of our own religious tradition.

I believe that we, Christians and Muslims, must recognize with joy the religious values that we have in common, and give thanks to God for them. Both of us believe in one God, the only God, who is all justice and all mercy; we believe in the importance of prayer, of fasting, of almsgiving, of repentance and of pardon; we believe that God will be a merciful judge to us at the end of time, and we hope that after the resurrection he will be satisfied with us and we know that we will be satisfied with him.

Loyalty demands also that we should recognize and respect our differences. Obviously the most fundamental is the view that we hold on the person and work of Jesus of Nazareth. You know that, for Christians, Jesus causes them to enter into an intimate knowledge of the mystery of God and into a filial communion by his gifts, so that they recognize him and proclaim him Lord and Savior.

Those are important differences, which we can accept with humility and respect, in mutual tolerance; this is a mystery about which, I am certain, God will one day enlighten us.

Christians and Muslims, in general we have badly understood each other, and sometimes, in the past, we have opposed and even exhausted each other in polemics and in wars.

I believe that today, God invites us *to change our old practices*. We must respect each other, and we must also stimulate each other in good works on the path of God.

With me, you know the reward of spiritual values. Ideologies and slogans cannot satisfy you nor can they solve the problems of your life. Only spiritual and moral values can do it, and they have God as their foundation.

Dear young people, I wish that you may be able to help in building a world where God may have first place in order to aid and to save mankind. On this path, you are assured of the esteem and the collaboration of your Catholic brothers and sisters whom I represent among you this evening. . . .

To the Delegation of the World Islamic Call Society
(Rome, January 15, 1990)

Since we are believers in God — who is Goodness and Perfection — all our activities must reflect the holy and upright nature of the one whom we worship and seek to obey. For this reason, also in the works of mission and *da'wah*, our actions must be founded upon a respect for the inalienable dignity and freedom of the human person created and loved by God. Both Christians and Muslims are called to defend the inviolable right of each individual to freedom of religious belief and practice.

There have been in the past, and there continue to be in the present, unfortunate instances of misunderstanding, intolerance and conflict between Christians and Muslims, especially in circumstances where either Muslims or Christians are a minority or are guest workers in a given country. It is our challenge as religious leaders to find ways to overcome such difficulties in a spirit of justice, brotherhood and mutual respect. Hence, by considering the proper means of carrying mission and *da'wah*, you are dealing with an issue which is important both for religious and for social harmony.

You have also been addressing the difficulties faced today by those who believe in God in their efforts to proclaim his presence and his will for mankind. As believers, we do not deny or reject any of the real benefits which modern developments have brought, but we are convinced nevertheless that without reference to God modern society is unable to lead men and women to the goal for which they have been created.

It is here too that Christians and Muslims can work together, bearing witness before modern civilization to the divine presence and loving Providence which guide our steps. Together we can proclaim that he who has made us has called us to live in harmony and justice. May the blessings of the Most High accompany you in your endeavors on behalf of dialogue and peace!

Message to the Faithful of Islam
at the End of the Month of Ramadan
(Rome, April 3, 1991)

Every year it is the custom of the Pontifical Council for Interreligious Dialogue to send a message of greetings, on behalf of the Catholics around the world, to Muslims on the occasion of your Feast of the Breaking of the Fast at the end of the month of Ramadan. This year, because of the tragic effects of the past months of conflict and war in the Middle East, and the continued suffering of so many, I have decided to send you these greetings myself.

First of all, I wish to express my sympathy and solidarity with all those who have lost loved ones. As you Muslims believe, so do we Christians affirm with hope that they have returned to the merciful judgment of God. May this time of mourning be tempered by the awareness that God's mercy and love are without limit. He alone knows "that which he has prepared for his chosen ones, what no eye has seen, no ear has heard, things beyond the mind of humans" (1 Corinthians 2:9).

To all Muslims throughout the world, I wish to express the readiness of the Catholic Church to work together with you and all people of goodwill to aid the victims of the war and to build structures of a lasting peace, not only in the Middle East, but everywhere. This cooperation in solidarity toward the most afflicted can form the concrete basis for a sincere, profound and constant dialogue between believing Catholics and believing Muslims, from which there can arise a strengthened mutual knowledge and trust, and the assurance that each one everywhere will be able to profess, freely and authentically, his or her own faith.

You who have completed the arduous month of fasting according to the dictates of your religion give to modern societies a needed example of obedience to God's will, to the importance of prayer and self-discipline, and to an ascetical simplicity in the use of this world's goods. We Christians have also recently completed our annual Lenten season of prayer and fasting, which is for us a time of repentance and purification. We Christians and Muslims share these values, according to our respective religious beliefs and traditions, and which we offer humanity as a religious alternative to the attractions of power, wealth and material pleasures.

The path of those who believe in God and desire to serve him is not that of domination. It is the way of peace: a union of peace with our Creator expressed in doing his will; peace within the whole created universe, by using its benefits wisely and for the good of all; peace within the human family, by working together to build strong bonds of justice, fraternity, and harmony within our societies; peace in the hearts of all individuals, who know from whom they have come, why they are on this earth, and to whom they will one day return. On this feast, my

Muslim brothers and sisters, our prayer is that God will grant his peace to you and to all who turn to him in supplication....

Injustice, oppression, aggression, greed, failure to forgive, desire for revenge and unwillingness to enter into dialogue and negotiate: these are merely some of the factors which lead people to depart from the way in which God desires us to live on this planet. We must all learn to recognize these elements in our own lives and societies, and find ways to overcome them. Only when individuals and groups undertake this education for peace can we build a fraternal and united world, freed from war and violence.

I close my greeting to you with the words of one of my predecessors, Pope Gregory VII, who in 1076 wrote to Al-Nasir, the Muslim Ruler of Bijâya, present-day Algeria:

"Almighty God, who wishes that all should be saved and none lost, approves nothing in us so much as that after loving him one should love his fellow man, and that one should not do to others, what one does not want done to oneself. You and we owe this charity to ourselves especially because we believe in and confess one God, admittedly in a different way, and daily praise and venerate him, the Creator of the world and ruler of this world" (*NA* 3).

These words, written almost a thousand years ago, express my feelings to you today as you celebrate *Id al-Fitr*, the Feast of the Breaking of the Fast. May the Most High God fill us all with his merciful love and peace!

To the Islamic Leaders of Senegal
(Dakar, February 22, 1992)

It is natural that *believers in God should meet in friendship and sharing*. Christians and Muslims, together with the followers of the Jewish religion, belong to what can be called "the tradition of Abraham." In our respective traditions Abraham is called "the intimate friend of God" (in Arabic, *Al-Khalil*). He receives this title because of his flawless faith in God. Leaving his native land to go where God was leading him, Abraham always held to the conviction that God alone is to be worshipped and adored. God alone is to be obeyed. Even when given difficult tasks to perform, Abraham remained the faithful and obedient servant of God.

At the Second Vatican Council, the bishops of the Catholic Church produced a solemn Declaration on the Church's attitude to people of other religions. Referring to Muslims, this document stated: "The Church has a high esteem for Muslims, who worship God, who is one, living and subsistent, merciful and almighty, the Creator of heaven and earth, who has also spoken to men. They strive to submit themselves without reserve to the hidden decrees of God, just as Abraham submitted himself to God's plan, to whose faith Muslims eagerly link their own" (*NA* 3).

As two religious communities who strive to submit ourselves without reserve to the will of God, we Christians and Muslims should *live together in peace, friendship, and cooperation*. I am happy to note that, since the arrival of the first Christians in this land, the people of Senegal have given the world a good example of this "sharing of life...."

I would like to support and encourage all these efforts at building a harmonious society because I am convinced that this is the way of God. Our Creator and our final judge desires that we live together. *Our God is a God of peace*, who desires peace among those who live according to his commandments. *Our God is the holy God* who desires that those who call upon him live in ways that are holy and upright. He is *a God of dialogue* who has been engaged, from the very beginning of history, in a dialogue of salvation with the humanity which he created. This dialogue continues to the present day, and will go on until the end of time.

We Christians and Muslims must be people of dialogue. As I have often said, and as the bishops of Senegal have repeated, this commitment to dialogue means, first of all, "a dialogue of life," a positive acceptance, interaction and cooperation by which we bear active witness, as believers, to the ideals to which God has called us.

But our commitment to do God's will leads us beyond the task of living together in harmony. Modern life has many problems. In dialogue, we who believe in the goodness of God have a special duty to address the problems of our people and search together for solutions which can make modern society more just, more human, more respectful of the rights, dignity and human freedom of each individual.

Some of the problems facing people today are *economic*. We who believe must give special attention to our countrymen and all those in today's world who live *in poverty*. A world where some people have more than they need, while others lack even the basic necessities of life, demands that Christians and Muslims study together the redistribution of resources according to *justice*. We must be attentive to the role of governments which have the responsibility to provide for the development of their country for the good of all. We must actively promote the values of honesty and respect for human life and its essential environment. We must see to it that all citizens without discrimination on grounds of race, religions, language or gender, have the same opportunities for good education and health care, and the chance to make their own contribution to the good of all.

One of the greatest scourges of humanity in the century now drawing to a close is that of *war*. How many lives have been lost, how much destruction has been caused, how much anger and resentment have come about due to these conflicts! How many men, women and children have lost their livelihood, residence, possessions and even homelands due to these wars! Christians and Muslims have a special duty *to work for peace*, to collaborate in building the social structures, national and international, for reducing tensions and to prevent them from escalating into violent conflicts. For this reason, I encourage Christians and Muslims to take an active part in interreligious meetings and organizations which have been working and praying for peace as their goal.

However, not all the needs of mankind are material. Those who worship God are the first to acknowledge this. There is much *moral suffering* in today's world. Many people today feel lonely, disoriented and confused, hopeless, lost and abandoned. Many have lost the sense of a God who cares about them, a God of love, a God who is merciful and compassionate. We for whom God is a reality, in fact the deepest reality of our lives, must never tire of bearing witness to God's presence at the center of human life. We do not believe in an angry God of whom people must be terrified, nor an absent God who has no interest in our affairs. We believe in a God who is good, a God who is present, a God who desires to guide us along the paths which are best for us. It is true, as I said at Casablanca, that "loyalty also demands that we *recognize and respect our differences*. The most basic is obviously the regard we have for the person and work of Jesus of Nazareth." We Christians receive the Spirit from him, and it is through Jesus that we enter into intimacy with God. We believe that Jesus is Lord and Savior.

Both groups believe that God is full of mercy for those who have strayed and return to him in a spirit of humility and repentance. This is good news, a message for those who are seeking a faith which can give meaning and direction to their life. In order to *make our specifically religious contribution to society*, we must develop dialogue between Christians and Muslims. We must be ready to speak openly and frankly to one another; we must listen to one another with attentiveness and respect. Last March, I received a beautiful letter from Dr. M. Hamid Algabid, secretary-general of the Organization of the Islamic Conference (OIC) in which he promised "the availability of the member nations of the OIC to work with the Holy See to foster peace and strengthen dialogue between Christians and Muslims." This offer of collaboration we gladly accept and we encourage all Christians everywhere in the world to work together with Muslims for these important goals.

Honesty impels me to admit that Christians and Muslims have not always treated each other in ways that reflect the immense goodness of God. In some parts of the world there are still tensions between our two communities and Christians are the victims of discrimination in several countries. Muslim-Christian dialogue still must develop before we arrive at a point of true *conviviality* to ensure mutual respect for freedom of conscience and worship, with equal treatment of both groups, no matter where they live. Once again I would like to recall to you the words of the Declaration *Nostra Aetate:* "Over the centuries many quarrels and dissensions have arisen between Christians and Muslims. The sacred Council now pleads with all to forget the past, and urges that a sincere effort be made to achieve mutual understanding; for the benefit of all people, let them together preserve and promote peace, liberty, social justice and moral values" (*NA* 3).

I repeat that appeal to you today. Let us together make a sincere effort to come to a *deeper mutual understanding*. Let our collaboration for humanity, in the name of God, be a blessing and benefit for all people!

4

John Paul II on Judaism

Address to Delegates to the Meeting
of Representatives of Episcopal Conferences
and Other Experts in Catholic–Jewish Relations:
Commission for Religious Relations with the Jews
(March 6, 1982)

The links between the Church and the Jewish people are founded on the design of the God of the Covenant and — as such — have necessarily left their traces in certain aspects of the institutions of the Church, particularly in her liturgy.

Certainly, since the appearance, two thousand years ago, of a new branch from the common root, relations between our two communities have been marked by the misunderstandings and resentments with which we are familiar. And if, since the day of the separation, there have been misunderstandings, errors, indeed offenses, it is now our task to leave these behind with understanding, peace, and mutual respect. The terrible persecutions suffered by the Jews in different periods of history have finally opened the eyes of many and appalled many people's hearts. Christians have taken the right path, that of justice and brotherhood, in seeking to come together with their Semitic brethren, respectfully and perseveringly, in the common heritage that all value so highly. Should it not be pointed out, especially to those who remain skeptical, even hostile, that this reconciliation should not be confused with a sort of religious relativism, less still with a loss of identity? Christians, for their part, profess their faith unequivocally in the universal salvific significance of the death and resurrection of Jesus of Nazareth.

Yes, the clarity and affirmation of our Christian identity constitute an essential basis if we are to have real, productive, and durable ties with the Jewish people. In this sense, I am happy to know that you dedicate much effort in study and prayer together, the better to grasp and formulate the sometimes complex biblical and theological problems which have arisen because of the very progress of Judeo-Christian dialogue. Work that is of poor quality or lacking in precision would be extremely detrimental to dialogue in this field. May God allow Christians and Jews really to come together, to arrive at an exchange in depth, founded on their respective identities, but never blurring it on either side, truly searching the will of God the Revealer.

Such relations can and should contribute to a richer knowledge of our own roots, and will certainly cast light on some aspects of the Christian identity just mentioned. Our common spiritual patrimony is very large.

To assess it carefully in itself and with due awareness of the faith and religious life of the Jewish people as they are professed and practiced still today can greatly help us to understand better certain aspects of the life of the Church. Such is the case of liturgy whose Jewish roots remain still to be examined in depth, and in any case should be better known and appreciated, by our faithful. The same is true of the history of our institutions which, since the beginning of the Church, have been inspired by certain aspects of the synagogue community organization. Finally, our common spiritual patrimony is particularly important when we turn to our belief in only one God, good and merciful, who loves men and is loved by them (cf. Wisdom of Solomon 24:26), Lord of history and of the destinies of men, who is our Father and who chose Israel, "the good olive tree onto which have been grafted the wild olive branches, those of the gentiles" (*NA* 4; cf. also Romans 11:17–24)....

It is ultimately on such a basis that it will be possible to establish — as we know is happily already the case — a close collaboration toward which our common heritage directs us, in service of man and his vast spiritual and material needs. Through different but finally convergent ways we will be able to reach, with the help of the Lord who has never ceased to love his people (cf. Romans 11:1), this true brotherhood in reconciliation and respect and to contribute to a full implementation of God's plan in history....

To Representatives of the Jewish Community of Rome
(April 13, 1986)

First of all, I would like, together with you, to give thanks and praise to the Lord who stretched out the heavens and laid the foundations of the earth (cf. Isaiah 51:16) and who chose Abraham in order to make him father of a multitude of children, as numerous "as the stars of heaven and as the sand which is on the seashore" (Genesis 22:17; cf. Genesis 15:5), to give thanks and praise to him because it has been his good pleasure, in the mystery of his Providence, that this evening there should be a meeting in your "Major Temple" between the Jewish community that has been living in this city since the times of the ancient Romans and the Bishop of Rome and universal Pastor of the Catholic Church. . . .

In the light of the Word of God that has just been proclaimed and that lives for ever (cf. Isaiah 30:8), I would like us to reflect together, in the presence of the Holy One — may he be blessed! (as your liturgy says) — on the fact and the significance of this meeting between the Bishop of Rome, the Pope, and the Jewish community that lives and works in this city which is so dear to you and to me.

I had been thinking of this visit for a long time. In fact, the Chief Rabbi was kind enough to come and see me, in February 1981, when I paid a pastoral visit to the nearby parish of San Carlo. In addition, a number of you have been to the Vatican more than once, on the occasions of the numerous audiences that I have had with representatives of Italian and world Jewry, and still earlier, in the time of my predecessors Paul VI, John XXIII and Pius XII. I am likewise well aware that the Chief Rabbi, on the night before the death of Pope John, did not hesitate to go to St. Peter's Square. Accompanied by members of the Jewish faithful, he mingled with the crowd of Catholics and other Christians, in order to pray and keep vigil, as it were bearing witness, in a silent but very effective way, to the greatness of soul of that Pontiff, who was open to all people without distinction, and in particular to the Jewish brethren.

The heritage that I would now like to take up is precisely that of Pope John, who on one occasion, as he passed by here — as the Chief Rabbi has just mentioned — stopped the car so that he could bless the crowd of Jews who were coming out of this Temple. I would like to take up his heritage at this moment, when I find myself not just outside, but, thanks to your generous hospitality, inside the Synagogue of Rome.

This gathering in a way brings to a close, after the Pontificate of John XXIII and the Second Vatican Council, a long period which we must not tire of reflecting upon in order to draw appropriate lessons from it. Certainly we cannot and should not forget that the historical circumstances of the past were very different from those that have laboriously matured over the centuries. The general acceptance of a legitimate plurality on the social, civil and religious levels has been arrived at with great difficulty. Nevertheless, a consideration of centuries-long cultural conditioning could not prevent us from recognizing that acts of discrimination, unjustified limitation of religious freedom, oppression also on the level of civil freedom in regard to the Jews were, from an objective point of view, gravely deplorable manifestations. Yes, once again, through myself, the Church, in the words of the well-known Declaration *Nostra Aetate,* "deplores the hatred, persecutions, and displays of anti-Semitism directed against the Jews at any time and by anyone"; I repeat: "by anyone" (*NA* 4).

I would like once more to express a word of abhorrence for the genocide decreed against the Jewish people during the last war, which led to the holocaust of millions of innocent victims.

When I visited the concentration camp at Auschwitz on June 7, 1979, and prayed for the many victims from various nations, I paused in particular before the memorial stone with the inscription in Hebrew and thus manifested the sentiments of my heart: "This inscription stirs the memory of the people whose sons and daughters were destined to total extermination. This people has its origin in Abraham, who is our father in faith (cf. Romans 4:12), as Paul of Tarsus expressed it. This people, which received from God the commandment: 'Thou shalt not kill,' has experienced in itself to a particular degree what killing means. Before this inscription it is not permissible for anyone to pass by with indifference."

The Jewish community of Rome, too, paid a high price in blood. It was surely a significant gesture that in those dark years of racial persecution the doors of our religious houses, of our churches, of the Roman seminary, of buildings belonging to the Holy See and of Vatican City itself were thrown open to offer refuge and safety to so many Jews of Rome being hunted by their persecutors.

Today's visit is meant to make a decisive contribution to the consolidation of the good relations between our two communities, in imitation of the example of so many men and women who have worked and who are still working today, on both sides, to overcome old prejudices and to secure ever wider and fuller recognition of that "bond" and that "common spiritual patrimony" that exists between Jews and Christians.

This is the hope expressed in the fourth paragraph of the Council's Declaration *Nostra Aetate,* which I have just mentioned, on the relationship of the Church to non-Christian religions. The decisive turning-point in relations between the Catholic Church and Judaism, and with individual Jews, was occasioned by this brief but incisive paragraph.

We are all aware that, among the riches of paragraph four of *Nostra Aetate,* three points are especially relevant. I would like to underline them here, before you, in this truly unique circumstance.

The first is that the Church of Christ discovers her "bond" with Judaism by "searching into her own mystery" (*NA* 4). The Jewish religion is not "extrinsic" to us, but in a certain way is "intrinsic" to our own religion. With Judaism, therefore, we have a relationship which we do not have with any other religion. You are our dearly beloved brothers and, in a certain way, it could be said that you are our elder brothers.

The second point noted by the Council is that no ancestral or collective blame can be imputed to the Jews as a people for "what happened in Christ's passion" (*NA* 4) — not indiscriminately to the Jews of that time, nor to those who came afterwards, nor to those of today. So any alleged theological justification for discriminatory measures or, worse still, for acts of persecution is unfounded. The Lord will judge each one "according to his own works," Jews and Christians alike (cf. Romans 2:6).

The third point that I would like to emphasize in the Council's declaration is a consequence of the second. Notwithstanding the Church's awareness of her own identity, it is not lawful to say that the Jews are "repudiated or cursed," as if this is taught or could be deduced from the Sacred Scriptures of Old or the New Testament (*NA* 4). Indeed, the Council has already said in this same text of *Nostra Aetate,* but also in the Dogmatic Constitution *Lumen Gentium,* referring to St. Paul in the Letter to the Romans (Romans 11:28–29), that the Jews are "beloved of God," who has called them with an "irrevocable calling."

Our present relations rest on these convictions. On the occasion of this visit to your Synagogue, I wish to reaffirm them and to proclaim them in their perennial value. This is the meaning which is to be attributed to my visit to you, to the Jews of Rome.

It is not of course because the differences between us have now been overcome that I have come among you. We know well that this is not so. First of all, each of our religions, in the full awareness of the many bonds which unite them to each other, and in the first place that "bond" which the Council spoke of, wishes to be recognized and respected in its own identity, beyond any syncretism and any ambiguous appropriation.

Furthermore, it is necessary to say that the path undertaken is still at the beginning. Therefore a considerable amount of time will still be needed, notwithstanding the great efforts already made on both sides, to remove all forms of prejudice, even subtle ones, to readjust every manner of self-expression and therefore to present always and everywhere, to ourselves and to others, the true face of the Jews and of Judaism, as likewise of Christians and of Christianity, and this at every level of outlook, teaching and communication.

In this regard, I would like to remind my brothers and sisters of the Catholic Church, including those living in Rome, that the guidelines for implementing the Council in this precise field are already available to everyone in the two documents published respectively in 1974 and in 1985, by the Holy See's Commission for Religious Relations with Judaism. It is only a question of studying them carefully, of immersing oneself in their teachings and of putting them into practice.

Perhaps there still remain between us difficulties of the practical order waiting to be overcome on the level of fraternal relations. These are the result of centuries of mutual misunderstanding, and also of different positions and attitudes, not easily settled, in complex and important matters.

No one is unaware that the fundamental difference from the very beginning has been the attachment of us Catholics to the person and teaching of Jesus of Nazareth, a son of your people, from which were also born the Virgin Mary, the apostles who are the "foundations and pillars of the Church" and the greater part of the first Christian community. But this attachment is located in the order of faith, that is to say in the free assent of the mind and heart guided by the Spirit, and it can never be the object of exterior pressure, in one sense or the other. This is the reason why we wish to deepen dialogue in loyalty and friendship, in respect for one another's intimate convictions, taking as a fundamental basis the elements of the revelation which we have in common, as a "great spiritual patrimony" (cf. *NA* 4).

It must be said, then, that the ways opened for our collaboration, in the light of our common heritage drawn from the Law and the prophets, are various and important. We wish to recall first of all a collaboration in favor of man, his life from conception until natural death, his dignity, freedom, rights, and self-development in a society which is not hostile but friendly and favorable, where justice reigns and where, in this nation, on the various continents and throughout the world, peace rules, the shalom hoped for by the lawmakers, prophets and wise men of Israel.

More in general, there is the problem of morality, the great field of individual and social ethics. We are all aware of how acute the crisis is on this point in the age in which we are living. In a society which is often lost in agnosticism and individualism and which is suffering the bitter consequences of selfishness and violence, Jews and Christians are the trustees and witnesses of an ethic marked by the Ten Commandments, in the observance of which man finds his truth and freedom. To promote a common reflection and collaboration on this point is one of the great duties of the hour.

Finally, I wish to address a thought to this city in which the Catholic community with its bishop, and the Jewish community with its authorities and its Chief Rabbi live side by side. Let this not be a mere "coexistence," a kind of juxtaposition, interspersed with limited and occasional meetings, but let it be animated by fraternal love.

The problems of Rome are many. You know this well. Each one of us, in the light of that blessed heritage to which I alluded earlier, is conscious of an obligation to work together, at least to some degree, for their solution. Let us seek, as far as possible, to do so together. From this visit of mine and from the harmony and serenity which we have attained may there flow forth a fresh and health-giving spring like the river that Ezekiel saw gushing from the eastern gate of the Temple of Jerusalem (cf. Ezekiel 47:1ff.), which will help to heal the wounds from which Rome is suffering.

In doing this, I venture to say, we shall each be faithful to our most sacred commitments, and also to that which most profoundly unites and gathers us together: faith in the one God who "loves strangers" and "renders justice to the orphan and the widow" (cf. Deuteronomy 10:18), commanding us also to love and help them (cf. Deuteronomy 10:18; Leviticus 19:18, 34). Christians have learned this desire of the Lord from the Torah, which you here venerate, and from Jesus, who took to its extreme consequences the love demanded by the Torah.

All that remains for me now, as at the beginning of my address, is to turn my eyes and my mind to the Lord, to thank him and praise him for this joyful meeting and for the good things which are already flowing from it, for the rediscovered brotherhood and for the new and more profound understanding between us here in Rome, and between the Church and Judaism everywhere, in every country, for the benefit of all.

Therefore, I would like to say with the Psalmist, in his original language which is also your own inheritance: *hodû la Adonai ki tob, ki le olam hasdô yomar-na Yisrael ki le olam hasdô yomerû-na yir'èh Adonai, ki le olam hasdô* (Psalms 118:1–2, 4).

"O give thanks to the Lord for he is good, his steadfast love endures for ever! Let Israel say, 'His steadfast love endures for ever.' Let those who fear the Lord say, 'His steadfast love endures for ever.'" Amen.

Address to the Jewish Community — West Germany
(November 17, 1980)

If Christians must consider themselves brothers of all men and behave accordingly, this holy obligation is all the more binding when they find themselves before members of the Jewish people! In the *Declaration on the Relationship of the Church with Judaism* in April of this year, the bishops of the Federal Republic of Germany put this sentence at the beginning: "Whoever meets Jesus Christ, meets Judaism." I would like to make these words mine, too. The faith of the Church in Jesus Christ, the son of David and the son of Abraham (cf. Matthew 1:1), actually contains what the bishops call in that declaration "the spiritual heritage of Israel for the Church," a living heritage, which must be understood and preserved in its depth and richness by us Catholic Christians.

The concrete brotherly relations between Jews and Catholics in Germany assume a quite particular value against the grim background of the persecution and the attempted extermination of Judaism in this country. The innocent victims in Germany and elsewhere, the families destroyed or dispersed, the cultural values or art treasures destroyed forever, are a tragic proof of where discrimination and contempt of human dignity can lead, especially if they are animated by perverse theories on a presumed difference in the value of races or on the division of men into men of "high worth," "worthy of living," and men who are "worthless," "unworthy of living." Before God all men are of the same value and importance.

In this spirit, during the persecution, Christians likewise committed themselves, often at the risk of their lives, to prevent or relieve the sufferings of their Jewish brothers and sisters. I would like to express recognition and gratitude to them at this moment. And also to those people who, as Christians, affirming they belonged to the Jewish people, traveled along the *via crucis* of their brothers and sisters to the end — like the great Edith Stein, called in her religious institute Teresa Benedicta of the Cross, whose memory is rightly held in great honor.

I would further like to mention also Franz Rosenzweig and Martin Buber, who, through their creative familiarity with the Jewish and German languages, constructed a wonderful bridge for a deeper meeting of both cultural areas. . . .

The depth and richness of our common heritage are revealed to us particularly in friendly dialogue and trusting collaboration. I rejoice that, in this country, conscious and zealous care is dedicated to all this. Many public and private initiatives in the pastoral, academic, and social field serve this purpose. . . .

It is not just a question of correcting a false religious view of the Jewish people, which, in the course of history, was one of the causes that contributed to misunderstanding and persecution, but above all of the dialogue between the two religions which — with Islam — gave the world faith in the one, ineffable God who speaks to us, and which desire to serve him on behalf of the whole world.

The first dimension of this dialogue, that is, the meeting between the people of God of the Old Covenant, never revoked by God (cf. Romans 11:29), and that of the New Covenant, is at the same time a dialogue within our Church, that is to say, between the first and the second part of her Bible. In this connection, the directives for the application of the conciliar declaration *Nostra Aetate* say: "The effort must be made to understand better everything in the Old Testament that has its own, permanent value . . . since this value is not wiped out by the later interpretation of the New Testament, which, on the contrary, gave the Old Testament its full meaning, so that it is a question rather of reciprocal enlightenment and explanation."

A second dimension of our dialogue — the true and central one — is the meeting between present-day Christian Churches and the present-day people of the Covenant concluded with Moses. It is important here "that Christians — to continue the post-conciliar directives — should aim at understanding better the fundamental elements of the religious tradition of Judaism, and learn what fundamental lines are essential for the religious reality lived by the Jews, according to their own understanding. . . . "

In the light of his promise and Abraham's call, I look with you to the destiny and role of your people among the peoples. I willingly pray with you for the fullness of *Shalom* for all your brothers in nationality and in faith, and also for the land to which Jews look with particular veneration. Our century saw the first pilgrimage of a pope to the Holy Land. In conclusion, I wish to repeat Paul VI's words on entering Jerusalem: "Implore with us, in your desire and in your prayer, respect and peace upon this unique land, visited by God! Let us pray here together for the grace of a real and deep brotherhood between all men, between all peoples! . . . May they who love you be blessed. Yes, may peace dwell in your walls, prosperity in your palaces. I pray for peace for you. I desire happiness for you" (cf. Psalms 122:6–9).

May all peoples in Jerusalem soon be reconciled and blessed in Abraham! May he, the ineffable, of whom his creation speaks to us: he, who does not force mankind to goodness, but guides it: he, who manifests himself in our fate and is silent; he, who chooses all of us as his people; may he guide us along his ways to his future!

"Relations with Non–Christian Religions" at General Audience
(June 5, 1986)

A special relationship — with non-Christian religions — is the one that the Church has with those who profess faith in the Old Testament, the heirs of the patriarchs and Prophets of Israel. The Council in fact recalls "the spiritual bond linking the people of the New Covenant with Abraham's stock" (*NA* 4).

This bond, to which we have already referred in the catechesis dedicated to the Old Testament, and which brings us close to the Jews, is again emphasized by the declaration *Nostra Aetate* when it refers to those common beginnings of faith, which are found in the patriarchs, Moses, and the Prophets. The Church "professes that all who believe in Christ, Abraham's sons according to faith, are included in the same patriarch's call. . . . [T]he Church cannot forget that she received the revelation of the Old Testament through the people with whom God in his inexpressible mercy designed to establish the ancient Covenant" (*NA* 4). From this same people comes "Christ in his human origins" (Romans 9:5), son of the Virgin Mary, as also his apostles are its sons.

All this spiritual heritage, common to Christians and Jews, constitutes an organic foundation for a mutual relationship, even though a great part of the children of Israel "did not accept the Gospel." Nevertheless the Church (together with the Prophets and the apostle Paul) "awaits the day, known to God alone, on which all peoples will address the Lord in a single voice and 'serve him with one accord'" (Zephaniah 3:9; *NA* 4).

Address to Jewish Representatives at Buenos Aires
(April 9, 1987)

Meeting representatives of the Jewish community has been a frequent occurrence during my visits to different countries from the beginning of my pontificate. This is not just a casual meeting, nor is it a mere expression of an obligation of courtesy.

You know well that, since the Second Vatican Council and its declaration *Nostra Aetate* (4), the relations between the Catholic Church and Judaism have been built on a new foundation, which is in fact very old, since it refers to the closeness of our respective religions, united by what the Council precisely calls a spiritual "bond."

The years that followed, and the constant progress of the dialogue on both sides, have deepened even more the awareness of that "bond" and the need to strengthen it always through mutual knowledge, esteem, and the overcoming of the prejudices which succeeded in separating us in the past. . . .

Address to Representatives of
the Jewish Community of Poland
(June 9, 1991)

Meetings with the representatives of the Jewish communities constitute a constant element of my apostolic journeys. This fact possesses its own meaning. It emphasizes a unique common faith, which connects the children of Abraham, who confess the religion of Moses and the Prophets, to those who also acknowledge Abraham as their "father in faith" (John 8:39) and accept in Christ, "son of Abraham and son of David" (cf. Matthew 1:1), the entire rich heritage of Moses and the Prophets as well.

A meeting with the Jews on Polish soil is particularly meaningful every time it occurs. Today, I would like to refer to all that I have said during previous meetings on this subject and which my faith and heart dictate. This magnificent, and at the same time, tragic past of almost one thousand years of common history on Polish soil comes together, as does the responsibility for today's world of those who believe in the one God, as well as hope for the future, as we aspire to change the world through the rebirth and renewal of people who are, to an equal degree, open to the voice of God and to the needs of their neighbor.

During my last meeting with the representatives of the Jewish community in Poland, at the residence of the Polish primates on June 4,

1987, which I recall with gratitude and with emotion, I expressed the thoughts and feelings with which I and, I think, the overwhelming majority of Poles powerlessly watched the terrible crime perpetrated against the entire Jewish people, sometimes without knowledge of what was taking place, because those who were doing it tried to hide it. I said then that we experienced it "in the spirit of profound solidarity with you. That which threatened you also threatened us. The threat to us was not fulfilled to the same extent as the threat to you; it did not have enough time to be fulfilled to the same degree. You bore the terrible sacrifice of destruction. It can be said that you bore this sacrifice for others, who were also supposed to be destroyed."

I heartily echo the words that I found in the pastoral letter of the Polish bishops dated November 30, 1990: "The same land was a common homeland for Poles and Jews for ages; the mutual loss of life, a sea of terrible suffering and of the wrongs endured should not divide, but unite us. The places of execution, and in many cases, the common graves, call for this unity."

The human past does not disappear completely. The history of the Poles and Jews, even though there are so few Jews currently living on Polish soil, is still very much present in the lives of Jews, as well as in the lives of Poles. I brought this to the attention of those of my countrymen who visited me in Rome on September 29, 1990. "The nation which lived with us for many generations has remained with us even after the horrible death of millions of its sons and daughters," I said. "Together, we await the day of judgment and resurrection."

Today it seems to be a thing of great importance that, on both sides, we try to perceive, salvage, and renew the good things that occurred in our mutual relations (and, after all, a lot of good things happened over the centuries). We should also try to find unity and friendship despite the evil, because there was also much evil in our mutual history.

Unfortunately, both the good and the evil that occurred between us was crushed by the genocide, inconceivable in its severity, to which the Jewish nation fell prey. One can at least say the unprecedented crime of killing an entire nation shocked Christian Europe and mobilized it to righting the wrongs that were perpetrated against the Jews and which were often written into the customs and way of thinking. After an interval of two thousand years, the Jews finally acquired their own state. The nations with a Christian civilization undertook the arduous task of rooting out from their mentalities all unjust prejudices against the Jews, as well as any manifestations of anti-Semitism. Christian churches, including the Catholic Church, actively participated in this task. . . .

Interview in ·*Parade* Magazine with Tad Szulc
(April 3, 1994)

[John Paul II:] The attitude of the Church toward the people of God's Old Testament — the Jews — can only be that they are our elder brothers in the faith.

It goes back to my youngest years, when, in the parish church of my native Wadowice, I listened to this psalm sung during evening Mass.

> O, Jerusalem, glorify the Lord:
> Praise Your God, O Zion!
> For He made the bars of your gates strong,
> And blessed Your children within You. . . . (Psalm 147)

I still have in my ears these words and this melody, which I have remembered all my life. And then came the terrible experience of World War II and the [Nazi] occupation, the Holocaust, which was the extermination of Jews only for the reason that they were Jews. It was a terrible upheaval that has remained in the memory of all the people who were close to these events.

But afterward, whenever I had the opportunity, I spoke about it everywhere — perhaps expressing it in the strongest fashion when I met the representatives of the Jewish community in Warsaw in 1987. I told them that they must bear witness to what happened to their people. . . .

It must be understood that Jews, who for two thousand years were dispersed among the nations of the world, had decided to return to the land of their ancestors. This is their right.

And this right is recognized even by those who look upon the nation of Israel with an unsympathetic eye. This right was also recognized from the outset by the Holy See, and the act of establishing diplomatic relations with Israel is simply an international affirmation of this relationship. . . .

Part Two

BUDDHIST RESPONSES

5

Pope John Paul II and Christian-Buddhist Dialogue

His Holiness, the XIVth Dalai Lama

AN INTERVIEW BY WAYNE TEASDALE

The following interview with the Dalai Lama by Brother Wayne Teasdale was part of a much longer conversation that took place in Dharamsala, Himachal Pradesh, India, on September 16, 1997. It addresses the relationship between Buddhism and Catholicism as understood by the Dalai Lama, his own personal relationship with the Pope, dialogue itself, the need for prophetic witness by the Catholic community, and the need for other world religions to speak out on the issue of Tibet's agony.

Catholic–Buddhist Relations and Dialogue

Wayne Teasdale: Your Holiness, do you feel that the Catholic Church, on the Vatican level, is sincere about its commitment to interreligious dialogue, or interfaith relations? I raise this question because there seem to be mixed signals from Rome at times.

Dalai Lama: As an organization, that is, in its Vatican structure, I don't really know. But among Christians I think there are two types. One type, or group, of Christians sincerely accept other traditions. There are some good things in the Buddhist tradition, and so, it deserves respect. In the second group, there are some Christians who do not respect Buddhism, and certainly they don't know it; they are ignorant of the Dharma. Then these Christians, in the name of their religion, want to fight, and they cause bloodshed. This problem doesn't only exist in the past, but is even happening today. Therefore, these Christians spread disunity among humanity in the name of religion itself, and they encourage that. The first group has some kind of genuine respect. Out of this respect they want closer relationships with us. This is good work, and very positive.

Normally, I think, not only on the Christian side, but the Buddhist side as well, there are these two types, or two groups. But the difference is that, on the Christian side, usually there is an influence that arises from a Western kind of mentality that has pursued world dominance.

WT: That's so true.

DL: Buddhists, I think, don't have that attitude or feeling. That's the primary difference. Buddhists sometimes criticize Christians, but they also understand and accept Christian values. When this happens then Christians and Buddhists become close friends. They learn certain things from each other. From our own tradition we may also have something to offer Christians. So, in that way I think the relationship is very positive and very good.

Another type of Christian does not have the quality of genuine respect, but rather sees dialogue, or interfaith relationships, as necessary, a necessary evil. They think, Buddhism exists, and we can't deny its reality. They realize they can't stop Buddhism (laughs).

WT: Yes, right!

DL: So, these Christians follow a diplomatic way, or something, you see. They say, better now deal with Buddhists.

WT: You mean they tolerate Buddhists?

DL: Yes, that's right. They say, better now to deal with them. That kind of attitude is not very common among Buddhists. So, you see, there are these two types.

WT: Yes, I agree! I agree! Tell me, Your Holiness, what are your personal impressions of Pope John Paul II?

DL: Oh, very good! Right from the beginning of our relationship I feel, and the reason for this is because of his personal background, that is, coming from a Communist, totalitarian, and antireligious sort of situation. So, you see, his history is very similar to my own. Therefore, right from the beginning, at once, there has existed some kind of personal close feeling that developed between us. Then some kind of unanimous agreement, total agreement between us on the value of spirituality emerged. There was also some concern for the younger generation, that they are losing interest in spirituality and its great value. In this, I think, we always found agreement. On several occasions he always mentioned these matters. Another point is that we always emphasized the importance of dialogue and closer relations.

WT: Did you find John Paul II easy to talk to and accessible?

DL: Oh, yes. I tried to inspire him to commit to a joint statement with me on the environment, and I gave him a lot of background information that other friends had given me. I presented these materials to him, and mentioned briefly the importance of ecology today, but he made no response; it seemed he had no interest in the environment. That, I think, represents one of our chief differences. This is a little disappointing. Otherwise, we enjoy very good relations.

WT: Was that experience in the 1980s?

DL: Yes.

WT: Well, he has since written on the importance of ecology, and perhaps this reflects your influence, among others. How do you find his English?

DL: His pronunciation is not very clear for me, but I think he also found my accent very difficult (laughs heartily).

WT: Well, that's something you both have in common! Yes. Do you think the Pope understands Buddhism? Does he have an adequate grasp of it? I ask you this question bearing in mind his comments about Buddhism in his book *Crossing the Threshold of Hope*. His remarks there about the Dharma have occasioned considerable criticism from Buddhist and even Christian scholars. He gives only a scant seven pages to Buddhism in this volume, and they seem to fall far short of any real depth in his approach to your tradition. He speaks of Buddhism's view of the world as seeing it as essentially bad, or evil, and then he comments that it has a "negative soteriology." Both of these statements are very problematic. What do you think?

DL: I have not felt that his view of Buddhism was very deep. His remarks about the Dharma in his book are both sad and amusing. They are sad because his approach moves in the direction of polemics, and amusing because so superficial. Buddhism does not regard the world as evil; the world itself is basically neutral. What is really a problem, or can be evil, is the attitude of grasping, or attachment, selfish attachment, stemming from ignorance. What does he mean by the word soteriology?

WT: The term soteriology concerns the doctrine of salvation, and in the case of Christianity, of Christ as the unique Savior of humankind, the Mediator between God and the human family. Christ is the way to salvation, in the Christian understanding of life.

DL: Of course in the Buddhist view there is no mediator because each one of us is responsible for his or her own salvation; it is a matter of individual determination and effort to achieve enlightenment and liberation from samsara, or the cycle of rebirth. The Buddha is a model of how to achieve these goals, but he cannot substitute his effort for our own; we are responsible for ourselves. It's up to us!

WT: Now, let me change the subject, or direction. The Gethsemani Encounter was a high point in Buddhist-Christian relations, the meeting that took place in July 1996 at the monastery where Thomas Merton lived for twenty-seven years. I was supposed to attend, you know, and I regret not coming, as a friend, Abbot James Connor, said I would. Tell me, what do you feel was accomplished in that meeting?

DL: There's no doubt this meeting promoted or advanced mutual understanding. I'm sure of it. Of course, there was one dissenting voice, a Buddhist monk from Sri Lanka who, as he expressed it, saw Buddhism as the best way, as the superior faith.

WT: I'm sure the Christians present were glad to hear that "good news." It was music to their ears! (We both laugh.)

DL: Such positions leave no room for dialogue, and are not based on genuine respect; dialogue then breaks down.

WT: It's clear why! What would you like to see happen as a follow-up to the Gethsemani experience? Do you have any ideas for joint projects between Christian and Buddhist monks and nuns? What would you like to see happen?

DL: I think more frequent meetings.

WT: You mean more regular meetings?

DL: Yes! That would be very beneficial in the long run; it would deepen dialogue and expand our friendship.

WT: What do you think of the possibility of a joint Christian-Buddhist community? It would be an experiment in existential dialogue. We could share life together, and study each other's tradition, while exploring spiritual practice in both our traditions.

DL: Yes! I like this idea very much, and it definitely should be tried, but on a small scale at first.

Tensions in the Relationship

WT: Your Holiness, there's no question of the Pope's support for interreligious dialogue; his many statements on various occasions attest to its depth, endurance, and seriousness. But there have been these mixed signals, especially emanating from statements by Cardinal Joseph Ratzinger, a Vatican official. He is the prefect of the Congregation for the Doctrine of the Faith, and he has made some insensitive and ill-conceived statements about Buddhism.

DL: What were these comments by Cardinal Ratzinger about the Dharma, that is, about the Buddhist tradition? What did he say?

WT: Well, it's terribly embarrassing. He said: "Buddhism is spiritually mental autoeroticism," or mental masturbation. Terrible! Do you understand?

DL: What's the meaning?

WT: I think he's trying to suggest that Buddhism is a kind of mind game, that it's focused on self-absorption.

DL: Does he mean illusion?

WT: That would be another way to express it. Yes, illusion, but again, as a mind game, a mental activity with no real relationship to reality, human life itself. That's what he means. What do you make of that remark? How would you respond to it?

DL: I don't know! (Laughs.) Well, it is true that, in the Buddhist perspective, the mental way is paramount. So, there is a certain truth to his statement, but surely not in the way he intends it. Buddhist practice requires a lot of mental work. So, there is a kind of truth to his unfortunate assertion. That's the only way to enlightenment, that is, through the nature of the mind, and getting control of oneself through an effort of the mind, or the will; will itself is also a mental function.

The whole Buddhist concept is peace of mind, or serenity of mind. Ultimately, lasting peace of mind or serenity is achieved only through the mind itself. But of course, it cannot be obtained through illusion in Cardinal Ratzinger's mistaken view. In his statement, there seems to be some negative feeling or emotional content that motivates and impels him to make such remarks. This might well be the background from which he regards the Buddhist tradition. That's really unfortunate! It's definitely not beneficial to the Christian-Buddhist relationship! Using such language only degrades the dialogue; it drags it down to the level of polemics, and that appears to be Cardinal Ratzinger's aim. What do you think?

WT: Well, I think his "off the cuff" remark was undoubtedly calculated. Vatican curial officials are not in the custom of making such statements unless they are meant for public consumption, or publication. Quite frankly, I believe it is fear and ignorance that motivated that insensitive outburst from such an important figure. The context of his slur on Buddhism — there is no other way to truthfully name it — was an interview. This interview was published in the French weekly *L'Express*. In that interview he states: "If Buddhism is attractive, it is only because it suggests that by belonging to it you can touch the infinite, and you can have joy without concrete religious obligations. This is spiritually self-indulgent autoeroticism." Then he went on to express his greatest fear: "In the 1950s someone said that the undoing of the Catholic Church in the twentieth century would not come from Marxism but from Buddhism. . . . They were right." What do you make of these statements?

DL: First, it is clear that he does not understand Buddhism! Buddhism is a way, as he himself suggests, "to touch the infinite," though we do not use such terms. It's a way to truth by overcoming obstacles within us. Some of these obstacles would include ignorance, fear, greed, and hatred. This process of overcoming these kinds of states and emotions leads in time to enlightenment. Enlightenment is profound understanding of reality united with freedom from all these states, emotions, and attachments, but also requires a deep-seated compassion that is wise and concrete, that is, is active.

Secondly, Buddhist practice, chiefly meditation, brings with it eventually a pervasive serenity, or peace of mind, because then we know what the nature of the mind is. The nature of the mind is consciousness itself, but an absolute, non-dual awareness, unified, and not primarily human. This consciousness is animated by an infinitely wise compassion, compassionate wisdom. This compassion is very profound, and it must bear fruit in some kind of service, or compassionate action as we see so clearly among Christians, Jews, and Muslims. This makes possible bliss or joy. There *are* also definite religious obligations, but these involve our relationship to the *sangha,* or community, and our personal commitment to spiritual practices.

WT: That is very beautifully expressed. Personally, I feel that Cardinal Ratzinger's comments constitute an overreaction, especially when he asserts that Buddhism would undo Catholicism. I don't believe that's the aim of Buddhism, nor is it possible because it cannot destroy Christ, nor his Church. One of the deep truths Buddhists can learn from Christians and other theists is that God *does* exist, that God is not merely a concept, or the result of a reasoning process, but is essentially experiential. The knowledge that this is the case is the fruit of mystical experience, and it is important to share this absolute truth with our Buddhist brothers and sisters. To further elaborate in connection with Cardinal Ratzinger's statement, because God exists, *is* existence itself, the Church, and any other form theism has assumed, cannot be destroyed, displaced, undone, or outgrown. That is my firm conviction.

DL: I understand and respect that. Although I do not personally accept the notion of a Creator, because we Buddhists follow the view of dependent arising, or the interdependence of all beings, I do feel that the experience of God is valid and true. There is definitely something to this theistic mysticism, and I strongly respect it. In fact, I want to learn more about it!

WT: Yes, well that is one reason why I gave you a copy of Evelyn Underhill's book, *Mysticism,* really to provide some background for you to understand our meaning when we speak of God, or the Divine Reality.

DL: Very good! I appreciate it very much!

WT: I wanted to mention that many in Rome do not agree with Cardinal Ratzinger's assessment of Buddhism, particularly Cardinal Arinze, who calls for mutual understanding and forgiveness. In his address this year [1997] commemorating the Buddhist *Vesakh,* or as you know, the time each year that draws attention to the Buddha's life and the important events in his very rich experience, he referred to Buddhism and Christianity as "communities of forgiveness and compassion."

DL: That's really very good! Very, very good! That's the approach we need.

Support for the Tibetan Cause

WT: Now I want to turn to the Tibetan issue. Your Holiness, what kind of support have religious and spiritual leaders given to you, and the cause of Tibet? You have received so much attention from the international group of World Parliamentarians, the media, Hollywood, recording stars, and the Catholic monastic community. What about the religious and spiritual leaders? How have they responded?

DL: To me privately, for example, the Pope is very sympathetic. Actually, one time I asked him for some funds to be used for educational purposes, and he immediately agreed, but then somehow it did not materialize. At that time, about fifty Tibetans were scheduled to go to Tibet as volunteer teachers, and this is why I requested the money from the Pope. This program didn't happen because of a lack of Chinese response. I had asked the Pope for $50,000. I'm sure if the program had gone forward, the Vatican would have given the money. So, you see, privately, there is very good support, but publicly, as you know, there has been almost nothing, neither from John Paul II, or any other Vatican official. But then among Christians, and some cardinals, archbishops in America, Europe, and Australia there has been some kind of support expressed.

Of course in many countries I have visited — practically everywhere — usually I have meetings with the higher authorities, both civil and religious, and they often express public support, especially in America, particularly Monastic Interreligious Dialogue (of which you are a member), and the various groups Lodi Gyari (the Dalai Lama's Special Envoy to the Americas) has organized. I remember that you have been present on many of these occasions, for instance, the meeting with Cardinal Bernard Law, the Archbishop of Boston in September 1995. Do you remember?

WT: Oh, yes, quite well, and I remember how you told him that the Pope, indeed the Catholic Church, have an absolute moral responsibility to speak out for Tibet. Cardinal Law said, I believe, that he would mention your concerns in Rome.

DL: Then with Hindus, in 1996 I met one young spiritual teacher, who was also a *sannyasi* (a monk), a master in the advaitic school of Vedantic mysticism. He really wanted to do more for the Tibetan cause. So anyway, I feel that religious and spiritual leaders can do more, and it is worthwhile. I personally feel the Tibetan issue in which I am involved is actually a struggle for the survival of spirituality, of human values. I am very much concerned with these human values! The highest priority for me, besides the planet itself and humankind, is Tibetan Buddhist culture; that is a profound human value. Concerning human values, and then Buddhism, another is spirituality. So, the Tibetan struggle is very much related to spiritual values. Six thousand of our monasteries have been destroyed by the Chinese, and more than a million and half Tibetans have been killed, while tens of thousands have been imprisoned and tortured over the years. You can easily see how this is a matter of human values and of spiritual culture.

I often say that the preservation of Tibetan Buddhist culture, and Buddhism itself, is not only for the benefit of six million Tibetans, but also for the larger community in this part of the world (Asia), and as far as the Tibetan Buddhist culture is concerned, I feel that humanity itself is also benefited by this tradition and culture. I believe Tibetan culture can make a contribution, to some extent, to humankind, especially to the happiness of the human family. It can be very beneficial here, I feel. It can enhance humanity.

WT: Yes, for the benefit of all humanity, I quite agree.

DL: And so, for these reasons, the spiritual leaders need to lend their support to the Tibetan issue.

WT: Let me ask you by way of clarification, what would be the level of support you want to see? What kind of support?

DL: Essentially the religions should support religious freedom. Everybody says the violence in Tibet must end, and there must be freedom of religion there. This violence in Tibet is very serious. In China proper, again it's a question of religious freedom for the Muslims, the Christians, the Buddhists. This is a very serious matter. So, the kind of support I want to see and would welcome is an expression of concern for religious freedom in Tibet and China. Then there should be efforts exerted behind the scenes. There was a small group of Christian brothers and sisters who visited China and Tibet. That is also very good! They visited some of the monasteries and convents. Simply to visit Tibetans in Tibet as a group with these Christian monks and nuns in their robes was a powerful witness. This type of act is an indication of solidarity. Isn't it?

WT: Well, you've got all the Christian monks and nuns on your side. You do, really!

DL: Really, I think in reality, yes. Whether they can influence a change of direction is another question. I do feel that, among non-Christians, I am one of the few people who has a very close relationship with Christians, especially with Catholic monastics.

WT: Yes, that is quite true! Absolutely. Yes!

DL: Yes, it really does seem so. I have often been received by these people very warmly, these monastics; all of them treat me with great respect.

WT: That's very true, and rightly so.

DL: They never show any reservation, or any sense that this is something un-Christian, that is, that I am un-Christian in their view, something outside their world. They never express that kind of attitude. Of course those monasteries, those places where I visited, they invited me. So, right from the beginning they have a different attitude; they are totally welcoming. (He laughs heartily.)

WT: But also they know you are a monk, you see, and that helps. Have you thought, perhaps, of asking the Pope in a letter to bring the issue of Tibet up in the United Nations? See, in the Gospel it recommends that we keep trying or being persistent in seeking and asking for justice.

DL: I think you are right about that.

WT: The Gospel sets a precedent, because Jesus says, keep asking; keep asking; keep knocking, and even an unjust judge will give you justice to get rid of you, if you keep asking. So, if you continue to ask, the door will eventually open!

DL: If you know someone who has good relations, personally, with the Pope, or some important person in the Vatican, then I think, to send a letter is OK. Otherwise, without a sort of proper channel, or way, if there is a reaction, it could be embarrassing, and I don't think that's good.

WT: So, you think person-to-person would be better?

DL: Yes, much better! OK.

WT: When are you next in Europe?

DL: Next year [1998]. Now, I think in this moment, people are very serious about religious freedom in Tibet. So, I think this is the right time for an initiative with Rome.

WT: I think Cardinal Arinze would be the right person to approach, the Nigerian cardinal. He's the president of the Pontifical Council for Interreligious Dialogue, the Vatican department in charge of the Catholic Church's relations with non-Christian religions. So, actually, relations with Buddhists come under his department. He would be the one to approach, Francis Cardinal Arinze. You've met him?

DL: Yes, I have.

WT: You would want to talk to him directly, or write him a letter. Actually, perhaps, you could suggest in a letter that you would like to talk to John Paul II about certain things.

DL: As I mentioned earlier, it should be someone who has a good, personal relationship with the Pope who initiates contact. Then, that may be better.

WT: OK, I see. That makes a lot of sense. I think Cardinal Arinze would be the logical choice, or even Cardinal Hume [of England]. Both are close to John Paul, and both are important voices. Another possibility is the Abbot Primate, Marcel Rooney. You know when you stay at San Anselmo in Rome, the Abbot Primate is the abbot of this monastery, and he is the head of the Benedictine Order. He has a very significant position. He has some access to the Pope. I knew his predecessor, but he died so suddenly. His successor is also an American. Perhaps, he might be the one to open this direct channel. He realizes that the monastic world of the Catholic Church has made a commitment to Tibet and to you personally. He would certainly be sympathetic and honor that commitment.

DL: Then I think it might work, but so far, no satisfaction. I will ask our representative in Geneva to make a special visit to the Vatican. She is also in charge of our relations with the Holy See. She knows Cardinal Arinze.

WT: Yes, I think he would be a good one to work with. I really do.

DL: This visit would come at the right time!

WT: Let me ask you, do you feel that the interfaith organizations, such as the Parliament of the World's Religions, the Temple of Understanding, the United Religions, have a responsibility to speak about Tibet?

DL: Oh, yes! Certainly. Everyone has this responsibility.

WT: Thank you, Your Holiness.

DL: You're welcome, Brother Wayne.

WT: This has been very interesting, and very useful. Thank you, Your Holiness.

6

The Intrareligious Realization

Ruminations of
an American Zen Buddhist

ROBERT AITKEN

I threw up my hands when I was invited to respond to pronouncements by His Holiness John Paul II on the subject of Buddhism. I felt
that his Christianity was so exclusive and evangelical, his views of Buddhism were so completely misinformed, and his words about prominent
Buddhist leaders were so condescending and patronizing that I would
not be able to reply from any kind of common ground. Here is his case
for Catholic Christianity:

> *Christ is absolutely original and absolutely unique.* If He were only a
> wise man like Socrates, if He were a "prophet" like Muhammad,
> if He were "enlightened" like the Buddha, without any doubt,
> He would not be what He is. He is *the one mediator between God
> and humanity.*[1]

The Vietnamese Buddhist teacher and poet Thich Nhat Hanh cites
this passage in his *Living Buddha Living Christ* and comments:

> Of course Christ is unique. Socrates, Muhammad, the Buddha,
> you, and I are all unique. The idea behind the statement, how-

---

This essay was edited by Nelson Foster and Greg Mello.

ever, is the notion that Christianity provides the only way of salvation, and all other religious traditions are of no use. This attitude excludes the dialogue and fosters religious intolerance and discrimination. It does not help.[2]

I agree. It is indeed an absolute, exclusive position. From there, His Holiness draws a bead on Buddhism:

> The "enlightenment" experienced by the Buddha comes down to the conviction that the world is bad, that it is the source of evil and of suffering for man. To liberate oneself from this evil, one must free oneself from this world. . . . The fullness of such a detachment is not union with God, but what is called nirvana, a state of perfect indifference with regard to the world.[3]

Quite the contrary, the Buddha did not declare the world to be the source of human misery. Instead the source can be found in the persistent, subjective errors that people make about the world and their place in it. It seems that in speaking of Buddhist notions of source and liberation, the Pope was referring to the Four Noble Truths and the Eightfold Path, a Buddhist teaching that forms the foundation of classical Buddhism and from which the many schools of Buddhism have evolved. In that basic teaching, The Buddha said that *dukkha* is everywhere. *Dukkha* is a Pali word which is variously translated as "unsatisfactoriness," "suffering," "anguish." This misery is everywhere among people. Its source is the human tendency to cling to notions of a permanent and exclusive self. Liberation from such erroneous attachment is nirvana and can be found on a path of practice that begins with right views of impermanence and interdependence and continues through eight steps of thought, speech, and action, ending with right meditation.[4]

The specific Zen Buddhist view about the human being and the world can be summed up in the final two lines of Hakuin Ekaku's "Song of Zazen": "This very place is the Lotus Land [Nirvana], this very body the Buddha."[5] This world, where people are so unhappy, can be experienced as Elysium itself. You and I are already so fulfilled. Our task is to realize such facts. One way or another, other Mahayana schools of Buddhism, and Vajrayana schools, too, would say something similar.[6]

Having said all this, I must also acknowledge that fine words butter no parsnips. His Holiness can be holier than we Buddhists, and we Buddhists can fall into the same kind of invidious rhetoric. There is, in fact, more than a trace of truth in his generalizations. Buddhist teaching is of this world, but it is not a teaching that is significantly *implemented* in the world, at least not in Europe and in the Americas. Thich Nhat Hanh urges compassionate attitudes and actions in his talks and his many books. Various others (I include myself) write essays or entire books that set forth social critiques that are Buddhist in orientation. However, there are few manifest exemplars who are actually engaged in challenging a culture of disassociation, displacement, and alienation. The Buddhist Peace Fellowship is a forum and coordinating agency for Buddhists interested in social change,[7] but the many Buddhist communities in the Americas and Europe are by and large left with little defense against the norms of consumerism, which can exert a far more telling and salient influence than their religious practice. Until practice becomes praxis, Western Buddhists cannot claim truly to be of this world.

Moreover, Buddhists generally do not match the passion with which John Paul II addresses the horrors of child labor, widespread interethnic murder and rape, and other large-scale depredations across the world. We cannot take much satisfaction in our metaphysics of mercy. For the most part, even interreligious dialogues are sponsored, not by Buddhists, but by Christians or by consortiums of scholars.

His Holiness invites dialogue with non-Christians in his writings and by reaching out to them in colloquia, such as the assemblies of leaders of major religions sponsored by the Vatican in 1984 and 1991. Probably no major religious leader has done more to bring high priests and eminent scholars of the many faiths together for the purpose of mutual understanding. These are not just exercises in comparative religion, but are explicitly intended as dialogues of spiritual experience.[8]

Even in the personal writings of His Holiness, so full of disingenuous perceptions of Buddhism, I can find an opening for communication. He cites with favor *Nostra Aetate,* a document of the Second Vatican Council on non-Christian religions:

> The Holy Spirit works effectively even outside the visible structure of the Church, making use of . . . *semina verbi* [seeds of the Word], that constitute *a kind of common soteriological root present in all religions.*[9]

"Seeds of the Word" would not be my expression, of course. But suppose it could refer to seeds of all religions in the spiritual womb in every person. An analogy would be the human talent for language. Like other people, I was born with the innate capacity to learn any language and happened to grow up in an English-speaking family. Cultivating my ordinary human talent, I have learned other languages. Also, I grew up in a Protestant Christian family, but with my natural capacity to understand the heart of other religions, I cultivated my Buddhist potential. I am enriched as one whose Buddhism informs his Christianity and whose Christianity informs his Buddhism.

Probably my upbringing in a tolerant setting has helped me to be this flexible. I am not an East European who battled for decades to protect his faith against benighted governments. I do not expect His Holiness to be able to embrace Buddhism as Ramakrishna could embrace Islam. I would simply hope that he might broaden and deepen his own Christian sympathy for others to the degree that he could, for example, allow Zen Buddhism a place among religions, rather than just a niche labeled "Eastern method of therapy."[10] The encounter of religions sponsored by the Vatican could then become enlarged. We could get down to cases and start to deal intimately and existentially with the possibilities of intrareligious realization.

Let me offer one such possibility from my perspective: I submit that the Holy Spirit, which in *Nostra Aetate* Pope John XXIII found working effectively outside the visible structure of the Church, is no other than the Bodhisattva Kuan-yin, not merely as a Christian angel of mercy in the guise of a Buddhist archetype, but Kuan-yin herself with her thousand hands serving the many beings[11] — even as this same spirit is no other than Jesus preaching the Gospel and dying on his cross for our sins, with no connection whatever to anything Buddhist. And there are other ways Christian metaphors could be expanded. *Nostra Aetate* declares:

> *There is only one community and it consists of all peoples.* They have only one origin, since God inhabited the entire earth with the whole human race. And they have one ultimate destiny, God, whose providence, goodness and plan for salvation extend to all.[12]

Suppose this image were enlarged: the one community could rather be one network made up of people whose destiny is a common potential for spiritual fulfillment, not necessarily just within a monotheistic religion, but in whatever religion the people find themselves. Moreover, the network could also include animals, plants, clouds, stars, and so on, all encouraged to find fulfillment in their own ways.

Conventional Christianity would have to be deepened, of course. At the end of the Gospel of Mark (16:15) we find Jesus saying:

Go into the whole world, preach the Gospel to every creature. He who believes and is baptized shall be saved, but he who does not believe shall be condemned.

The Gospel of Mark has gone through many translations, but the essential message of this passage can still be discerned. We accept the Good News of liberation, our obligation to love selflessly, and our intimacy with our own wellsprings, or we are condemned to a living death, not by an angry God, but by the nature of reality and the human heart. That is just how it is.

World events and modern technology press these truths upon us. Chinese, Rwandans, Chileans — all of us — speak to one another as though we were in the same room. In fact, we are indeed in the same room. It is not only possible but imperative to uncover our love for the many others. We either cultivate and implement profound reconciliation of outer differences once and for all, or by the crushing pressure of political, economic, and technological implosion we shall surely squash each other into a bloody pudding.

Reconciliation of seemingly implacable religio–political positions that divide our world is a matter of seeing into the metaphors of the other, sharing our own metaphors, and living the truths which theirs and ours illuminate. Far deeper, and far more inspiring, than the literal, the motifs of folk stories, myths, and poetry are cognate the world over. When I find the words of Jesus to his disciples to be my own truths, my misunderstanding of Christianity falls away. However, if I were to treat such words verbatim and interpret them within a closed system, I would be just reinforcing the bulwarks of institutional religion and ethnic justification.

All colleges offer a course in logic, as indeed they should. All colleges, and all secondary and primary schools and nurseries as well, should also teach metaphor as the Tao of liberation through folk stories, myths, and poetry. When a young adult can be guided, say, to experience a wild duck as a thought, flashing out of sight in the mind of the boundless skull, the world will be saved in that moment — for that moment. All things will spring to infinite possibilities within their own spheres. The human skin will no longer be impervious, but will enclose all bodies. Alienation will for the duration of the realization be the only alien. Thereafter, the way to prove the experience again and again in praxis will be clear.

There is a venerable history of communication by metaphor. Long before Alexander the Great brought his troops to the kingdoms that are now Pakistan, tales and legends were carried by merchants, travelers, and pilgrims from India to Turkey to Greece and back. They found common ground with their hearers. We find the same stories, which is to say, the same experiences, in *Aesop's Fables* and the *Jataka Tales*. The Buddha himself appears in the communion of Christian saints in the guise of Saint Josaphat, a prince who left his palace in search of enlightenment.[13]

Intimacy between religions and their metaphors also developed in the oasis towns along the silk route connecting China with India and Persia. Archaeologists have discovered Nestorian writings dating from the eighth century that apply Buddhist terminology to Christian principles. Christian texts in Chinese call themselves sutras and employ Mahayana imagery and notions "almost to the point of losing their identity."[14]

Yet by the time Jesuits entered Japan and China in the sixteenth century, no trace of understanding between Christians and Buddhists remained. Even knowledge of each other had died out. In Japan there was a brief interval of harmonious misunderstanding, but both sides were disillusioned very quickly. Eventually, for political reasons, Christianity was proscribed, with torture and violent death for the faithful. In China it became clear to the Mandarins that the Christians were interested in conversion, not in metaphorical interchange, and the mission that was established with such high hopes had to accept a tiny, marginal place in the panoply of Chinese religious culture.

In the nineteenth century, however, when Asian texts began to be available in European translations, thinkers from Emerson and Thoreau to Schopenhauer found inspiration in Buddhist and Hindu metaphors. The reverse took place in Asia, particularly with the acceptance of Christian social and educational ideals. Now at the end of the twentieth century, well-established societies of Buddhist-Christian interchange from the scholarly to the monastic flourish in Asia, North America, and Europe. Interest in the practice of Buddhism is also widespread in Western countries. *Buddhist America*, a standard directory, lists more than five hundred Buddhist practice centers in the United States and Canada, almost all of them with lay membership. They represent the three major Buddhist schools: Mahayana, Vajrayana, and Theravada. Spot-checking, I find that many prominent centers are not listed, so it seems that five hundred is probably too low a figure.[15] As His Holiness remarks, "Today we are seeing a certain *diffusion of Buddhism in the West*."[16] Indeed.

I can speak only for Zen Buddhism (with some hesitation, for even Zen is by no means monolithic). We can trace the "diffusion" of Zen among Roman Catholics in Europe and the Americas to the influence of Thomas Merton, Hugo Lassalle, Aelred Graham, David Steindl-Rast,

William Johnston, Thomas Hand, and other Catholic monks, priests, and nuns who explored Zen practice to one degree or another and shared the experiences. Thomas Merton, through his friendship and correspondence with the Japanese Zen Buddhist scholar D. T. Suzuki and through his writings about Zen, was particularly inspiring to his fellow Cistercians. I remember taking tea after a Zen retreat with Catholics in Washington state about 1980. By way of introducing himself, a Trappist monk peeled off his robe to expose his T-shirt, on which was inscribed in bold letters, "Thomas Merton Monk."

In my own work, however, I find myself closest to Father Lassalle — Hugo Makibi Enomiya-Lassalle (1898–1990). A Jesuit priest, he was a lifetime resident and naturalized subject of Japan who first explored the possibilities of Zen Buddhism in 1943, then took up the practice with Harada Sogaku Roshi of Hosshin Monastery in Fukui Prefecture. After Harada Roshi died in 1961, Father Lassalle continued his Zen Buddhist study with his heir, Yasutani Haku'un Roshi, then with Yamada Koun Roshi, Yasutani Roshi's heir in turn, whose little center in Kamakura during the 1970s and early 1980s was crowded with Catholic priests and nuns who had been influenced by Father Lassalle's example.

Father Lassalle was a Christian who sought ways to become a better Christian through his practice of Zen Buddhism. Stephen Batchelor, in his cogent study *The Awakening of the West*, points out that Lassalle recommended Zen Buddhist practice for Christians as a way to the central experience of *kensho*, a realization that Lassalle viewed as "neither Buddhist nor Christian nor necessarily connected with any religious confession."[17] He made it clear that he regarded *kensho* as a refined psychological experience that could lead to a vision of God.[18]

Some twelve Christians who were influenced by Father Lassalle and became heirs of Yamada Roshi are teaching Zen Buddhism in large communities in Europe and also in Dallas, Manila, and Madras. They are part of the Sanbo Kyodan (Order of the Three Treasures) that emerged from the Harada-Yasutani line and that is administered from the temple that Yamada Roshi founded in Kamakura. Most of these Christian teachers are Roman Catholic priests and nuns, but one is a Protestant minister, one a lay Catholic, and one a former priest.

Father Lassalle might have been their inspiration, but not all of them hew to his line. One who was inspired, Father Willigis Jäger, now a central figure among Sanbo Kyodan teachers in Germany, insists that Zen itself is beyond any religion.[19] It is on this very point that controversy has erupted among the Sanbo Kyodan teachers. The range of opinion seems to reflect the emphasis some teachers place upon *kensho* as an experience that leads one back to deeper Christianity, and the importance others place upon lifetime Zen practice — preparing the way for *kensho* and clarifying and integrating it thereafter. Teachers at this latter end of the spectrum affirm the unique nature of *kensho* in the fields of organized religion and the place of Zen as a Buddhist tradition. Thus in a relatively small network, in a fairly recent tradition, there is complex diversity.

My own community, the Diamond Sangha, is another relatively recent tradition. Rooted in the Sanbo Kyodan, it is organizationally independent. At Diamond Sangha centers in the Americas, Australasia, and Europe, there is rarely an overt sign of Christianity. It is not absent, however. Speaking personally, as a teacher of Zen Buddhism in the Diamond Sangha tradition, I am a Buddhist, yet nonetheless I am also a Protestant Christian who never converted, in the decisive sense of that term, to Buddhism. I find the metaphorical language of Jesus and Old Testament figures rising to my mind when I speak to my students. Somehow such expressions as "Love never faileth" and "The Kingdom of Heaven is within you" maintain their archetypal power in the depths of my mind. I know that Jesus Christ is indeed the redeemer of all humankind. It is essential that we take up his cross and follow him. If everybody does, then the whole world will be redeemed. With my lineage as a Diamond Sangha master, I too am conducting a Buddhist-Christian dialogue at a certain place on the spectrum. Moreover, I and other Diamond Sangha teachers find Christians among our members, and indeed two of the Diamond Sangha teachers with full transmission are themselves Christian clerics, one Catholic and one Protestant: Father Patrick Hawk of Amarillo, Texas, and the Reverend Dr. Rolf Drosten of Leverkusen, Germany.

Some Catholic priests and sisters who are teachers of Zen Buddhism also lead Christian contemplative retreats. They too have become elements of Buddhist-Christian interchange. The participants in these retreats, unlike their counterparts fifty years ago, no longer sit in chairs with their chins on their chests. They sit up straight and count their breaths in good Buddhist style while they settle into their Christian meditation. They commonly sit on *zafus,* the Zen Buddhist cushions, in line along the wall on two sides of the room, leaving a third side free for the entrance and the fourth for the altar, very much like Zen Buddhist meditation halls in Japan.

Thus Zen Buddhist teachers who are Christian are breaking new ground, and there are other possibilities. The Diamond Sangha has

enlarged itself to include an "Affiliate Master," a Catholic sister and retired community director, Pia Gyger, of St. Katharina-Werk in Basel,
Switzerland. Unlike Zen Buddhist teachers with Dharma transmission
who are also Catholic or Protestant, she is a Catholic superior who is
also fully qualified as a Zen Buddhist teacher. The difference is subtle
but real, and she may ultimately be viewed as the founder of a new
tradition within the edifice of the Church itself.

Under Sister Pia's influence, the members of St. Katharina-Werk not
only have integrated Zen training into their Catholic community, but
have also spun off programs to bring young people of warring areas
of the world together for reconciliation, to work with the poor in the
slums of Manila, and to speak truth to power in the halls of the United
Nations. If Buddhism as a religion of this world lacks exemplars in the
Americas and Europe, the religion of St. Katharina-Werk, by whatever
name, offers one of its own.

There is still another model — scholars of the Buddhist-Christian
dialogue who inform and in many ways guide both Buddhists and
Christians. Their translations, commentaries, and original thinking offer
invaluable insight and orientation to those of us sitting in our meditation halls. There is something far more visceral than academic research
and learned exchange involved in the Society for Buddhist-Christian
Studies, with its substantial journal full of cogent disquisitions and its
hugely successful conferences. One of its leaders, John Cobb, has said
that Buddhists "lack something of supreme importance when they do
not incorporate Jesus Christ into their Buddhism." Such eminent Buddhist scholars as Masao Abe and Keiji Nishitani argue that *shunyata,*
the potent vacancy realized in Zen Buddhist practice, is a positive rem-
edy for the discouraging, if not terrifying, nihility that some Christians
reach in their devotions.[20]

I understand Cobb, Abe, and Nishitani to be saying that a radical
commitment to relate to and take in metaphors of the other serves
not just the cause of the Buddhist-Christian interchange, but also the
profound human process of integration and peace. But perhaps there
is a limit to such interchange. I have heard that after meeting for dialogue annually for a period of ten years, Christians and Buddhists in
Kyoto found that they had nothing more to talk about. By unanimous
agreement, they established an ecumenical program of prison visitation.
This would be another model of applying the intrareligious realization: a community enlarged to include Christians, Buddhists, Muslims,
and Jews working side by side in the prison, the hospice, the political
demonstration, and the school.

Integration in the realms of practice, interchange, and shared social endeavor is not a blend or a concoction. More than a millennium
ago, Nestorian Christianity apparently attempted a kind of blanc-mange
of religion, in which distinctions between Christianity and Buddhism
were blurred. It died out, as it must inevitably, for the archetypal
metaphors of both sides were obscured and inspiration was thus lost.
Though occasionally one will see conflation in contemporary Christian-
Buddhist settings, it is generally deplored. I have heard, for example, that
"Dharma," in its meaning "Buddhist teaching," was translated as "Good
News" ("Gospel") by one Sanbo Kyodan teacher, and this was roundly
condemned by others. The intrareligious realization encompasses: it is
not a mixture. Christianity and Buddhism — not to mention Islam,
Judaism, the various Yogas, Taoism, Confucianism, Shinto, and indige-
nous practices — each can mature the human heart-mind of the sincere
student of religious mystery.

In the realm of mytho-history, the Buddhist-Christian dialogue began with the visit to the baby Jesus by the Wise Men from the East.
Forgotten for so many centuries, it has revived and is taking a fascinat-
ing, complex course. How can the process be summed up? Where do
we stand, and what might the future hold? It is evident that we have
come to the place where John Cobb could feel comfortable in suggesting that Buddhists should learn Jesus and where Masao Abe and Keiji
Nishitani were safe in suggesting that Christians should learn that the
twenty kinds of emptiness are themselves empty. The interchange and
intrachange move on from there. Buddhists are beginning to experiment
with co-housing and to stand with Catholic Workers and Plowshare ac-
tivists in challenging the acquisitive system. Christians experiment with
zazen and realize the dynamic and timeless oneness and its boundless,
fertile ramifications.

Still, the end is by no means yet. For the most part, Buddhists
and Christians are still in a dialogue phase. Moreover, in the context
of Buddhist-Catholic interchange, it is crystal clear that we will stay
where we are officially, at least for a while. See, for countless examples,
*Interreligious Dialogue: The Official Teaching of the Catholic Church (1963–
1995)*, a collection of 199 pronouncements by John Paul II and his
immediate predecessors, plus a number of other Church documents.[21]
Not only is the same patronizing message of Catholic faith repeated
over and over, but it does not deviate a bit from the historical method
and purpose of missionizing which the Church has maintained for centuries. In 1982, at the fourth centennial of the establishment of Matteo
Ricci's mission in China, John Paul II cited with favor a comment in a

letter from Father Ricci's companion, Michael Ruggieri: "We have become Chinese . . . to win the Chinese to Christ."[22] Four hundred years have passed. In most ways we live in a different world, but fundamentally the way of Matteo Ricci and his colleagues has changed only in methods of technology and communication.

Make no mistake. Ramakrishna became a Muslim to become a Muslim, and thus enlarge his Hinduism. If he had a missionizing message, it was that enlarging is good for one's own religious practice. John Paul II has a very different kind of missionizing in mind, and we must await a sea-change in the Church and its patriarchy before intrareligious realization can be possible on any scale.

Notes

1. John Paul II, *Crossing the Threshold of Hope* (New York: Alfred A. Knopf, 1994), 42–43. Emphases in this and subsequent quotations from this book are in the original.

2. Thich Nhat Hanh, *Living Buddha Living Christ* (New York: G. P. Putnam's Sons, 1995), 193.

3. John Paul II, *Crossing the Threshold of Hope*, 85–86.

4. Walpola Rahula, *What the Buddha Taught* (New York: Grove Weidenfeld, 1974). This standard manual is a commentary on the Four Noble Truths and the Eightfold Path.

5. Cited in Robert Aitken, *Encouraging Words: Zen Buddhist Teachings for Western Students* (San Francisco: Pantheon Press, 1993), 180.

6. *Mahayana* is a Sanskrit term that means "Great Vehicle." It refers to the Buddhism which arose five hundred years after Shakyamuni; it is practiced in China, Japan, Korea, and, together with Theravada (the modern development of classical Buddhism), Vietnam. Tibetan Buddhism is often considered to be Mahayana. *Vajrayana* is a Sanskrit term that means "The Way of the Adamantine Truth." It refers to the Buddhism which arose in Tibetan culture areas of western Asia in the seventh century.

7. The Buddhist Peace Fellowship and its journal, *Turning Wheel*, can be reached at P.O. Box 4650, Berkeley, CA 94704.

8. Pontifical Office for Non-Christians [now the Pontifical Council for Interreligious Dialogue], "Dialogue and Mission: Thoughts about the Attitude of the Church toward the Adherents of Other Religions," *Osservatore Romano*, August 24, 1984, 10–11.

9. John Paul II, *Crossing the Threshold of Hope*, 81.

10. Cardinal Joseph Ratzinger, "Letter to the Bishops of the Catholic Church on Some Aspects of Christian Meditation" (The Vatican, 1989), introduction, 2, n. 1.

11. *Kuan-yin* (Chinese), *Kannon* (Japanese) — derived from the Indian Buddhist archetype *Avalokiteshvara* ("one who hears the sounds of the world"; the Bodhisattva of Mercy).

12. Cited in John Paul II, *Crossing the Threshold of Hope*, 78.

13. Malcolm David Eckel, "Perspectives on the Buddhist-Christian Dialogue," in *The Christ and the Bodhisattva*, ed. Donald S. Lopez Jr. and Steven C. Rockefeller (Albany: State University of New York Press, 1987), 55–56. See also Stephen Batchelor, *The Awakening of the West: The Encounter of Buddhism and Western Culture* (Berkeley, Calif.: Parallax Press, 1984), 32–34.

Tolstoy mentions the story of St. Josaphat in *My Confession* (London: J. M. Dent, 1904), 79. We may conjecture that Tolstoy's act of leaving home at the very end of his life to die in a lonely railroad station was his way of embodying the archetypal story. I like to think that he knew it was the story of the Buddha setting out to find his spiritual fortune. Tolstoy's last pilgrimage, however misguided, would then be a classic case of playing out an intrareligious realization.

14. Hans-J. Klimkeit, "Christians, Buddhists and Manichaeans in Medieval Central Asia," *Buddhist-Christian Studies* 1 (1981): 47–48.

15. Don Morreale, ed., *Buddhist America: Centers, Retreats, Practices* (Santa Fe: John Muir Publications, 1988). *Theravada* is a Pali term meaning "The Way of the Elders." It refers to modern Buddhism of South and Southeast Asia.

16. John Paul II, *Crossing the Threshold of Hope*, 85.

17. Batchelor, *Awakening of the West*, 212, citing Hugo Enomiya-Lassalle, *Zen Way to Enlightenment* (London: Sheed and Ward, 1966), 35.

18. Cited in Batchelor, *Awakening of the West*, 214.

19. Willigis Jäger, "Zen and Religion," *Blind Donkey* 9, no. 1 (January 1987): 13–24.

20. See Lopez and Rockefeller, eds., introduction to *Christ and the Bodhisattva*, 37.

21. Pontifical Council for Interreligious Dialogue, *Interreligious Dialogue: The Official Teaching of the Catholic Church (1963–1995)*, ed. Francesco Gioia (Boston: Pauline Books, 1997).

22. Ibid., 259.

7

On John Paul II's View of Buddhism

MASAO ABE

In his book *Crossing the Threshold of Hope*, we find John Paul II's essay "Buddha?" This is the best essay to know the Pope's view of Buddhism. At the beginning of the essay the Pope states:

> [F]rom a certain point of view, like Christianity, [Buddhism] is a religion of salvation. Nevertheless, it needs to be said right away that the doctrines of salvation in Buddhism and Christianity are opposed.

The Buddhist doctrine of salvation is, according to him,

> almost exclusively *negative soteriology*. The "enlightenment" experienced by Buddha comes down to the conviction that the world is bad, that it is the source of evil and of suffering for man. To liberate oneself from this evil, one must free oneself from this world.

These statements touch the core of the present issue. And the crucial point lies in the term "detachment." Detachment is the negation of attachment or overcoming of attachment. This is the necessary condition for Buddhist salvation. Detachment from the world is sine qua non for Buddhist salvation. However, it is not sufficient. For Buddhist salvation, not only detachment from the world but also detachment from detachment itself is necessary. True detachment is dynamic, including detachment from the world and freedom from detachment. However important the detachment from the world may be, one should not attach to "the detachment from the world." Detachment must be realized even from "the detachment from the world." Rigid indifference to the world is simply another form of attachment, that is, attachment to detachment.

Although Buddhism emphasizes the importance of detachment, Buddhism is not a negative soteriology, as the Pope suggests, because Buddhism's emphasis on detachment includes detachment from detachment.

Buddhist detachment is a dynamic and creative detachment. For the sake of detachment from the world, Buddhists can work in the world without being limited by secular conditions. Buddhists can make social commitments freely.

In this connection, it would be helpful for us to return to the Buddha's teaching of the Middle Path:

Avoiding both of the two extremes such as hedonism and asceticism, Buddha showed the Middle Path as the way of salvation: the Middle Path is not a mere middle point of two extremes. It leads us to go beyond the duality itself and to the higher knowledge *(Abbiñña)*.

With this higher knowledge one is no longer enslaved by the duality of attachment and detachment, but realizes a master dynamic and creative detachment.

In his essay "Buddha?" the Pope states that

Buddhism is in large measure an *"atheistic"* system. We do not free ourselves from evil through the good which comes from God; we liberate ourselves only through detachment from the world, which is bad. The fullness of such a detachment is not union with God, but what is called nirvana, a state of perfect indifference with regard to the world.

The Pope understands Buddhism to be "in large measure an 'atheistic' system" probably by taking Christianity and Judaism as the standard of judgment. Unlike Christianity and Judaism, Buddhism is not a monotheism which is based on the belief in one absolute God who is creator, lawgiver, judge, and redeemer. Instead, Buddhism is based on the law of *pratitya-samutpada*, or dependent co-origination.

This law indicates that everything in and out of the world is completely interdependent, that is, co-arising and co-ceasing; nothing is self-existing. Even the divine is interdependently realized with the human. The fullness of the law of dependent co-origination is not becoming one with God, but the realization that everyone and everything is respectively the manifestation of the absolute Reality. Buddhism is not an atheism, but a religious realism beyond monotheism.

Mahayana Buddhists take samsara (endless transmigration of living and dying) in itself as "Death" in its authentic sense. Death in its authentic sense is not death as distinguished from life. If we grasp the process of transmigration not from the outside (objectively), but from within (subjectively or existentially), then we are always living and yet always dying at every moment. Without living, there is no dying; without dying, there is no living. Living and dying are nondualistically one in our existential realization. Since living and dying are two opposing principles, this antinomic oneness of living and dying itself is the greatest suffering: Death. In this existential realization, the endless transmigration of living-dying as such is realized as the Great Death.

The realization of the Great Death has a double connotation: negative and positive. On the one hand, the Great Death is negative in that it entails the antinomic oneness of living and dying as the greatest suffering — the most serious existential problem which must be solved to attain emancipation. On the other hand, the Great Death is positive in that it entails the resolution of the problems of suffering and the realization of the Great Life. This double connotation and the accompanying shift from the negative to the positive connotation are possible because the Great Death is a total, holistic, and existential realization of the endlessness of living-dying in which one becomes identical with the Great Death and thereby overcomes the endlessness of living-dying. Once we come to this existential realization, we can say with justification that samsara and nirvana are identical. Thus the realization of the Great Death is the crucial point for the seemingly paradoxical Mahayana doctrines.

Ethically speaking, Buddhists clearly realize that good should conquer evil. However, through the experience of their inner struggle, Buddhists cannot say that good is strong enough to overcome evil. Good and evil are completely antagonistic principles, resisting each other with equal force, yet inseparably connected and displaying an existential antinomy as a whole. However imperative it may be from the ethical point of view, it is, according to Buddhism, illusory to believe it possible to overcome evil with good and thereby to attain the highest good. Since good and evil are mutually negating principles with equal power, an ethical effort to overcome evil with good never succeeds and results in a serious dilemma. Realizing this existential dilemma innate in human existence and characterizing it in terms of original sin, Christians have propounded the necessity of faith in God, who delivers man from sin through God's redemptive activity. From a Christian perspective, God himself is Good with a capital G, as can be noted in the biblical statement, "No one is good, but God alone" (Mark 10:18; Luke 18:19). Since the law is the expression of God's will, obedience and disobedience to the law constitute human good and evil. Moreover, it is emphasized, "Do not be overcome by evil, but overcome evil with good" (Romans 12:21).

In Buddhism, on the contrary, what is essential for salvation is not to overcome evil with good and to participate in the supreme Good, but to be emancipated from the existential antinomy of good and evil and to awaken to Emptiness prior to the opposition between good and evil. In the existential awakening to Emptiness, one can be master of, rather than enslaved by, good and evil. In this sense, the realization of true Emptiness is the basis for human freedom, creative activity, and ethical life.

Thus, the following aspects of Buddhist salvation must be noted: (1) Buddhism is primarily concerned with salvation of a human being as a person who, unlike other living beings, has self-consciousness and free will and thereby alone has the potential to become aware of and emancipated from the transience common to all things in the universe. This is the existentialistic and personalistic aspect of Buddhism. (2) However, a cosmological dimension is the necessary basis for this Buddhist salvation, because in Buddhism salvation is not from sin as rebellion against God, but emancipation from the cycle of birth and death, which is part of the transience of the universe. This is the cosmological aspect of Buddhism. These two aspects are inseparable — the more cosmological the basis of salvation, the more existentially thoroughgoing the salvation. In this sense, the Buddhist cosmology which is the basis of nirvana is an existential cosmology, and Buddhist existentialism or personalism may be called "cosmo-existentialism" or "cosmo-personalism."

Mahayana Buddhism has always emphasized, "Do not abide in nirvana" as well as "Do not abide in samsara." This means that one should not abide in transmigration nor abide in the emancipation from transmigration, that is, nirvana. The reason is that if one abides in so-called nirvana by transcending samsara, one is not yet completely free from attachment, that is, attachment to nirvana, and that one is still confined by the duality of nirvana and samsara. It must also be said that one is still selfishly concerned with one's own salvation, forgetting the suffering of others in samsara. On the basis of the idea of the Bodhisattva, Mahayana Buddhism thus criticizes and rejects nirvana as the transcendence of samsara and teaches true nirvana to be the returning to samsara by negating or transcending "nirvana as the transcendence of samsara." Therefore, nirvana in the Mahayana sense, while transcending samsara, is nothing but the realization of samsara as samsara, no more no less, through the complete returning to samsara itself. This is why, in Mahayana Buddhism, it is often said of true nirvana that "samsara as-it-is is nirvana." This paradoxical statement is again based on the dialectical character of true nirvana, which is, logically speaking, the negation of negation (that is, absolute affirmation) or the transcendence of transcendence (that is, absolute immanence). True nirvana is, according to Mahayana Buddhism, the real source of both *prajna* (wisdom) and *karuna* (compassion). It is the source of *prajna* because it is entirely free from the discriminating mind and thus is able to see everything in its uniqueness and distinctiveness without any sense of attachment. It is the source of *karuna* because it is unselfishly concerned with the salvation of all others in samsara through one's own returning to samsara.

For the sake of wisdom, do not abide in samsara; for the sake of compassion, do not abide in nirvana. This is the meaning of life in Buddhism.

8

A Buddhist Response
to John Paul II

JOSÉ IGNACIO CABEZÓN

In the latter half of the twentieth century religions find themselves being pulled in two opposed directions by two distinct sets of competing forces. On the one hand, there are the conservative forces of tradition that exert pressures on religions by compelling them to maintain their independence and assert their uniqueness. These forces, acting like the survival instinct in organisms, cause religions to view each other antagonistically, as competitors in the spiritual jungle. On the other hand, especially in the last few decades, we see at work a new set of forces that cause these same traditions to view themselves as members of a common human family (a society) of religions. These latter forces, irenic in nature, impel religions in the direction of greater mutual respect and cooperation. To use a Freudian analogy, we might say that these two sets of forces function for traditions the way the id and superego function for individuals. A healthy tradition, like a well-rounded individual, is one that learns to balance these forces, neither succumbing to the temptation to annihilate competitors, nor allowing itself to be swallowed up by them. I propose to respond to John Paul II's views of Buddhism by analyzing how he has attempted to balance the two sets of forces just described in some of his published works, and by offering some critical judgments concerning his efforts in this regard.

Irenic Tendencies

In perusing the documents pertinent to the present topic, one is struck almost immediately by the sheer number and diversity of Buddhist visitors the Pope has received, both in Rome and on his numerous visits to countries with sizable Buddhist populations. John Paul II has met with more Buddhist leaders and laypeople from a wider range of Buddhist cultures than any Pope before him. He not only has been passively welcoming of Buddhists, but has actively sought to bring about interreligious encounters, both in the Asian countries he has visited, and, for example, in his convening of the World Day of Prayer for Peace in Assisi in 1986. The importance for interreligious dialogue of sheer human, face-to-face contact cannot be overestimated, and in this regard the efforts of John Paul II have been exemplary.

As witnessed by his constant reference to these documents, it is clear that the texts of the Second Vatican Council serve in many ways as the theological ground for the Pope's thought and actions regarding interreligious dialogue. Hence, it is clear that John Paul II, at least in the early years of his papacy, concurs with positive depictions of Buddhism in those texts, such as the one in *Nostra Aetate*, that state of Buddhism that it "testifies to the essential inadequacy of this changing world. It proposes a way of life by which men can, with confidence and trust, attain a state of perfect liberation and reach a state of supreme illumination either through their own efforts or by the aid of divine help."[1] It is also evident that he sees his attempts to reach out to adherents of different faiths, Buddhism among them, as fulfilling the call in such documents for entering "with prudence and charity into discussions and collaborations with members of other religions" (*NA, ID* 38), and to treat all people "in brotherly fashion, . . . to be at peace with all men" (*NA, ID* 40). Such attitudes and activities on the part of Catholics, the documents state, are appropriate because of the essential unity of humankind — "All men form but one community" (*NA, ID* 37)[2] — and because of the similarities that exist between religions in seeking to address the "unsolved riddles of human existence": the nature of man, sin, virtue and the afterlife, the purpose of life, the origin of suffering, and the path to happiness (*NA, ID* 37).[3] Hence, John Paul II reiterates on many occasions that "the Catholic Church rejects nothing of what is true and holy in these religions. She has a high regard for the manner of life and conduct, the precepts and doctrines which, although differing in many ways from her own teaching, nevertheless often reflect a ray of truth which enlightens all men" (*NA, ID* 38).[4]

Many of the documents of Vatican II, however, are often cautious both in regard to other religions and in regard to the way in which Catholics should engage in the task of interreligious dialogue. This caution is reflected in the wording of these texts, and is present as well in the writings of John Paul II. Hence, *Nostra Aetate* speaks of other religions often (not always) reflecting a ray (not the totality) of truth. John Paul reiterates this on several occasions and adds that other religions contain "the 'traces' or 'seeds' of the Word" (not the Word itself) (*ID* 341). *Lumen Gentium* is willing to grant the possibility of eternal salvation to "those who, through no fault of their own, do not know the gospel of Christ or his Church" (*LG, ID* 42), but is silent about those who actively and self-consciously repudiate theism (and therefore Christianity) in favor of other religious options, as most Buddhists do. It speaks of passive non-Christians as seeking God through "shadows and images" (*LG, ID* 42) (not through the light of truth that is Christ), and though it is willing to grant the existence of good and truth in other religions, it is explicit that these are, even in these religions, the gift of Christ, and "a preparation for the Gospel" (*LG, ID* 42). For example, the need for asceticism and contemplation, states *Ad Gentes*, has "been sown by God in certain ancient cultures before the preaching of the Gospel" (*AG, ID* 52), and it goes on to encourage the careful study of these traditions to see how they "might be incorporated into the Christian life." The good "found down in the minds and hearts of men or in the rites and customs of people" is to be "preserved from destruction," but it is also to be "purified, raised up and perfected for the glory of God" (*LG, ID* 43; see also *AG, ID* 47, 49).

Caution is exhibited in these sources, and in John Paul's own writings, not only as regards the place of other religions and their doctrines vis-à-vis the Church, but also as regards the very process of dialogue. Cooperation with other religions, both for the clergy and for the laity, as mentioned in *Apostolicam Actuositatem*, is not only desirable, it is often imperative, and yet this cooperation should be "prudent" (*AA, ID* 44; and also *NA, ID* 38). This prudence or caution is exhibited in John Paul II's own statement prior to the Assisi conference:

> What will take place at Assisi will certainly not be religious syncretism but a sincere attitude of prayer to God in an atmosphere of mutual respect. For this reason, the formula chosen for the gathering at Assisi is: being together in order to pray. Certainly we cannot "pray together," namely to make a common prayer, but we can be present while others pray. (*ID* 341; see also *ID* 365)

Hence, caution or prudence in the action of dialogue involves at the very least the repudiation of syncretism[5] — the maintenance of the boundaries of tradition[6] — both in regard to attitude and in regard to religious ritual.

All of this is to say, although not of course in so many words, that truth belongs ultimately and in its entirety to the Church alone. To the extent that truth and good exist in other religions and cultures (e.g., the contemplative and ascetic tradition of Buddhism), it exists there as a gift of God,[7] though even then it needs to be adapted (purified and perfected) so that it may properly serve the Church. Some Buddhists may see in these qualifications a kind of elitism and even paternalism. They may balk at being characterized as having "an implicit faith in Him [Christ]" (*Crossing the Threshold of Hope* [hereafter: *CTH*] 83). They may sense in the notion of "prudence" a nascent paranoia, but as a method of perceiving and interacting with other religions, I see little that is objectionable here. Every religion that seeks to maintain the uniqueness and integrity of its tradition must find some meaningful way of situating other traditions vis-à-vis its own. It would be absurd to demand that in this process the other should emerge as superior to, or even on a par with, one's own tradition. Buddhist attempts to situate itself vis-à-vis Christianity for the purposes of interreligious dialogue are no less elitist.[8] Such is the nature of the beast we call tradition. No matter how infused it is with qualifications that seek to preserve the integrity, uniqueness, and even the superiority of the Catholic Church's own tradition, the overall tenor of most of John Paul II's interreligious rhetoric is irenic in tone: "We know what we believe to be the limits of these religions, but that does not take away from the fact that they possess even outstanding religious values and qualities" (*ID* 341).[9]

John Paul II thus sees within Buddhism, if not truth in a pure form, at least "religious elements at the service of truth" (*ID* 410). While in some early missives he has implied that Buddhist monasticism represents a "flight from society" (*ID* 260), elsewhere he recognizes that the spiritual search of Buddhist monks is "similar in some respects" to that of Christian monks (*ID* 418), and in general John Paul II has been supportive of the Buddhist-Christian monastic/contemplative dialogue (see *ID* 377–78). Citing *Redemptoris Missio*, he makes it clear that Buddhism does have something to teach the Catholic Church, when, for example, he exhorts the bishops of Thailand to see in other religions "a challenge for the Church," one that forces her "to examine more deeply her own identity" (*ID* 455).[10] "Dialogue with the great religious traditions of Asia recalls for us the universal values of self-discipline, silence and contemplation in developing the human person" (*ID* 458). And again, when addressing religious representatives in Japan in 1980, he expresses the Church's "esteem for your high spiritual values, such as purity, detachment of heart, love for the beauty of nature, and benevolence and compassion for everything that lives" (*ID* 222). At times the Pope has gone so far as to tell Buddhists that he knows that they "understand the heart. And the aspirations of our hearts are pointing in the same direction" (*ID* 245). This rhetoric, irenic in tone, is the rule, rather than the exception, in the Pope's writings on Buddhism up to the early 1990s.

Agon Rising

In the early 1990s, however, there is a significant shift in the Pope's rhetoric concerning Buddhism. This culminates in the polemic against Buddhism found in his 1994 book *Crossing the Threshold of Hope*. Three years earlier, in 1991, the Pope cautions the bishops of North Africa regarding "some limits to dialogue." "It is difficult if certain partners," he says, "are not capable of seeing the other religion as it really is, but rather let themselves be influenced by prejudice" (*ID* 466). This, I would suggest, is precisely the limit of the Pope's reaction to Buddhism as it is found in his 1994 volume. We find there not the generally positive, albeit cautious, depiction of Buddhism that is found in most of John Paul II's other writings, but rather a negative depiction of Buddhism that I believe emerges out of the Pope's inability to see the other "as it really is."

The doctrines of salvation in Buddhism and Christianity are not simply different, states John Paul II — they "are opposed" (*CTH* 85). The Buddhist soteriology, "the only point of this system," is a negative one: "[T]he world is bad. . . . [I]t is the source of evil and of suffering for man" (*CTH* 89). Buddhist enlightenment, the Pope states, requires separating oneself from — becoming indifferent to — the world, distancing oneself from what is essential to our human, psychic, and bodily existence (*CTH* 85–86). Although detachment is conducive to salvation even in Christianity, Christian detachment, unlike its Buddhist counterpart, is not an end in itself, having as its goal not negative indifference, but positive union with God. Buddhist contemplative methods may bring about a certain level of purification, and so serve a function similar to the preparatory (purification) stage in Christian mysticism, but the Buddhist techniques are incomplete insofar as, being directed at that negative goal, they cannot lead "the human soul to be permeated with the living flame of love" (*CTH* 87).

Christian mysticism has "built up" Christianity, the Church, and even Western civilization precisely because of its positive soteriology (*CTH* 88). We are thus left to wonder whether the negative soteriology of Buddhism can sustain any *real* religion — any *meaningful* form of civilization — at all, since it is "fundamentally contrary to the development of both man himself and the world" (*CTH* 88). Christians, who should in any case "know their own spiritual heritage well, and consider whether it is right to set it aside lightly" (*CTH* 90), must therefore be cautious of how they attempt to appropriate Buddhist techniques of meditation.

Such a position regarding Buddhism clearly represents a departure from Church doctrine in recent decades. It calls for a detailed reply from Buddhist theologians, which unfortunately is beyond the scope of this essay. It would be irresponsible of me, however, not to offer some response to what is probably the most lengthy assessment of Buddhism in the history of the papacy, and so I offer the following brief comments.

John Paul's tactics in these few pages of *Crossing the Threshold of Hope* are clearly meant to portray Buddhism as a kind of world-denying gnosticism.[11] If by the *world* we mean all that exists, then certainly Buddhism cannot be characterized as world-denying, since such a world includes the state of ultimate human perfection Buddhists call enlightenment. Now Buddhism does maintain that the world of nonenlightened beings is filled with suffering. But "the evil" that is the source of this suffering, though a part of the world, is neither the world itself, nor is it caused by the world. That the world is the "theater" in which sentient beings experience suffering does not make the world evil, nor does it require Buddhists to abandon it. What *is* to be abandoned is the suffering and the causes of suffering, not the world. The evil that is the principal cause of suffering is ignorance, and its elimination leads to the state of permanent peace and fulfillment known as enlightenment. Enlightenment is achieved only *in* this world, and not apart from it. It requires *understanding* the world, not flight from it. Christians too maintain that there is something to be abandoned. They call it sin. But this no more makes of Christianity a negative soteriology than the notion of abandoning ignorance does of Buddhism. Clearly, there are both negative and positive aspects to the soteriology of both religions. It is no more the case that Buddhism's theory of salvation is completely negative than it is that Christianity's is wholly positive.

What positive elements exist in Buddhists' depictions of enlightenment? Buddhas — that is, perfected beings, beings who have attained enlightenment — are said not only to have abandoned all negative qualities (*spang bya*), but to have acquired all positive ones (*sgrub pa'i chos; yon tan*).[12] Among the most important positive qualities of buddhas mentioned in the Mahayana Buddhist texts are wisdom (*prajna*),[13] the understanding of the world as it is, and altruism (*byang sems*), which in buddhas manifests as the desire — based on pure, impartial love and compassion — to free all beings from suffering.[14] These positive qualities exist in a seminal state in all beings (both human and nonhuman), which is to say that all beings have the capacity for perfection as part of their nature.[15] The attainment of enlightenment, far from requiring of human beings that they abandon what is natural to them, is precisely the actualization of what is truly natural to them. Attaining enlightenment is what allows beings to interact in the world in truly authentic, spontaneous, and loving ways. The Buddhist sources claim that love for beings in the minds of buddhas is so profound that it literally causes them to become embodied, to enter the world for the sake of helping beings. Hence, the very bodies of buddhas are the physical manifestation of their love for others. So much for the claims that Buddhism lacks positive aspects to its soteriology, that it requires the abandonment of what is natural to human beings, and that it falls short of having a fully developed notion of love.

In addition to what might be characterized as a *theological* opposition to Buddhism, just described, there is also evident in *Crossing the Threshold of Hope* what can only be called a kind of *annoyance*, this directed at the fact that Buddhist leaders like the Dalai Lama are bringing "Buddhism to the people of the Christian West, stirring up interest both in Buddhist meditation and in its methods of praying" (*CTH* 85). John Paul II also seems disturbed at seeing Western Buddhist monks in the entourage of the patriarch of Thailand (*CTH* 85). To this annoyance at the presence of Buddhism in Western culture, one can only reply, I suppose, that in this age of radical pluralism there *is* no longer any such thing as the *Christian* West. The West no more belongs to Christianity (or to Judaism or to Islam) than the East does to Hinduism or Buddhism or Confucianism. Moreover, if Westerners find some consolation and spiritual nourishment in the teachings of Asian religions like Buddhism, is this not a cause for rejoicing, especially if the alternative for many of these people is, as I think is clear, secular atheism? In any case, if there is interest in the spiritual path of Buddhism in the West, it is largely because Westerners have not seen their own religious traditions as sources of such nourishment. So if annoyance is to be the response, perhaps it is better directed at those Western (including Catholic) religious leaders who, lacking such spiritual grounding themselves, fail in their task of inculcating the foundations for the spiritual path in others.

The distorted picture of Buddhism in John Paul's more recent writings arises from what is an increasing fear of Buddhism as a competitor in the spiritual, especially the contemplative, sphere. As mentioned above, papal documents in the early years of the present papacy exhibited a cautious admiration of Buddhism. Although a 1992 statement by John Paul II praises "the religions of Asia, especially Hinduism and Buddhism," for their "contemplative spirit, their methods of meditation and asceticism," there is already evident in that same document a concern regarding individuals who "have lost their roots in their own tradition and are looking to other sources for spiritual support and enrichment" (*ID* 499). The threat is identified in that text not as Buddhism, however, but as "new or alternative religious movements," which are "a challenge . . . to the Christian communities of Asia" (*ID* 500). By 1994, as we have seen, the Pope is declaring *Buddhism itself* to be the threat, and now a threat not to Asia but to the Christian West. Fear of Buddhism in the Catholic Church can be seen most recently in a 1997 interview given to the French weekly *L'Express* by Cardinal Joseph Ratzinger, the head of Vatican's Congregation for the Doctrine of the Faith, and a close theological adviser to the Pope.[16] There, Ratzinger states that "in the 1950s someone said that the undoing of the Catholic Church in the twentieth century wouldn't come from Marxism but from Buddhism. . . . They were right." Ratzinger's remarks — fueled, no doubt, by the statements in the Pope's book — border on paranoia, and represent a considerable departure from the Church's position on Buddhism in the 1970s and 1980s.

Certainly, it is the right (and even duty) of any religion to criticize what it considers to be false or dangerous in another religion. And whether or not it is right, it is certainly natural for a religious tradition to protect itself from what it considers the threat of another religious tradition using all rhetorical means at its disposal. But for such rhetoric to be convincing, it should be based on fact, not fiction, error, and mischaracterization. Personally, I have great faith in the power of dialogue — in its ability to correct misperceptions and to assuage fears. It is my hope that this present, difficult period in Buddhist-Catholic relations will quickly come to an end, but this will occur only through the understanding that is brought about by dialogue. I end, therefore, with this prayer: that hearts everywhere may be open to the truth that is the fruit of dialogue.

Notes

1. *Nostra Aetate* (hereafter *NA*), in Francesco Gioia, ed., *Interreligious Dialogue: The Official Teaching of the Catholic Church (1963–1995)* (hereafter *ID*) (Boston: Pauline Books, 1997), 38. For an implicit reference to Buddhism in the writings of John Paul that reflects the views of *NA*, see *ID* 371–72.

2. This sentiment is echoed repeatedly in the writings of John Paul II; see, for example, *ID* 393. The nature of the unity, however, is not always theologically neutral, but decisively Christian in nature. Consider John Paul's words to the Roman Curia: "Accordingly, there is *only one* plan for every human being who comes into this world (cf. John 1:9), one single origin and goal, whatever may be the color of his skin, the historical and geographical framework within which he happens to live and act, or the culture in which he grows up and expresses himself. The differences are a less important element, when confronted with the unity which is radical, fundamental and decisive" (*ID* 361).

3. See also John Paul's statement at the conclusion of the Assisi conference, in which he identifies the two most important similarities between the various religions represented at that meeting: the preservation and dignity of life and the realization that peace is ultimately to be sought in the reality beyond this life (*ID* 349).

4. This one passage of *NA* is cited repeatedly in the work of John Paul II. See, for example, *ID* 287, 341, 364, 470, and *Crossing the Threshold of Hope* (New York: Alfred A. Knopf, 1994) (hereafter: *CTH*), 80.

5. "Not only syncretism, but also the appearance of syncretism which is totally contrary to real ecumenism" (*ID* 433).

6. This commitment to one's own tradition is sometimes spoken of as a commitment to "truth," "the voice of conscience," or "adherence to the truth of one's convictions," which John Paul sees not only as a precondition for dialogue, but as something which "by its very nature makes dialogue with others both necessary and fruitful" (*ID* 422). On the importance of safeguarding "the uniqueness of each religious tradition," see also *ID* 379.

7. "The Spirit who 'blows where he wills' (cf. John 3:8) is the source of inspiration for all that is true, good and beautiful. . . . 'Every truth, no matter who says it, comes from the Holy Spirit' " (*ID* 445).

8. For example, some Buddhists may find it disturbing and paternalistic when their traditions are characterized by John Paul, following *Evangelii Nuntiandi*, as "carrying within them the echo of thousands of years of searching for God, a quest which is incomplete but often made with great sincerity and righteousness of heart" (*ID* 409), but no more so, I suppose, than Christians are when they are characterized by Buddhists as devoting their lives to the worship of a nonexistent entity, or worse, of a whimsical mundane deity.

9. There are times at which one might have hoped for greater sensitivity in the Pope's words, as, for example, when he describes the religious leaders at

Assisi as "turning, all of us, toward God, in order to implore this gift [of peace] from him" or when he describes their common aspiration as a "journey toward one final end, God" (*ID* 368). Wherever other religious leaders may have been turning, it is clear that Buddhists were neither turning nor journeying toward God! But even in that same text, there is discernment that not all of those present share a belief in "a personal God who is all-powerful" (*ID* 369; see also 371–72).

10. A similar sentiment is expressed in his very first statement to the Secretariat for Non-Christians in 1979. See *ID* 216.

11. It is interesting that John Paul II should mention gnosticism at the conclusion of his discussion of Buddhism, not by identifying Buddhism as a kind of gnosticism, but by claiming that the latter is the underlying philosophy of "so-called New Age" movements (*CTH* 90). I find this a bit disingenuous, however, for in substance, if not in name, the kind of theological position that is ascribed to Buddhism in the preceding pages is precisely that of gnosticism, or at least that of certain branches of gnosticism.

12. For a detailed treatment of the Mahayana Buddhist notion of enlightenment, see John J. Makransky, *Buddhahood Embodied: Sources of Controversy in India and Tibet* (Albany: State University of New York Press, 1997).

13. Wisdom, at least for Indian and Tibetan Mahayana Buddhists, refers to the understanding of emptiness, on which see Jay Garfield, *The Fundamental Wisdom of the Middle Way: Nagarjuna's* Mulamadhyamakakarika (New York: Oxford University Press, 1995); C. W. Huntington Jr. and Geshé Namgyal Wangchen, *The Emptiness of Emptiness: An Introduction to Early Indian Madhyamika* (Honolulu: University of Hawaii Press, 1989); Jeffrey Hopkins, *Meditation on Emptiness* (Boston: Wisdom Publications, 1993); and José Ignacio Cabezón, *A Dose of Emptiness: An Annotated Translation of the* sTong thun chen mo *of mKhas grub dGe legs dpal bzang* (Albany: State University of New York Press, 1992).

14. See Harvey Aronson, *Love and Sympathy in Theravada Buddhism* (Delhi: Motilal Banarsidass, 1980); and the Dalai Lama, *The World of Tibetan Buddhism*, translated, edited, and annotated by Geshe Thubten Jinpa (Boston: Wisdom Publications, 1995), part 2.

15. This doctrine is known in Mahayana Buddhism as the doctrine of buddha-nature (*tathagatagarbha*). See David Seyford Ruegg, *La théorie du tathagatagarbha et du gotra: Études sur la soteriologie et la gnoséologie du Bouddhisme* (Paris: École Française d'Extrême Orient, 1969). For a more concise and lucid synopsis of the doctrine, see Paul Williams, *Mahayana Buddhism: The Doctrinal Foundations* (London: Routledge, 1989), chapter 3.

16. I base the remarks that follow on a syndicated article by Christopher P. Winner, "Cardinal Warns of Buddhism," *Denver Post*, March 26, 1997, 27a, which appeared originally in *USA Today*.

Part Three

JEWISH RESPONSES

9

John Paul II and the Jews

DAVID M. GORDIS

At the time of this writing, His Holiness Pope John Paul II is in
Poland, revisiting, perhaps for the last time in view of his failing health
and advancing years, the country of his birth. He is now in the city of
Cracow, the intellectual center in which he was formed and where he
lived during World War II, where he became Bishop and then Cardinal.
Though accounts of his trip dwell both on its personal nature (he will
visit his parents' graves) and on its potential impact on Polish politics
and on the overwhelmingly Catholic populations of Poland, no Jewish
observer of the Pope and his career can be unmoved by this journey's
special resonance for Jews. No Pope in all of the history of the papacy
has focused on the Church's relationship to Jews and to Judaism as has
John Paul II. He has been most outspoken of all Popes in renouncing
Church teaching of contempt for Jews. Undoubtedly, his rejection of
the "teaching of contempt" and his concern for Jews and Judaism were
forged in the crucible of World War II, in that city so close to Auschwitz. As he returns there now, the moment is a good one for reflection
on the intellectual and spiritual journey he has taken in shaping his and
the Church's conception of Jews and Judaism.

The account of the revolutionary transformation of the relationship
of the Church both to Judaism and to Jews must, of course, begin
with His Holiness Pope John XXIII and the Second Vatican Council.
Pope John XXIII was a remarkable leader of the Catholic Church, who
set out on a twofold journey of restructuring the relationship of the
Church to the Jews and Judaism; he set in motion a reconsideration of
doctrinal and liturgical formulations, and he introduced a new pattern

of interrelationships between Catholics and Jews. It has been noted that in choosing the name that would mark his papacy, John Paul II was deliberately associating himself with his predecessors, John XXIII, whose Vatican II gave birth to *Nostra Aetate,* the declaration on the Church and the Jews; Pope Paul VI, who established the Holy See's Commission for Religious Relations with the Jews; as well as John Paul I, who reigned briefly and sustained at least the tone of what had preceded him but whose impact was abbreviated along with his reign.[1]

John XXIII reshaped the world of the Church through *aggiornamento,* a period of renewed seeking of God's presence in the world, and Paul VI created instruments to articulate and pursue the transformation. But it has been John Paul II who has made the relationship of the Church with the Jews a central feature of his papacy. What are the central themes of his journey? What has been accomplished, and what remains to be done? Drawing on the collected texts of the Pope's statements[2] and on the excellent work of Eugene Fisher and others, I will review central themes and venture some observations on the implications of the Pope's vision for Catholic-Jewish relations in particular and for interreligious relationships in general.

The principal themes in the Church's reconsideration of its relations with Judaism and the Jewish people are familiar and, as expected, recur as motifs in the statements of John Paul II, modulated and recast but reappearing in the tens of pronouncements made in the course of meetings with Jewish groups of all kinds at the Vatican and in many other world cities: a repudiation of anti-Semitism; the rejection of supersessionism, the doctrine that the covenant with the Church supplanted the covenantal relationship of God with the Jewish people, and the affirmation of the latter's continuing validity; and the vision of a "joint social action and witness to the One God and the reality of the Kingdom of God as the defining point of human history."[3]

The fullest articulation of these themes took place on the extraordinary occasion of the Pope's visit to the Synagogue of Rome on April 13, 1986. This was an epochal event, of great symbolic power and emblematic force as well as substantive importance. Even those who did not understand a word of what was said on that day were overwhelmed by the image of the white-clad Pope and the Chief Rabbi of Rome, Elio Toaff, also clad in white, embracing at the impressive Moorish-style synagogue. The Jewish community of Rome was there physically in impressive numbers, but all there assembled felt also the symbolic presence of Italian and European Jewry who had perished in the Holocaust. For them this visit came too late.

Beyond the imagery, the Pope used the occasion of his visit to make his most extensive and thorough statement of his position on Jews and Judaism. The statement is central to our theme and deserves full and careful study and analysis.

The Pope began his address on that occasion by placing his visit into a historical and theological context:

> First of all, I would like, together with you, to give thanks and praise to the Lord who stretched out the heavens and laid the foundations of the earth and who chose Abraham in order to make him father of a multitude of children, as numerous "as the stars of heaven and as the sand which is on the seashore" (Genesis 22:17) — to give thanks and praise to him because it has been his good pleasure, in the mystery of his Providence, that this evening there should be a meeting in this, your "Major Temple," between the Jewish community which has been living in this city since the times of the ancient Romans and the Bishop of Rome and universal Pastor of the Catholic Church.

The Pope's intent was clearly to suggest that the occasion of his visit was a significant event both in sacred history as well as in the unfolding drama of Catholic-Jewish relations. He made reference to the long gestation period of his visit: "I had been thinking of this visit for a long time." He referred to the frequency of meetings of Jews with his predecessors Paul VI, John XXIII, and Pius XII. The passing reference to John XXIII was not meant to suggest a lack of recognition of the extraordinary role of that Pope in the unfolding drama. John Paul II proceeded to state explicitly:

> The heritage that I would now like to take up is precisely that of Pope John, who on one occasion, as he passed by here — as the Chief Rabbi has just mentioned — stopped the car so that he could bless the crowd of Jews who were coming out of this very temple. And I would like to take up this heritage at this very moment, when I find myself not just outside, but, thanks to your generous hospitality, inside the Synagogue of Rome.[4]

John Paul then proceeds to refer to *Nostra Aetate* and the historic change that it represented. The general acceptance of a "legitimate plurality on the social, civil and religious levels has been arrived at with great difficulty."[5] What brought about this recognition? It was not any adjustment of belief patterns or theological stance. Rather, the change was a necessity of history, a requirement in view of the tragic historical record. Despite the difficulty in adjusting to a change of attitude toward the "other," the change was a historical necessity:

> Nevertheless, a consideration of centuries-long cultural conditioning could not prevent us from recognizing that acts of discrimination, unjustified limitation of religious freedom, oppression also on the level of civil freedom in regard to the Jews were, from an objective point of view, gravely deplorable manifestations. Yes, once again, through myself, the Church, in the words of the well-known declaration *Nostra Aetate,* "deplores the hatred, persecutions, and displays of anti-Semitism directed against the Jews at any time and by anyone." I repeat: "by anyone."[6]

The Pope then proceeds from the general category of persecution to the specific horror of the Holocaust: "I would like once more to express a word of abhorrence for the genocide decreed against the Jewish people during the last war, which led to the *holocaust* of millions of innocent victims."[7]

This papal statement is obviously heartfelt, but it is also carefully crafted, and reveals as well as any of the formulations I have read or heard the characteristics of the papal repudiation of historical anti-Semitism. Careful analysis is useful and will allow me to suggest one major thesis of my discussion: the Pope is genuinely and profoundly moved by the agonies of history and seeks to change that history for the better. At the same time he is constricted by theological rigidity, and, more important, by the nature of traditional religious assertions of truth compounded by a hierarchically structured church and the implicit and explicit doctrine of infallibility, and is therefore unable to make certain critical leaps in his formulation.

The Pope speaks of a "plurality on the social, religious and civil levels." I do not believe that he is speaking of religious pluralism, that is, the affirmation of the legitimacy and truth claims of other traditions. Rather, the existential reality is that the social, civil, and religious orders are diverse. The lack of acceptance of that reality has led to the deplorable manifestations of discrimination and persecution against the Jews. These were gravely deplorable "from an objective point of view," a phrase which is slightly puzzling. "Objective" as opposed to what? To subjective? Religious? There is a coolness in the repudiation, despite its obvious heartfelt quality, an unwillingness to state that from the religious and moral perspective of Christianity these manifestations are deplorable. Why the acceptance of "plurality"? Not the awareness of the danger inherent in claims to absolute truth and to the authority to proclaim that truth as absolute. That claim and that authority remain intact. It is the historical record which makes necessary a repudiation of the discrimination. The attitude toward the truth claims of others and the historical link between Christian doctrine and Christians in fomenting that historical record are never adequately addressed. Never is it clearly stated there that much of the deplorable record was of persecutions directed against Jews by Christians in the name of Christianity. The Pope commonly moves to the passive voice in talking of the acts, avoiding confronting the issue of the perpetrators. On a number of occasions, including the Rome synagogue visit, John Paul II deplores acts of persecution against Jews committed "by anyone." This is a good deal weaker than an explicit reference to perpetration "by Christians" and "in the name of Christianity" would have been.

Another frequently reiterated theme in papal statements is the close relationship between Judaism and Christianity and the dependency of the latter on the former. In the Rome address he refers to this relationship in the context of a visit to Auschwitz:

> When I visited in June 1979, the concentration camp at Auschwitz and prayed for the many victims from various nations, I paused in particular before the memorial stone with the inscription in Hebrew and thus manifested the sentiments of my heart: "This inscription stirs the memory of the people whose sons and daughters were destined to total extermination. This people has its origin in Abraham, who is our father in faith (cf. Romans 4:12), as Paul of Tarsus expressed it. Precisely this people, which received from God the commandment, 'Thou shalt not kill,' has experienced in itself to a particular degree what killing means. Before this inscription it is not permissible for anyone to pass by with indifference."[8]

This is a genuinely moving recollection. John Paul II himself was clearly profoundly affected by the experience, and his audience cannot have helped but be deeply affected as well. After introducing the theme of the bond between Jews and Christians, he proceeded to elaborate on that bond and spoke of his hopes for its articulation:

> Today's visit is meant to make a decisive contribution to the consolidation of the good relations between our two communi-

ties, ... to overcome old prejudices and to secure ever wider and fuller recognition of that "bond" and that "common spiritual patrimony" that exists between Jews and Christians.[9]

In emphasizing the bond between Christianity and Judaism, John Paul II is doing more than paying tribute to the Jewish sources of Christianity, which he is, of course, doing. The Pope is dealing with anti-Judaism by asserting that Judaism fits into the Christian theological scheme. This is a major step forward in view of the historical record. It is a legitimation of Judaism in Christian terms. It suggests that Christians should accept Jews because of the horror of the historical record and because Judaism can fit into the Christian theological structure. But, significantly, the Pope never deals explicitly with Christian doctrinal anti-Judaism, or the record of Christian anti-Semitism. The Christianity of Christian anti-Semites is passed by in silence. The failure to speak of Christian perpetrators is particularly striking in view of the frequent references to Christian rescuers. Typically, at the Rome synagogue:

> And it was surely a significant gesture that in those dark years of racial persecution the doors of our religious houses, of our churches, of the Roman seminary, of buildings belonging to the Holy See and of the Vatican City itself were thrown open to offer refuge and safety to so many Jews of Rome being hunted by their persecutors.[10]

The impression of the Vatican organized as a vast rescue network may be considered something of an exaggeration, despite the welcome acts of heroism and rescue which did in fact take place. In any event, references to rescuers abound. Coming to terms with Christian perpetrators never takes place.

Further, the acceptance of plurality is not the assertion of pluralism, and is rooted not in religious obligation or moral necessity. It is historically required, particularly because of the bond between Jews and Christians. I remain haunted by the question: What if the historical record had not developed as it did? What if there were no bond between Judaism and Christianity? What, then, would be the proper relationship between Christians and "others," including Jews? Does even this moving and welcome progress represent a highly selective memory and something short of genuine pluralism?

Let me define my terms: diversity is a reality in the world. We are, in fact, different from one another. Tolerance is certainly better than intolerance in dealing with the other, but it still maintains the stance of our own centrality and our appropriate role in judging the legitimacy of the other. Pluralism means coming to terms with the truth claims of the other and an adjustment of one's own claims to truth. Pluralism requires a degree of "epistemological modesty," and is uncommon in the historical record of all religions and in the doctrines of virtually all faiths. The Pope's moving statements, of enormous power and historical importance, still fall short of pluralism.

Nostra Aetate's fourth paragraph is a focus of the Pope's Rome synagogue address. He draws three major points from that paragraph and reiterates them. First, again relating to the "bond" with Judaism, he states:

> [T]he Church of Christ discovers her "bond" with Judaism by "searching into her own mystery." The Jewish religion is not "extrinsic" to us, but in a certain way is "intrinsic" to our own religion. With Judaism, therefore, we have a relationship which we do not have with any other religion. You are our dearly beloved brothers and, in a certain way, it could be said that you are our elder brothers.[11]

In view of our understanding of the intensity of emotions within families, and, particularly, between siblings, some discussion of the complexity of the history of that fraternal relationship would have been extraordinarily useful. We never are offered that sort of analysis of history.

The second major point from paragraph four of *Nostra Aetate* relates to the charge of deicide:

> [N]o ancestral or collective blame can be imputed to the Jews as a people for "what happened in Christ's passion." . . . So any alleged theological justification for discriminatory measures or, worse still, for acts of persecution, is unfounded.[12]

What, then, is the believing Christian to make of the Gospel accounts? Certainly, raising the issue of the historicity of the Gospel accounts would be too much to expect from the Bishop of Rome. However, some contextualization of those accounts by the Pope would have been bold, significant, and ultimately of great power in pointing the way to a new pattern of interrelationship. But that was not to be.

Finally, building on the second point, the Pope addresses the issue of supersessionism:

> The *third* point that I would like to emphasize in the Council's declaration is a consequence of the second. Notwithstanding the Church's awareness of her own identity, it is not lawful to say that the Jews are "repudiated or cursed," as if this were taught or could be deduced from the sacred Scriptures of the Old or the New Testament.[13]

The Pope goes on to cite an earlier portion of *Nostra Aetate* in which there is a reference to the Romans 11 characterization by Paul of the Jews as "beloved of God, who has called them with an irrevocable calling." Romans 9 to 11 constitutes an important but ambivalent text on Paul's attitudes to Judaism. It is good to have them cited by the Pope for good and positive reasons. But this is an exercise in selective reading. The truth is that the teaching that Jews were repudiated and cursed was for centuries read in and deduced from the Christian Bible. The New Testament accounts continue to contribute to the teaching of contempt. The Pope repudiates the teaching of contempt but provides little guidance in dealing with the offensive scriptural characterizations which gave rise to them.

At the risk of belaboring the point, let me refer to one further formulation used by the Pope in his Rome synagogue address. After pointing out that the path to Jewish-Christian understanding is not an easy one, and bearing in mind that "each of our religions, in the full awareness of the many bonds which unite them to each other, ... wishes to be recognized and respected in its own identity, beyond any syncretism and any ambiguous appropriation," John Paul II continues:

> No one is unaware that the fundamental difference from the very beginning has been the attachment of us Catholics to the person and teaching of Jesus of Nazareth, a son of your people from which were also born the Virgin Mary, the apostles who were the "foundations and pillars of the church," and the greater part of the first Christian community. But this attachment is located in the order of faith, that is to say, in the free assent of the mind and heart guided by the Spirit, and it can never be the object of exterior pressure, in one sense or the other. This is the reason why we wish to deepen dialogue in loyalty and friendship, in respect for

another's intimate convictions, taking as a fundamental basis the elements of the revelation which we have in common, as a "great spiritual patrimony" (cf. *NA, 4*).[14]

Once again, I find myself both grateful for the Pope's words but disappointed. The repudiation of forced conversion is welcome. But is missionary activity repudiated in light of its tragic history? Not at all. It might be ungracious of me to suggest that the very opposite is put forward here. The reason why the Church wishes to deepen dialogue is that embracing faith in Jesus must be "an assent of the mind and heart guided by the Spirit." How welcome it would have been to have heard the Pope say that "respect for one another's intimate convictions" requires the acceptance of the legitimacy of the other's search for truth and the abandonment of the attempt to transform the other into a theological copy of one's self. Such a repudiation of missionary activity, despite the agonies of history, never appears.

Though most of the themes of the transformed relationship of the Church to the Jews and Judaism are referenced in the Rome synagogue address, one major achievement of John Paul's papacy had not yet occurred: the establishment of diplomatic relations with the State of Israel. From the start, virtually every visiting Jewish delegation had stressed the significance of this issue for Jews throughout the world. The comments of Howard I. Friedman, then President of the American Jewish Committee, during an audience in 1985 in which I had the privilege of participating, were typical. After citing the Pope's apostolic letter *Redemptionis Anno*, which had referred to the special ties between the Jewish people and the city of Jerusalem, Friedman stated:

> Your Holiness, we recognize the complexity of the problems involved, but we dare to hope that the spirit that inspired your apostolic letter will lead to steps that will formalize the diplomatic ties between the Holy See and the State of Israel and her people.[15]

Significantly, the Pope did not refer to this comment in his response. A decade later, in December 1993, the Vatican established diplomatic ties with the State of Israel. Of profound historical and theological significance, the move was appropriately hailed as a major concrete indication of the new Vatican attitude to the Jewish people. The comments of the Pope when he received the first Israeli ambassador to the Holy See on September 29, 1994, are interesting. After reviewing the substantial contacts between the Vatican and Israeli representatives that preceded the formal recognition and speaking at some length of the peace process and the interest of the Church in protecting its holy places, John Paul II commented:

> The particular nature of the relations between the State of Israel and the Holy See quite obviously stem from the unique character of this land which is the focus of attention for the majority of believers, Jews, Christians, and Muslims, throughout the world. This land was sanctified by the One God's revelation to men; it continues to bear the mark and does not cease to be a place of inspiration for those who can make a pilgrimage there.[16]

Certainly, the unique character of the land sacred to three faiths is relevant to the nature of the relationship between the Church and the State of Israel. But of much greater significance for the importance of the establishment of these diplomatic relations is the historical relationship of the Church to Jews and Judaism. The reestablishment of Jewish national existence in the land of Israel and the consequent return of the Jewish people to an active role on the stage of world history were dissonant with the expectation that a degraded Jewish community was to remain witness to Jewish perfidy in rejecting Jesus and participating in his execution. The doctrinal and theological impediments to the recognition of Israel are not referred to by John Paul II, except in elliptical fashion. He goes on to state:

> Mr. Ambassador, you yourself have insisted on the historical significance of this ceremony, over and above the usual diplomatic conventions. Indeed, a new age is dawning in relations between the Holy See and the State of Israel, by a persevering dialogue and by active collaboration in the areas I have just mentioned. All this will help intensify the dialogue between the Catholic Church and the Jewish people of Israel and of the whole world.[17]

For many Jews, the issues that are left unstated are the most significant ones. Once again, the historical record is passed over in silence.

How then should one evaluate the overall accomplishments of John Paul II in his journey of reconciliation with the Jewish people and in nurturing the relationships of the Church he heads with the Jewish people? His pronouncements are profoundly moving; his achievements are remarkable; the task remains, however, uncompleted.

Critical observers of the Vatican and its relations to the Jewish people have frequently pointed to the Vatican's passivity during the Holocaust, a passivity that Vatican authorities have vehemently denied. I do not wish to enter that debate here. If the Vatican did less than it might have done to prevent the atrocities, so did virtually every government and every community, including the Jewish community at that time. Yet, a gnawing question remains: Why, in John Paul's remarkable record of reaching out and reconciliation, is there no effort to date to deal forthrightly with the historical record in which Church teaching is so deeply implicated? Referring to the alleged silence surrounding the Church and the Holocaust, James Carroll writes:

> On his visit to the synagogue, John Paul II recalled the 1943 fate of Roman Jews, but he made no reference to the Vatican's silence. After Hochhuth's play, the Vatican had released documents showing that many thousands of Jews had been rescued by various officials of the Catholic Church, but such heroes were almost always members of the lower clergy or were stationed outside of Rome. John Paul II, having refrained from mentioning Pius XII, went on immediately to praise the Roman priests, monks, and nuns who in 1943 "offered refuge and safety to so many Jews of Rome," opening their convents, seminaries, and the buildings "of Vatican City itself." The Pope had dared to mention the modern Church's greatest ignominy but had then taken comfort in the noble memory of the exceptions.... A Pope had been silent once again — this time about the silence of a Pope.[18]

While the record of the Vatican during the Holocaust may still be debated, the silence to date of John Paul II regarding the historical record of Christian anti-Semitism is incontrovertible. Why the silence on the part of an obviously well-intentioned and virtuous man whose achievements in moving Catholic-Jewish relations forward are nothing less than spectacular? James Carroll finds the answer to this question in the doctrine of papal infallibility, which he reports discussing with Hans Küng, the distinguished Catholic theologian who has frequently criticized the Pope. Küng reflected on his difficulties with Josef Cardinal Ratzinger, the conservative theologian who advises John Paul II on doctrinal matters:

> "They all told me, 'If you keep quiet, you can be what you want. But keep quiet!'" Küng said, "Of course, when I saw that, I had

to say, 'Well, I cannot just keep quiet about infallibility,' and now we see more and more that it is the crux of the whole system. It is the main reason why they are unable to correct themselves." [Carroll then comments:] Not only about women, I realized, but about their silence during the Holocaust. The doctrine of infallibility is like a virus that paralyzes the body of the church.[19]

Carroll goes on to quote further from Küng:

In the balance of the Council [Vatican II], I wrote that Nazi anti-Semitism would have been impossible without two thousand years of Christian anti-Judaism. It was not racial. It was religious.[20]

Küng's observation is correct, and full reconciliation will not be possible until the Church comes to terms fully with the truth of that assertion. That is why alongside our admiration for the progress in Catholic-Jewish relations which John Paul II has shaped, there is reason to keep in mind also the incompleteness. Carroll quotes Küng's book on Judaism:

I am concerned with the past which will not go away, a past which still continues to determine the present and which is still virulent today among large sectors of the nations. A repressed past easily becomes a curse.[21]

For a church in which confession represents an essential component of personal conciliation and salvation and which is a hierarchical structure, one must hope for the fullest coming to terms with history for the purposes of effecting genuine conciliation from the figure who stands at the head of the Church, the Pope. Papal infallibility is doubtless part of the problem in that admission of error in Church teaching and earlier papal behavior calls that infallibility into question. But the very hierarchical structure of the Church makes possible the advent of a Pope who might follow up on the progress of John Paul II with a real coming to terms with the realities of history. Hans Küng makes this point, but does so too harshly: "But I think it [the papacy] could survive in a very beautiful way, if we could have a John XXIV — and not a John Paul III. If we get a John Paul III, I think we can forget the Papacy."[22]

In terms of the relationship of the Church to Jews, Küng's characterization is overly critical. John Paul II's achievements in this area have been remarkable and impressive. Küng's judgments relate, of course, to disputes of a more far-reaching nature than Catholic-Jewish relations,

and we have no interest here in entering into those issues. In the journey of reconciliation between the Church and the Jews, John Paul II
has moved ahead impressively, though much that is critical remains to
be done.

Though the failure to come to terms with the Christian history
of anti-Judaism may be associated both with the Church's hierarchical
structure and with the doctrine of infallibility, more profound issues are
at stake in the search for true interreligious reconciliation. Each of our
traditional religions, not only Catholicism, sees itself as the exclusive
repository of truth and views the outsider as lacking that truth. Religious identity is commonly formed through invidious comparison with
those who are outside the fold and who are commonly demonized and
vilified. None of our religious traditions has been immune. At best,
efforts are made to forcibly bring the outsider into the fold; at worst,
the outsider is eliminated through even harsher means. The history of
Christian-Jewish relations is a special case because of the close relationship between the two faiths, but it is nevertheless an illustration of this
phenomenon. Claims to exclusive access to absolute truth reduce and
diminish the "other" to something less than one's self and open the door
to hatred and persecution. If what is sought is not simply civility, but
a transformation of the very soul of interreligious relationships, such
claims will have to be abandoned by all sides. Ironically, that may be both
more difficult for the Catholic Church because of the doctrine of infallibility, but more possible because of the capacity for leadership of the
papacy. Ultimately, the need to abandon absolutist claims is a challenge
to all religious traditions, and is not unique to the Catholic Church.

It is precisely because of the difficulty in radically transforming the
nature of one's own truth claims and crediting the truth claims of others
and the limitations on true reconciliation which exist unless such a
transformation takes place that one must ultimately be enormously impressed with what a conservative theologian like John Paul II has been
able to achieve. Again quoting Carroll: "That John Paul II has reasserted
the idea of infallibility, on the one hand, while demonstrating an unprecedented and genuine sympathy for Jews, on the other, is the great
paradox of his papacy."[23]

The next steps in Catholic-Jewish relations may require a John XXIV.
But if what we seek is a world of authentic interreligious understanding, in which religious traditions will not contribute to the pathologies
of hatred, vilification, and persecution but to their alleviation, then each
of our religious communities will require such a figure, combining the
good will of a John Paul II with a prophetic vision and courage. Until

those figures emerge, we can be grateful for John Paul II's considerable achievements.

Notes

1. Eugene J. Fisher, "Pope John Paul II's Pilgrimage of Reconciliation," in *Spiritual Pilgrimage: Texts on Jews and Judaism 1979–1995: Pope John Paul II,* ed. Eugene J. Fisher and Leon Klenicki (New York: Crossroad, 1995), xx.

2. See Fisher and Klenicki, eds., *Spiritual Pilgrimage.*

3. See Fisher, "Pope John Paul II's Pilgrimage," xxxvii.

4. See Fisher and Klenicki, eds., *Spiritual Pilgrimage,* 61.

5. Ibid., 62.

6. Ibid.

7. Ibid.

8. Ibid.

9. Ibid.

10. Ibid.

11. Ibid., 63.

12. Ibid.

13. Ibid.

14. Ibid., 64.

15. Cited in ibid., 46.

16. Ibid., 194.

17. Ibid.

18. James Carroll, "The Silence," *New Yorker,* April 7, 1997, 56.

19. Ibid., 60.

20. Ibid.

21. Ibid.

22. Ibid.

23. Ibid., 67.

10

John Paul II's Catholic Theology of Judaism

BYRON L. SHERWIN

Relationships among religions are shaped by attitudes that presume specific epistemological postures, for example:

1. A religion may either be true or false. Since my religion represents absolute truth, your religion must be false. This is the dominant position of medieval scholastic philosophical theology.

2. Truth is relative. There is no absolute truth. My religion is true for me; your religion is true for you. While all religions may contain truth, none has the monopoly on truth. This is a typically modern position that makes possible the posture of religious pluralism.

3. Absolute truth may exist, but it is beyond the ken of human comprehension. "The truth is a noun only for God, for humans however it is an adjective" (Franz Rosenzweig). Religions contain truth. However, some contain more truth than others. My religion contains more truth than yours.

4. There are truths and there is falsehood. Some religions contain truth, but others are false. My religion contains truth while your religion may contain truth or it may be false.

5. There is absolute truth, relative or incomplete truth, and there is falsehood. My religion is true; your religion either may contain truth or may be false. This position affirms the possibility of religious plurality, but not the posture of religious pluralism.

Nostra Aetate, the primary document of the Second Vatican Council that deals with the relationship of the Roman Catholic Church toward non-Christian religions (adopted October 27, 1965), moved the Church from its historical rootedness in attitude number 1 to a new position characterized by attitude number 5.[1] While this new position is one that acknowledges the legitimacy of religious *plurality*, it is not one that affirms religious *pluralism*. For *Nostra Aetate*, truth is contained in some other religions, while still others rest upon false and unenlightened doctrines. The truth is embodied in the Catholic faith. Other religions contain truth only insofar as they reflect the truth of Catholic doctrine. Catholic truth serves as the ultimate arbiter of whether other religions contain truth. With regard to non-Christian religions, *Nostra Aetate* states (para. 2):

> The Catholic Church rejects nothing of what is true and holy in these religions. She has a high regard for the manner of life and conduct, the precepts and doctrines which, although differing in many ways from her own teaching, nevertheless often reflect a ray of that truth which enlightens all men. Yet she proclaims and is duty bound to proclaim without fail, Christ who is "the way, the truth and the life" (John 14:6).[2]

With specific regard to Judaism, the dominant doctrinal stance of the pre-Vatican II Catholic Church was that Catholicism is true while Judaism is false (i.e., attitude number 1). But since Christianity had emerged out of Judaism, this attitude toward Judaism differed from the Church's attitude toward other non-Christian faiths. According to this view, Judaism had once been true, as it was rooted in a covenant made by God with the people of Israel. However, the people of Israel rejected the covenant, as evidenced by their sinful behavior. God sent Jesus to redeem them. They rejected Jesus and his teachings. They crucified Jesus, thereby committing the most heinous of sins — deicide. Consequently, God rejected the Jews and abrogated the covenant with them that was originally made with their ancestors. God held the Jews to be reviled and accursed because of their sins and punished them with perpetual wandering and degradation. Their only hope became accepting baptism, converting to Christianity, and embracing Christ, whom they had rejected. The Church, therefore, has a "mission to the Jews" to convert them to Christianity, to bring them the "good news," the Truth. Having rejected and nullified the "old" covenant, and the "old" people of the covenant, God established a "new" covenant, a New Testament with the "new Israel," now the "people of God," the universal Church, the Catholic Church. In theological parlance, aspects of this position came to be known as the "supersessionist doctrine" and the "displacement doctrine" — that is, Christianity supersedes Judaism, and the "new Israel" displaces the "old Israel" as the covenanted people of God. The truth of the old covenant is similarly superseded and displaced by the new covenant. These doctrines served through the centuries as a theological foundation for Christian anti-Semitism, which, according to numerous historians, served as a contributing cause of the Holocaust.[3]

An example of the pre-Vatican II claim that Judaism had once been a true religion that had relinquished that status may be seen in the typical pre-Vatican II *Baltimore Catechism* (question 391):

> Why did the Jewish religion, which up to the death of Christ had been the true religion, cease at that time to be the true religion? [Answer]: The Jewish religion . . . was only a promise of the redemption and figure of the Christian religion, and when the redemption was accomplished and the Christian religion established by the death of Christ, the promise and the figure were no longer necessary.

Nostra Aetate altered the former teachings of the Church regarding Judaism and the Jews, while deliberately offering the impression that the new teaching of the Church had always been the teaching of the Church. In very subtle terms, the "displacement doctrine" was virtually expunged, while a revised version of the "supersessionist doctrine" remained. *Nostra Aetate* rejects the "displacement doctrine" by affirming that God's covenant with the people of Israel was not revoked because that covenant is irrevocable "since God does not take back the gifts he bestowed or the choice he made." Yet a version of the supersessionist doctrine remains in the claim that, despite the fact that the covenant with the people of Israel remains in force, "it is true that the Church is the new people of God." Yet, the idea of "mission to the Jews," which had been a critical component of the supersessionist doctrine, is noticeably absent from the text of *Nostra Aetate*.[4] The integrity of Jews as Jews and of Judaism as a religion is now affirmed. No longer is Judaism depicted as an obsolete religion. No longer are Jews primarily defined as potential Christians.

The displacement doctrine is rooted in the claim that the Jews killed Jesus and that they are therefore accursed. *Nostra Aetate* rejects this claim by affirming that the Jews as a group are not responsible for the crucifixion and the death of Jesus: "Neither all Jews indiscriminately at that time, nor Jews today, can be charged with the crimes committed during his [Jesus'] passion." Consequently, "the Jews should not be spoken of as rejected or accursed, as if this followed from Holy Scripture." Anti-Semitism is therefore now deplored: "[The Church] deplores all hatreds, persecutions, displays of anti-Semitism leveled at any time or from any source against the Jews." Rather than enmity, "mutual understanding and appreciation" of the "common spiritual heritage" of Christians and Jews are now encouraged by the Church.

Nostra Aetate not only redefined the Church's attitude to non-Christian religions, but also affirmed that the relationship between Judaism and Catholicism is uniquely different from that which the Church has with any other non-Christian religion. This affirmation was further expressed in Paul VI's establishment in 1974 of the Pontifical Commission for Religious Relations with the Jews, while all other non-Christian religions are dealt with through the Pontifical Council for Interreligious Dialogue.

Within a decade after *Nostra Aetate*, in December 1974, the Commission for Religious Relations with the Jews issued "Guidelines and Suggestions for Implementing the Conciliar Declaration *Nostra Aetate* (para. 4)."[5] Building upon *Nostra Aetate,* the "Guidelines" both amplified and expanded the positions taken in the Vatican II document.

Nostra Aetate means "in this age of ours." By beginning with these words, the authors wanted to emphasize that the Church's reconsideration of its relationship with other religions takes place within the context of recent history and the present historical situation. This awareness is expanded in the "Guidelines" by its opening statement, which squarely places Jewish-Catholic dialogue within the context of the immediate post-Holocaust era. While this document restates a condemnation of anti-Semitism, it fails to acknowledge or to express contrition for beliefs or acts of Christian anti-Semitism. In a sense, this is surprising, since the initial impetus for *Nostra Aetate* (as well as for Vatican II) came from John XXIII, who was well aware of the social and historical impact of earlier anti-Jewish Church doctrine on anti-Semitic acts throughout the centuries.

Two factors clearly stimulated John XXIII to encourage the Church to alter its teachings about the Jews and Judaism. The first was the impact of his having read Jules Isaac's study of the history of Christian anti-Semitism, *The Teaching of Contempt,* in which the author demonstrates the irrefutable link between Church doctrine regarding the Jews and the centuries-long persecution of Jews by Christians with doctrinal sanction.[6] That Christian anti-Semitism was a contributing cause of the Holocaust was not lost on John XXIII. A second factor that informed John XXIII's intentions was his own activities as a member of the Vatican's diplomatic corps during World War II. Though he never publicly criticized either the sometimes pro-German attitudes and actions of his immediate predecessors, or their apparent apathy to the fate of European Jewry during the Holocaust, his own actions during that period — possibly in opposition to official Vatican policy — demonstrate his legion attempts to save Jews during the Holocaust. We know, for example, that while serving in Bulgaria, he was instrumental in convincing the Bulgarian government — an ally of Nazi Germany — not to accede to German demands to round up and to deport Bulgarian Jews to the death camps. While serving in Turkey, he personally helped save a few hundred Jewish children. At a diplomatic reception in Turkey, he was approached by the German ambassador, who asked if the Holy See could issue a statement condemning the atheistic Communists whom the Germans were then fighting. In blunt and undiplomatic language, he replied, "What shall I tell them about the millions of Jews your countrymen are murdering in Germany and Poland?"[7] As will be discussed below, these issues of Christian anti-Semitism and Holocaust awareness became pivotal as Catholic-Jewish relations continued to develop during the pontificate of John Paul II.

A second issue stressed in the "Guidelines" is the recognition of Judaism, not as a religion defined only in Christian theological categories, but as a religion with its own integrity, grounded in its own self-definition: "Christians must therefore strive . . . to learn by what essential traits the Jews define themselves in light of their own religious experience. . . . Dialogue demands respect for the other as he is; above all, respect for his faith and his religious convictions." Here one finds an acknowledgment that Judaism is not an obsolete nor a fossilized (Toynbee) religion, but a living faith — another theme that will develop in subsequent Church teachings about relations with Judaism. The link between the rejection of the displacement doctrine and the recognition of the integrity of Judaism was further strengthened in the Holy See's 1985 document "Notes on the Correct Way to Present the Jews and Judaism in Preaching and Catechesis in the Roman Catholic Church." Issued to mark the twentieth anniversary of *Nostra Aetate*, this document emphasizes the ongoing and contemporary vibrancy of Jewish faith. Unlike earlier teachings that described Judaism as being relegated to obsoletism after the destruction of the Second Jewish Commonwealth in the year 70 as a punishment for the sin of deicide, the new teaching proclaims (para. 25) that "the history of Israel did not end in 70.... It continued, especially in numerous Diasporas which allowed Israel to carry to the whole world a witness.... The permanence of Israel (while so many ancient people have disappeared without a trace) is a historical fact and a sign to be interpreted in God's design."[8]

A third issue developed by the "Guidelines" relates to "mission to the Jews." While affirming the missionary nature of Christianity, the "Guidelines" express careful sensitivity to "religious liberty" and to the "offense" that missionizing Jews causes members of the Jewish people. The "Guidelines" are implicitly aware that many Jews remain suspicious that the Church's initiatives for dialogue might really have a hidden missionary agenda. As one Vatican document clearly puts it, one obstacle to interreligious dialogue is that "the weight of history makes proclamation [of the Gospel] more difficult, as certain methods of evangelization in the past have sometimes aroused fear and suspicion on the part of followers of other religions."[9]

A fourth issue developed by the "Guidelines" is the need for the Church to examine various liturgical, canonical, catechetical, educational, and other texts it utilizes and promulgates to help ensure that such texts are correlative with post–Vatican II teachings on Judaism and the Jewish people.

Since his election to the papacy in 1978, John Paul II's teachings regarding the Church's relationship with Judaism and the Jewish people have been primarily shaped by two factors: (1) Vatican statements such as *Nostra Aetate* and the subsequent "Guidelines," and (2) the Pope's personal experiences in his native Poland. Indeed, probably no Bishop of Rome since St. Peter has lived in closer proximity to Jews than John Paul II.[10]

The Pope's native Poland had been a major spiritual and demographic epicenter of Jewish life for centuries. At the time of his birth in 1920, there were about 3.5 million Jews in Poland, representing about 10 percent of the total population. In his town of Wadowice, the Jewish population was about 25 percent. Despite the considerable escalation of anti-Semitism in interwar Poland, and despite the often openly anti-Semitic teachings of the Polish Church, the young Karol Wojtyla seemed remarkably immune to either social or doctrinal anti-Semitism.[11] He did not hear it from his local priest. His father (who raised him after his mother's death) had only cordial relationships with local Jews. When one of the future Pope's Jewish friends announced that she would be emigrating to Palestine because of the rise of Polish anti-Semitism in the 1930s, his father said to her, "Not all Poles are anti-Semitic. You know I am not." Reflecting upon this event almost a half-century later, Karol's boyhood friend, Ginka Beer Riesenfeld, recalled that she said to Karol's father that "very few Poles were like him." She further remembered that the young Karol was even more upset during this exchange than was his father.[12]

In the building where the young Wojtyla lived and in the schools he attended, there were Jews who befriended him and whom he befriended. Foremost among them was Jerzy Kluger, the Pope's lifelong friend, whose father served as president of the Jewish community of Wadowice. After losing track of one another after World War II, they were reunited in Rome, where Kluger went to live after the war. Tad Szulc, in his biography of John Paul II, writes, "Clearly, the pope misses the contact with his childhood friends and Wadowice. . . . To chat informally in Polish [with Jerzy Kluger] about the past and mutual friends, and away from papal protocol, may be the most important form of mental relaxation for the overworked Wojtyla."[13] Kluger was the first person received by the new Pope in private audience after his election in 1978.[14]

In 1989, John Paul II asked Kluger to represent him in placing a commemorative plaque on the site of the synagogue in Wadowice that had been destroyed by the Nazis. The Pope wrote:

> Many of those who perished, your co-religionists and our fellow countrymen, were our colleagues in our Elementary School and, later, in the High School where we graduated together, 50 years ago. All were citizens of Wadowice, the town to which both you and I are bound together by our memories of childhood and youth. I remember very clearly the Wadowice Synagogue, which was near to our High School. I have in front of my eyes the numerous worshippers, who during their Holidays passed on their way to pray there.[15]

From his courtyard, Karol Wojtyla would watch Jews enter the synagogue to celebrate the Jewish holy days. At least once, he attended religious services there on Yom Kippur, the Day of Atonement.[16] When the students in their high school would play soccer, they would constitute a Jewish team and a Catholic team. Because the Jewish team was usually undermanned, the young Wojtyla often would play for the Jewish team.[17]

In various addresses delivered throughout the world, John Paul II reflects upon his experiences in Poland of sharing both the joys and the tragedies of his Jewish countrymen. For example, in his first visit as Pope to the United States in October 1979, John Paul II reminded the Jewish community of New York, "As one who in my homeland has shared the suffering of your brethren, I greet you with the word taken from the Hebrew language: *Shalom!*" Speaking about the Holocaust to Jewish leaders in Warsaw in 1987, he said, "The Polish pope has a particular relationship with all this, because, along with you, he has in a certain sense lived all this here, in this land." In his later address to the Jewish community in Poland in 1991, the Pope lamented that "that which threatened you also threatened us. The threat to us was not fulfilled to the same extent as the threat to you. . . . You have the terrible sacrifice of destruction. . . . [A] sea of terrible suffering and of the wrongs endured should not divide, but unite us. The places of execution, and in many cases, the common graves, call for this unity." Reflecting on his meeting with Jews in Poland, the Pope said, "The Pope's meeting with Jews on Polish soil was very cordial because it called to mind and renewed the personal bonds formed at the time of his youth and the difficult years of the occupation."[18] However, most telling is the Pope's reflection on Judaism and the Jewish people in his book *Crossing the Threshold of Hope*. Here, the direction for Catholic-Jewish relations set down in *Nostra Ae-tate* and the Pope's experiences in his native Poland converge to serve as a framework for his perspective on Judaism and on Catholic-Jewish relations:

> The words of the Council's Declaration [i.e., *Nostra Aetate* 4] re-flect the experience of many people, both Jews and Christians. They reflect *my personal experience* as well, from the very first years of my life in my hometown. I remember, above all, the Wadow-ice elementary school, where at least a fourth of the pupils in my class were Jewish. I should mention my friendship at school with one of them, Jerzy Kluger — a friendship that has lasted from my school days to the present. I can vividly remember the Jews who gathered every Saturday at the synagogue behind our school. Both religious groups, Catholics and Jews, were united, I presume, by the awareness that they prayed to the same God. Despite their dif-ferent languages, prayers in the church and in the synagogue were based to a considerable degree on the same texts.

> •

> Then came the Second World War, with its concentration camps and systematic extermination. First and foremost, the sons and

daughters of the Jewish nation were condemned for no other reason than that they were Jewish. Even if only indirectly, whoever lived in Poland at that time came into contact with this reality.

Therefore, this was also a personal experience of mine, an experience I carry with me even today.... A few years ago Jerzy came to me to say that the place where the synagogue had stood should be honored with a special commemorative plaque. I must admit that in that moment we both felt a deep emotion. We saw faces of people we knew and cared for, and we recalled those Saturdays of our childhood and adolescence when the Jewish community of Wadowice gathered for prayer....

The words of *Nostra Aetate*, as I have said, reflect the experience of many. I think back to *the time of my pastoral work in Krakow*. Krakow, and especially the Kasimierz neighborhood, retain many traces of Jewish culture and tradition.... As Archbishop of Krakow, I was in close contact with the city's Jewish community. I enjoyed very cordial relations with the head of that community, which continued even after I came to Rome.

After my election to the See of Saint Peter, I have continued to cherish these deeply significant ties. On my pastoral journeys around the world I always try to meet representatives of the Jewish community. But a truly exceptional experience for me was certainly my *visit to the synagogue of Rome*.... During that memorable visit, I spoke of the Jews as our *elder brothers in the faith*. These words were an expression both of the Council's teaching, and a profound conviction on the part of the Church. The Second Vatican Council did not dwell on this subject at length, but what it did affirm embraces an immense reality which is not only religious but also cultural....

I am pleased that my ministry in the See of Saint Peter has taken place during the period following the Second Vatican Council, when the insights which inspired the Declaration *Nostra Aetate* are finding concrete expression in various ways. Thus the way two great moments of divine election — the Old and the New Covenants — are drawing closer together.[19]

Because of the Pope's close personal associations with Jews during his formative years, and because of his painful empathetic awareness of the plight of Jews during the Holocaust, particularly in Poland, the improvement of Catholic-Jewish relations has emerged as one of the leading non-Church issues that has preoccupied John Paul II during his papacy.[20] In his many journeys, the "traveling Pope" has made a point of meeting with representatives of local Jewish communities wherever there is one, even if it is not large. He is the first Pontiff to visit a synagogue, that is, the Synagogue of Rome in 1986.[21] In 1993, he personally interceded in the Auschwitz convent controversy — which had become a grating obstacle to the stability of Catholic-Jewish relations — by ordering the convent's nuns to relocate.[22] In April 1994, he hosted a concert at the Vatican in memory of the victims of the Holocaust, and later that year,[23] through his direct influence, the Holy See established full diplomatic relations with the State of Israel.[24]

The Vatican's establishment of diplomatic ties with Israel is a concrete and specific expression of the Church's rejection of the displacement doctrine. By recognizing the Jewish state, the Holy See implicitly sets aside the claim that the loss of Jewish political sovereignty in the Holy Land was a punishment for the sin of deicide. In concrete terms, it eliminates the earlier claim that the Jews have been punished and are accursed with perpetual wandering and humiliation. With regard to the Vatican's official diplomatic recognition of Israel, as with so many issues related to Catholic-Jewish relations, John Paul II posits a continuity of Church policy rather than the initiation of a new Church policy. He offers the impression that such initiatives and innovations merely make explicit long-standing implicit Church policy and doctrine.[25] For example, in *Crossing the Threshold of Hope*, he writes, "As for the recognition of the State of Israel, it is important to reaffirm that I myself never had any doubts in that regard."[26] Furthermore, as early as 1980, the Pope clearly recognized a link between the Holocaust and the establishment of the State of Israel: "The Jewish people, after tragic experiences connected with the extermination of so many sons and daughters, driven by the desire for security, set up the State of Israel."[27]

When Karol Wojtyla was elected Pope at the comparatively young age of fifty-eight, the Catholic Church was in disarray. The Vatican was in fiscal and spiritual chaos. The long pontificate of Paul VI had ended with a plethora of proposed new policies and procedures that had come out of Vatican II. Conservatives in the Church aimed at stifling these proposed changes. Reformers wanted immediate and sometimes radical implementation. Moderates called for prudence and slow going. Some characterized the immediate post–Vatican II period as a train that had no idea of which track to follow and where to go. John Paul I's election had promised stability and balance, but weeks after his assent to the papacy, John Paul I suddenly died. Upon his election on October 16, 1978, John Paul II found the Church in a quandary. Could it, would it, should it fully implement the teachings of Vatican II? What would they mean in terms of actual implementation? What would the implications of such implementation be?[28]

It is beyond the scope of this essay to discuss John Paul II's handling of these challenges. However, of all the issues posed by Vatican II, particularly those that do not directly relate to the direct governance of the Church, John Paul II has clearly paid inordinate attention to the issues regarding Catholic-Jewish relations as shaped by one paragraph in one document of Vatican II, that is, paragraph 4 of *Nostra Aetate*.

Both in itself, and in view of the many challenges facing the Pope throughout his pontificate, John Paul II's legion efforts in combating anti-Semitism and furthering Catholic-Jewish relations have been nothing less than remarkable. Many representatives and leaders of the Jewish community have acknowledged, applauded, and lauded John Paul II's efforts in improving Catholic-Jewish relations. However, the largely secular Jewish communal leadership tends to evaluate these achievements from the often myopic perspective of the Jewish communal agenda. What they fail to realize is that the Pope's teachings on Catholic-Jewish relations emerge out of a framework of faith, that is, out of a particular Catholic theological perspective. John Paul II's mission is to articulate Catholic doctrine to Catholics. His views on Judaism and the Jewish people, despite the influences of his personal experiences, represent a Catholic theology of Judaism that he desires to define and to convey to Catholics. While his views on the Jewish people often dovetail with Jewish communal interests, they must be understood primarily in theological terms. While the impetus for and the direction of Catholic-Jewish relations during the papacy of John Paul II may have been stimulated by his personal experiences, his theology of Judaism has been shaped and defined by Catholic doctrinal teachings. His Catholic theology of Judaism may be viewed as an amplification of and as a commentary on *Nostra Aetate* and various subsequent Vatican documents and episcopal pronouncements.

When John Paul II ascended to the papacy, it became his challenge and his responsibility to steer a huge institution seeking direction, one which was fragmented and threatened by instability. The Pontiff clearly understood that the institution he led — rooted in long-standing ancient and medieval traditions, yet operating under a mandate for change — could only effectively implement change when it was integrated into the continuity of tradition. Change had to be interpreted not as a break with the past, but as flowing out of the doctrinal teachings and the historical experiences of the past. Otherwise, change could bring a rupture of the continuity of the tradition and, consequently, could pose a further threat to an already fragile institutional structure. The American penchant for change for the sake of change finds little resonance in fundamentally European institutions such as the Holy See.

The teachings of *Nostra Aetate* regarding Judaism and the Jewish people proclaimed a doctrinal change of direction from the past. However, these changes often have been treated by the Holy See and by John Paul II as if they represent doctrinal continuity with the past. The Pope often evokes a claim of theological continuity in his vigorous attempt to steer his Church from a position of condemnation of Judaism to one of reconciliation with Judaism. As the Pope has said, "the relations between the Catholic Church and Judaism have been built on a new foundation which is in fact very old, . . . a spiritual bond."[29]

Paul VI made an unprecedented breakthrough in ecumenical relations by using such terms as "fraternal" to refer to Orthodox and Protestant Christians.[30] John Paul II extended use of this terminology to Jews. Here, too, there is an attempt to initiate radical change under the guise of continuity. Classical Christianity used the biblical motif of Israel as the "older brother" to fortify the displacement doctrine. In Hebrew Scriptures, older brothers (e.g., Esau) were displaced in favor of younger brothers (e.g., Jacob).[31] Historically, the Church (i.e., the younger brother) saw itself as displacing the Synagogue (i.e., the older brother), and as the rightful heir of the inheritance of the true faith. Now, John Paul II was reiterating the term "older brother," but infusing it with a positive meaning, rather than using this image to illustrate the displacement doctrine. Undoubtedly, he was influenced in this regard by the great Polish poet Mickiewicz's positive use of the term "elder brother" when referring to the Jewish people.

Ironically, both the displacement doctrine and its rejection underscore the unique relationship between Judaism and Christianity. Christianity developed out of Judaism. This is a relationship which Christianity has with no other religion. As John Paul II has acknowledged on numerous occasions, "With Judaism, therefore, we have a relationship which we do not have with any other religion." But now, this relationship is no longer adversarial, but integral. "The Jewish religion is not 'extrinsic' to us, but in a certain way is 'intrinsic' to our own religion."[32]

In a way, John Paul II has embraced a version of the "dual covenant theory," formulated in the early twentieth century by the German-Jewish philosopher Franz Rosenzweig.[33] While Rosenzweig uses this approach to find a place for Christianity within Jewish theology, John Paul II seems to utilize it in order to formulate a theology of Judaism within a Catholic framework. From his perspective, there is the Jewish covenant and the Christian covenant. The Jewish covenant (following the 1974 "Guidelines") is established by God and is shaped by how Jews define themselves, by Jewish theological self-understanding. Judaism is no longer viewed by the Church as a religion that had become obsolete in the first century, but rather as a "living heritage" rooted in the past and vibrantly alive in the present. It is with the living and contemporary Jewish people — heirs to an irrevocable and enduring covenant — that the Church enters into fraternal dialogue.[34]

The Christian covenant is now seen, not as replacing, but as continuing and amplifying the covenant made with Israel. Consequently, theological anti-Semitism, rather than being integral to Christian teachings, becomes anathema to it. However, from the Pope's theological perspective, rejection of the displacement doctrine and its replacement with a recognition of the permanence of the covenant with Israel lead not only to a recognition of the theological integrity of Judaism, but also to the integration of the covenant with the Jews into the process of Christian self-identity. Precisely because Christianity emerged from Judaism — because the original "Jewish" covenant is understood to be an integral part of the Christian covenant, because Jesus and the apostles identified themselves as Jews, because of liturgical and other influences of Judaism upon Christianity — Christian identity has now become irrevocably and integrally related to an encounter with Judaism.[35] These themes have been expressed by John Paul II in a number of ways on numerous occasions. Almost as a commentary on *Nostra Aetate's* brief reference to "the spiritual ties that link the people of the New Testament to the stock of Abraham," John Paul II has substantially amplified the original meaning of this phrase. For example, rather than seeing Jesus as a barrier for Christians to encounter Judaism, he perceives Jesus as a conduit to an encounter with the traditions and the beliefs of Jesus' people: "Whoever meets Jesus Christ meets Judaism."[36] No longer is there a fissure between Judaism and Christianity, but rather a familial continuity, an organic relationship.[37]

Yet, despite his affirmation of the "old" covenant, the Pope, as might be expected, sees the old covenant as a prelude and anticipation of the "new" covenant. The new covenant is described as the fulfillment of the old, and in a real sense is described as surpassing and fulfilling, if not also superseding (while not displacing), the old.[38] The old covenant is the necessary premise of the new covenant, which is its inevitable fulfillment. Here we see an extension of *Nostra Aetate's* rejection of the displacement doctrine, although along with the perpetuation of a version of the supersessionist doctrine. The Pope, however, seems not to see an endemic tension between the claims of the two covenants, though he admits that contradictions between them, especially on issues such as messianism and Christology, will be resolved in favor of Christian truth, in the eschatological future. Surely, when the Pope speaks of the one faith of humankind in the eschaton, he is referring to Catholic faith.[39] However, until the eschaton, during historical times, the two covenants coexist.

While the Christian covenant remains largely irrelevant for Jewish self-identity, the Jewish covenant takes on a pivotal role in Christian self-identity. This view of the organic development of Christianity out of Judaism, this claim of the extension of Christianity beyond Judaism, this virtual absorption and incorporation of aspects of Judaism into Christianity, is not considered by John Paul II to be inimical either to Judaism or to Catholic-Jewish dialogue. Rather, it is understood to be part of an internal dialogue *within* Christianity about the mystery of its own nature.[40] A vital feature of the Pope's Catholic theology of Judaism is that it is directed not at or to the Jews, but rather to Catholics seeking religious self-understanding and identity. On one level, John Paul II has articulated and has enacted a theological framework, directed both at Jews and at Catholics, for enabling Catholic-Jewish dialogue to proceed and to flourish. However, on another level, he has formulated a Catholic theology of Judaism that is directed at Catholics in search of spiritual self-understanding. Consequently, a review and an analysis of John Paul II's teachings about Judaism and the Jews must be understood on both levels.

Removal of the displacement doctrine serves as the theological foundation for the Church's repudiation of anti-Semitism and for the rejection of the claim that the Jews are collectively responsible for the death of Jesus.[41] John Paul II has consistently rejected the deicide claim and has vigorously condemned anti-Semitism throughout his pontificate.[42] Considering the gravity which the Catholic Church assigns to sin, it is especially significant that John Paul II has identified anti-Semitism as a specific sin.[43] Inextricably related to John Paul II's unequivocal and harsh condemnation of anti-Semitism is his personal and theological preoccupation with the Holocaust.

For John Paul II, the Holocaust is no abstractly evil event. Rather, it is a historical experience that "surpass[es] in horror anything that can be imagined."[44] It is a tragedy that he witnessed as it unfolded in his native Poland. He saw the Jews of Poland, including the families of many of his friends, disappear before his very eyes. Throughout his writings and his speeches, the experience of the Jews during the years of World War II is a constant referent. Besides the citation above from *Crossing the Threshold of Hope*, the following examples may be cited.

During his historic visit to the Synagogue of Rome in 1986, John Paul II reiterated what had by then become a common theme in this thinking: "I would like once more to express a word of abhorrence for the genocide decreed against the Jewish people during the last war, which led to the Holocaust of millions of innocent victims."[45]

The Pope's reflections on the Holocaust, delivered in Poland, have a special poignancy. Until recent years, Poles have focused primarily on their own suffering during the Nazi occupation, often ignoring or suppressing memories of the plight of Polish Jewry. Often, when discussing the war years, Poles would treat the experience of Jews as a matter of a competitive martyrology, with Poles seen as the primary victims of the German occupation.[46] To the Pope's great credit, he always has acknowledged that Jewish suffering during the Holocaust was unsurpassed by any group, even though this must have roused the ire of many of his fellow Poles. For example, while on pilgrimage to Auschwitz in 1979, John Paul II emphasized the plight of the Jewish victims who met their deaths there, despite the then current policy of the Polish Communist government not to do so. Referring to a Hebrew inscription at the site of the former death camp, the Pope said, "This inscription stirs the memory of the people whose sons and daughters were destined to total extermination. . . . This people, which received from God the commandment: 'Thou shalt not kill,' has experienced in itself to a particular degree what killing means. Before this inscription it is not permissible for anyone to pass by with indifference."[47] In an apostolic letter on the fiftieth anniversary of the outbreak of World War II, the Pope stated that "the Jews of Poland, more than others, lived this immense suffering."[48]

John Paul II consistently has condemned anti-Semitism, has linked that condemnation to his close personal awareness of the unique experience of the Jews during the Holocaust, and has considered a confrontation with the Holocaust to be a critical item on the agenda of Catholic-Jewish dialogue: "No dialogue between Christians and Jews can overlook the painful and terrible experience of the *Shoah*."[49] Nonetheless, in his statements on the Holocaust, the Pope offers a historiography and theology of the Holocaust that are problematic, especially for Jews.

Though the Pope readily acknowledges the activity, complicity, and apathy of Christians with regard to the Holocaust; though he recognizes correlative guilt of such individuals; and though he has called for their contrition, repentance, and reconciliation toward the Jewish people, John Paul II has nonetheless apparently refused to acknowledge the role of Christian doctrinal anti-Semitism as a contributing cause of the Holocaust, and he has not explicitly confronted the less than admirable behavior of the Holy See during the Holocaust. In an address to the German ambassador to the Holy See, the Pope said, "For Christians the heavy burden of guilt for the murder of the Jewish people must be an enduring call to repentance; thereby we can overcome every form of anti-Semitism and establish a new relationship with our kindred nation of the Old Covenant."[50] Yet in a 1988 address to the Jewish community of Vienna, the Pope said, "It would be, of course, unjust and untrue to put the blame for those unspeakable crimes on Christianity."[51]

It might be unreasonable to expect the Pope to condemn the Holy See for its behavior during World War II, even though as a Pole he has much to condemn.[52] Rather, one might expect the Pope simply to be silent with regard to the Church's behavior during the war years. Instead, we find John Paul II portraying Pius XI and Pius XII as advocates for the Jews, despite the historical record to the contrary.[53] We find him emphasizing out of proportion the actual help given to Jews during the war years by local churches.[54]

The Pope circumvents all possible links between Christian anti-Semitism and the Holocaust. He similarly sidesteps the problematic historical issue of the behavior of the Church during the war years. Instead, he tries to forge continuity between the supposedly pro-Jewish doctrines and actions of the Church before Vatican II and the actually pro-Jewish doctrines and actions of the Church during his own pontificate. This, then, gives the Pope an opening to identify what he considers to be the source of the ideology that engendered the Holocaust as well as many subsequent assaults against human life and dignity: *secular atheism*. Using the Holocaust as a paradigmatic and supreme example of dehumanization, the Pope identifies secular humanism as the primary cause of the Holocaust and of other horrors in recent history. For example, speaking about the Holocaust, he observes that "it is precisely an absence of faith in God . . . which can easily bring about such disasters."[55] Speaking in Germany in 1987 about Nazism, John Paul II said, "Let us pause . . . to reflect on the terrible consequences which can arise from a denial of God. . . . [We must] remain alert for new forms of anti-Semitism, racism, and neo-pagan religious persecution."[56] Similarly, in a 1987 letter to Archbishop May of St. Louis, the Pope wrote, "Reflection upon the *Shoah* [i.e., the Holocaust] shows us to what terrible consequences the lack of faith in God and a contempt for man created in his image can lead."[57] John Paul II perceives the secularism that propelled Nazism to be a "new paganism" aimed both against the Jews and against Christianity as well.[58] He depicts Marxism as such an ideology.[59] He links this ideology with all the "Auschwitzes of our time," including the practice of abortion.[60]

For John Paul II, one of the driving forces behind interreligious dialogue is the attempt to forge an interreligious alliance against a common enemy and challenge, that is, atheism, secularism, and materialism, which he sees as being at the root of dehumanization and as inimical to human life, dignity, and freedom. While John Paul II never minimizes the extent of Jewish suffering during the Holocaust, he nonetheless sees Holocaust awareness as a foundation for a universal moral theology and as a stimulus for a program of social action.[61]

John Paul II always has found great meaning and virtue in suffering. This view is consonant both with Catholic teaching and with a particularly Polish-Catholic proclivity for "messianic" self-understanding.[62] It is not surprising, therefore, that the Pope applies such a theological attitude to his understanding of the Holocaust. In the catastrophe that befell the Jews, the Pope finds multifaceted meaning. Such suffering, he contends, is simultaneously vicarious, purifying, pedagogic, and redemptive. It is a way in which Jews can bear witness to their "irrevocable calling" by God. "After all," says the Pope quoting the Gospel of John (4:22), "salvation is from the Jews."[63] Addressing Jewish leaders in Warsaw in 1987, the Pope said:

> It was you who suffered this terrible sacrifice of extermination. One might say that you suffered it also on behalf of those who were in the purifying power of suffering. The more atrocious the suffering, the greater the purification. The more painful the experience, the greater the hope. . . . Because of this terrible experience, you have become a loud warning voice for all humanity, for all nations, all powers of this world, all systems and every person. More than anyone else, it is precisely you who have become this saving warning. I think that in this sense you continue your particular vocation.[64]

Echoing motifs usually reserved by Catholics for Christ and by Poles for Poland — "the Christ of the nations" — John Paul II describes Jewish suffering during the Holocaust as having been vicarious suffering for humankind and therefore redemptive. Using the Christological motif of "sacrifice," he states: "You bore this sacrifice for others who were also supposed to be destroyed."[65] Elsewhere, he says that when confronting the horrors of the Holocaust, "we hear the voice of Christ."[66]

While affirming the irrevocable election of Israel by God, John Paul II sees suffering as an endemic component of that election, an election that the people of Israel, in his view, share with one of their sons — Jesus. "This extraordinary people continues to bear signs of its divine election. . . . Israel has truly paid a high price for its election. Perhaps because of this, Israel has become more similar to the Son of man, who, according to the flesh, was also a son of Israel."[67]

John Paul II's reflections on the Holocaust integrate not only past but now recent Jewish experience into his Catholic theology of Judaism. He attempts to infuse meaning into horror. He wants to elicit reconciliation between Jews and Catholics, especially between Jews and Poles, from an event that has evoked hostility and mistrust between these two groups. His comparisons of Jewish suffering to the passion of Christ can only be seen as intending to further such reconciliation. Nonetheless, from a Jewish perspective, the Pope's understanding of the Holocaust is problematic.

Classical Jewish theology recognizes the virtue of martyrdom. Jewish commentaries on the biblical text describing the "suffering servant" (Isaiah 53) relate it to the people of Israel. However, post-Holocaust Jewish thought is strongly resistant to discerning redemptive meaning from the systematic murder of one-third of the Jewish people, including over one million Jewish children. To ascribe meaning is to offer justification, to assign a reason for why so many had to suffer so many unspeakable horrors. To ascribe meaning to this catastrophe could readily lead to the view that what happened was inevitable, that the perpetrators were the agents of destiny or even of God. As Elie Wiesel has put it, "Suffering does not lead to saintliness. I think suffering is evil. Man is not created in order to suffer. If this were so, then God could not be holy. God does not want man to suffer; man suffers against God. We believe that suffering is not the answer; suffering is only the question."[68] Jews do not aspire to be "the Christ of the nations." It is told of a Hasidic master that during a time of persecution, he prayed to God, "We've had enough of suffering. If to be Your chosen people means that we are chosen to suffer, then choose someone else."

Particularly problematic for Jews has been the Pope's 1987 beatification (and the 1998 subsequent canonization) of Edith Stein, a Jewess who went to her death during the Holocaust as a baptized Jew, as a Catholic nun. In stating that her "baptism was by no means a break with her Jewish heritage," John Paul II reiterates his Catholic theology of Judaism which, in effect, absorbs Judaism into the continuum that culminates in Christian faith.[69] Here we see another example of how *Nostra Aetate* rejects the displacement doctrine while retaining aspects of the supersessionist doctrine. The integrity of Judaism is affirmed, but the hope and even the expectation of the conversion of the Jews are expressed by John Paul II on various occasions. While "mission to the Jews" as an aggressive or coercive task is no longer considered viable, the hope for the baptism of Jews remains, and the lauding of those, such as Edith Stein, who have taken this road, continues. Indeed, most Jews would find offensive the Pope's statement that "[o]n the strength of Christ's willingness to sacrifice himself for others she [i.e., Edith Stein] saw in her seeming impotence a way to render a final service to her people," like the biblical figure of Esther.[70] From the Pope's Catholic point of view, Edith Stein is a saint, a "Catholic Jew" who found fulfillment in Jesus Christ and who died a sacrificial death like her adopted Savior. But for Jews, Edith Stein was a Jewish apostate who abandoned the faith of her ancestors, who elected to receive that which Jewish martyrs throughout the centuries had perished rejecting. For many Jews, some of the teachings of the faith she accepted were a contributing cause of the event that claimed her life and the lives of millions of others of the faith she rejected. Those who took her life, and the lives of millions of others, were practicing adherents of the faith she embraced.

To be sure, evangelization is central to the mission of the Church.[71] It would be unreasonable to expect the Church to renounce a doctrine so central to its mission in the world. However, under John Paul II, the Church has revised its doctrine of evangelization from one of aggressive coercion to more benign forms in which the individual joins the Church through a free expression of conscience and conviction.[72] Long before Vatican II, John Paul II practiced what he was later to preach. A variety of sources have confirmed, for example, that in 1949, in Poland, a woman came to the young Father Wojtyla asking him to baptize her adopted son. From questioning her, Wojtyla learned that the child was Jewish. His parents had given him into the safekeeping of that woman during the Nazi occupation. They had explicitly requested that the child remain a Jew and be sent to his mother's family after the war, should they not survive. The parents were both killed. Wojtyla refused to baptize the child, respecting the will of his parents. He told the foster mother to arrange for the child to go to America to be reunited with his family and with his faith. Despite the pain of separation from her adopted son, the woman complied.[73]

As has been noted, John Paul II's social agenda rests upon his understanding of Catholic moral theology and his fierce opposition to secularism. While he has linked specific moral positions, such as his views of abortion, to his understanding of the Holocaust, this perspective is not largely shared by the representatives of most Jewish organizations with which the Church has been engaged dialogically. Here, one of the many incongruities in Catholic-Jewish dialogue as it is actually practiced becomes evident. While the Pope finds abortion, birth control, most forms of infertility treatment, and many positions endorsed by feminists to be immoral, it is precisely these issues that most of the Jewish organizations involved in dialogue with the Church are advocating, for example, a pro-choice stance on abortion. This incongruity deepens when one realizes that Catholic-Jewish dialogue in practice mostly obtains between the Church — a religious institution — and secular Jewish organizations that identify with the ideology the Pope has depicted as the archenemy of religion: namely, secular humanism. On the Catholic side of the dialogue there is a hierarchical Church, grounded in theology, and usually represented in interfaith dialogue by theologians who are clergy, or at least by clergy. On the Jewish side, there is a plethora of voluntaristic Jewish agencies, usually secular in nature, being represented by managerial staff and lay leaders untutored in theology and often of a secular or even an antireligious bent. The Catholic "language" of expression is theological. The Jewish "language" is often liberal secularism. The Catholic framework for discussion is theological. The Jewish framework is primarily informed by the Jewish communal agenda. As the present President of the Holy See's Commission for Religious Dialogue with Judaism, Cardinal Edward Cassidy, has put it, "We are not two humanitarian societies; far less are we two debating clubs. We are two faith communities and as such we are being called to respond to a common challenge."[74]

When Catholic-Jewish dialogue began in the United States, Catholics and Jews shared a social agenda. Both groups suffered social and economic discrimination and exclusion in Protestant America. As Catholics (primarily Irish and Italian) and Jews became integrated into the American fabric, as anti-Catholic and anti-Jewish discrimination abated, the social and political agendas of Catholic-Americans and Jewish-Americans diverged. Furthermore, the "official" position of the Church on human sexuality, abortion, euthanasia, and other issues finds little resonance in the predominantly liberal and highly secularized Jewish communal structure. Outside of North America, especially in largely Catholic countries, Jewish communities find themselves often too small to effectively participate in dialogue with the Catholic Church. The questions of who is the Church's actual and most appropriate partner in religious dialogue with Judaism and how authentic theological dialogue can be maintained are often problematic.

The Church desires dialogue not simply with Jews, but with Judaism. As the name of the Vatican Commission for *Religious* Relations with the Jews suggests, it seeks *religious*, theological dialogue between two "faith communities," and not primarily social dialogue. It perceives social issues as being inextricably related to matters of faith and theology, and not simply as agenda items for intergroup relations. The commission has called for a real "theological dialogue," that is, a dialogue on theological issues by those competent on both sides to do so. Perhaps the present incongruity in Catholic-Jewish theological dialogue is what the Pope had in mind when he warned that "[w]ork [of Catholic-Jewish dialogue] that is of poor quality or lacking in precision would be extremely detrimental to dialogue in this field."[75]

The incongruity of religious dialogue between the Church and Jewish social advocacy groups has created a situation in which one side is speaking theological discourse while the other is speaking from the framework of a specific group's communal agenda. This is not a dialogue, but two monologues speaking different languages. While theological concerns have been of paramount importance to the Church, and while the Church has recast its theology in terms of its relationship to Judaism, and while John Paul II has formulated a Catholic theology of Judaism, there has been little reciprocity from the Jewish side. Little attention has been paid in the Jewish academic, religious, or communal arenas to recasting the often negative classical Jewish theological attitudes and views of Christianity.[76] Few efforts have been expended to revise negative popular Jewish stereotypes of Christianity and of Christians. Changes in how Jews are portrayed in the catechism, liturgy, and Catholic textbooks reflect the Church's new understanding of the Jews and of Judaism. Yet such changes have not been reciprocated by the Jewish community in terms of how Catholics and Catholicism ought to be understood by Jews. Little has been done by the Jewish community to make Jews aware of post–Vatican II teachings about Jews and Judaism. As Cardinal Cassidy has bluntly put it, "I am truly amazed at times to read Catholic teaching and doctrine explained in Jewish publications in such a way that no Catholic would recognize them as part of his or her faith."[77] He further expresses dismay at the widespread lack of Jewish interest in and knowledge of the evolution of Catholic self-understanding with regard to Judaism and the Jewish people.

The Church's strong affirmation of Hebrew Scriptures and of the Jewish identity of Jesus, Mary, and the apostles has led to a veritable explosion of Catholic scholarship and education aimed at understanding and reclaiming aspects of Judaism at the time of Jesus and even some of the rituals of ancient and contemporary Judaism. The identity of Jesus as a Jew has been embraced by the Pope and by Catholic doctrine. However, scant attention has been paid by the Jewish community to the identity of Jesus as a Jew. Few attempts have been made by Jewish scholars and theologians to rethink and to recast the largely negative portrait of Jesus and the apostles found in classical Jewish religious thought and in popular Jewish attitudes.

Under the influence of John Paul II, the Church has developed a Catholic theology of Judaism that has been translated programmatically in a manner that immeasurably has improved Catholic-Jewish relations. As has been indicated above, this Catholic theology of Judaism is both promising and problematic from a Jewish perspective. For Catholic-Jewish relations to build on the substantial progress already achieved, and for the work of dialogue and reconciliation to proceed further, a new Jewish theology of Christianity is a *desideratum*, including a rethinking of Jewish attitudes toward Jesus and the apostles.

In various official documents, the Holy See has addressed most concerns of the Jewish communal agenda that relate to Catholic-Jewish relations. Anti-Semitism has been summarily condemned and defined as a sin against God. Holocaust awareness has heightened. Israel has been recognized by the Holy See, and full diplomatic relations have been achieved. Vatican recognition has triggered substantial positive effects for Israel diplomatically, politically, and economically. As a result of Israel's recognition by the Holy See, formerly closed diplomatic channels and economic opportunities in Catholic countries have opened up.

The Church is now calling for "a *theological* dialogue with Jewish representatives." The major item on the agenda that will determine the future complexion of Catholic-Jewish dialogue is whether the Jewish community is prepared to enter into serious and authentic *theological* dialogue with the Church. The Church, especially under the leadership of John Paul II, has moved boldly and comparatively rapidly in recasting and reshaping its theology, policies, and activities with regard to Judaism and the Jewish people. Whether reciprocity in the areas of theology, policy, liturgy, education, and related programming will take place within the Jewish community currently remains an unanswered question.[78] But underlying the sacred work of Jewish-Catholic dialogue are both a prayer and a hope. In the words of John Paul II:

As Christians and Jews, following the example of the faith of Abraham, we are called to be a blessing for the world. This is the common task awaiting us. It is therefore necessary for us, Christians and Jews, to first be a blessing to one another.[79]

Notes

1. The text of *Nostra Aetate* may be found in Francesco Gioia, ed., *Interreligious Dialogue: The Official Teaching of the Catholic Church (1963–95)* (Boston: Pauline Books, 1997), 37–40 (henceforth: Gioia). See John T. Pawlikowski, "*Nostra Aetate:* Its Impact on Catholic-Jewish Relations," *Thought* 67 (December 1991): 371–84.

2. See also Gioia, 239, 499, 547.

3. For good summaries of the "displacement doctrine," see Franklin Littell, *The Crucifixion of the Jews* (New York: Harper and Row, 1975), 28–32; Rosemary R. Ruether, *Faith and Fratricide: The Theological Roots of Anti-Semitism* (New York: Seabury Press, 1974) (henceforth: Ruether); Joseph Cardinal Bernardin, *A Blessing to Each Other* (Chicago: Liturgy Training Publications, 1996), 146–55 (henceforth: Bernardin).

4. The eminent Jewish theologian Abraham Joshua Heschel was deeply involved in negotiating the final draft of para. 4 of *Nostra Aetate.* In meetings with Cardinal Augustin Bea and with Paul VI he fought for the exclusion of any mention of "mission to the Jews" in that document. When such a reference appeared in an early draft, he issued a strong rebuke, saying, "I'd rather go to Auschwitz than give up my religion." As Heschel said in an interview, "I succeeded in persuading the Pope. . . . He personally crossed out a paragraph in which there was a reference to conversion or mission to the Jews. The Pope [i.e., Paul VI] himself. And the declaration published by the Ecumenical Council — if you study it carefully, you will notice the impact of my effort. There isn't the slightest reference to mission to the Jews" (see Heschel, *Moral Grandeur and Spiritual Audacity* [New York: Farrar, Straus and Giroux, 1996], 405). On the revised attitude of the Catholic Church on "mission to the Jews," see Eugene Fisher, "Is There a Christian Mission to the Jews?" in Clark Williamson, ed., *A Mutual Witness* (St. Louis: Chalice Press, 1992), 15–33.

5. The "Guidelines" were published on December 1, 1974, over the signature of Johannes Cardinal Willebrands, President of the Commission for Religious Relations with the Jews. The text of the "Guidelines" is found in Eugene J. Fisher, *Seminary Education and Christian-Jewish Relations* (Washington, D.C.: National Catholic Educational Association, 1983), 81–86.

6. Jules Isaac, *The Teaching of Contempt* (New York: Holt, Rinehart and Winston, 1964).

7. See Louis Michaels, *The Humor and Warmth of Pope John XXIII* (New York: Scribner, 1965), 53. On John XXIII's help to Jews during the Holocaust, see Lawrence Elliott, *I Will Be Called John* (New York: Berkley, 1973), 159–65.

8. Cited in Bernardin, 151–52.

9. See Gioia, 635.

10. See Carl Bernstein and Marco Politi, *His Holiness: John Paul II and the Hidden History of Our Time* (New York: Doubleday, 1996), 30 (henceforth: Bernstein).

11. On attitudes of the Polish Church toward the Jews in the immediate years before World War II, see Ronald Modras, *The Catholic Church and Antisemitism, Poland 1933–1939* (Chur, Switzerland: Harwood Academic Publishers, 1994). On Polish-Jewish relations between the world wars, see Yisrael Gutman et al., eds., *The Jews of Poland between Two World Wars* (Hanover, N.H.: University Press of New England, 1989). On attitudes of the Polish Church immediately after the war, see Aryeh Josef Kochavi, "The Catholic Church and Anti-Semitism in Poland Following World War II as Reflected in British Diplomatic Documents," *Gal-Ed* (1989): 116–28.

12. Bernstein, 44.

13. Tad Szulc, *Pope John Paul II: The Biography* (New York: Pocket Books, 1995), 74–75 (henceforth: Szulc). On John Paul II and Kluger, see also relevant references in Bernstein and in Gian Franco Svidercoschi, *Letter to a Jewish Friend* (New York: Crossroad, 1994) (henceforth: Svidercoschi). Also, Darcy O'Brien, *The Hidden Pope* (New York: Daybreak Books, 1998).

14. Szulc, 305.

15. Cited in Svidercoschi, 93.

16. Bernstein, 31.

17. Bernstein, 32; Szulc, 66.

18. Most of John Paul II's statements regarding Judaism and the Jewish people — many delivered at meetings with representatives of various Jewish communities throughout the world — have been collected in Eugene J. Fisher and Leon Klenicki, eds., *Spiritual Pilgrimage: Texts on Jews and Judaism 1979–1995: Pope John Paul II* (New York: Crossroad, 1995) (henceforth: *Pilgrimage*). For citations noted here, see 8, 99, 151, 153–54.

19. John Paul II, *Crossing the Threshold of Hope* (New York: Alfred A. Knopf, 1994), 98–100 (henceforth: *Threshold*).

20. See James Carroll, "The Silence," *New Yorker*, April 7, 1997, 66 (henceforth: Carroll).

21. See *Pilgrimage*, 60–73; Bernstein, 443–44.

22. See *Pilgrimage*, 167–69. On the "convent controversy," see Wladyslaw T. Bartoszewski, *The Convent at Auschwitz* (New York: George Braziller, 1990); Carol Rittner and John K. Roth, eds., *Memory Offended: The Auschwitz Convent Controversy* (New York: Praeger, 1991).

23. See *Threshold*, 188–91; Szulc, 494–96.

24. See *Threshold*, 191–99, 203–8; Szulc, 489–93.

25. See, e.g., *Pilgrimage*, 36, 46, 187.

26. *Threshold*, 100.

27. *Pilgrimage*, 12.

28. On the situation of the Church at the time of John Paul II's election, see Szulc, 338–59; Bernstein, 96–98, 155–60.

29. *Pilgrimage*, 89.

30. See *Pilgrimage*, xxii. John XXIII in his first meeting with Jewish representatives as Pope introduced himself as "Joseph, your brother" (Genesis 45:4).

31. The story of Cain and Abel is also relevant here. Earlier Church teachings compared the Jews to the fratricidal Cain, and Jesus and the Church to Abel. The "displacement doctrine" placed the "mark of Cain" and his punishment of eternal wandering upon the Jews. See Ruether, 133–34.

32. *Pilgrimage*, 63. See also the *Catechism of the Catholic Church* (Mahwah, N.J.: Paulist Press, 1994) (henceforth: *Catechism*), issued during the pontificate of John Paul II and endorsed by him: "The Jewish faith, unlike other non-Christian religions, is already a response to God's revelation in the Old Covenant" (para. 839, p. 233). Note John Borelli, "The Catechism and Interreligious Dialogue: The Jews and World Religions," in Bernard L. Marthaler, ed., *Introducing the Catechism of the Catholic Church* (New York: Paulist Press, 1994), 72–87.

33. See Franz Rosenzweig, *The Star of Redemption*, trans. William H. Hallo (New York: Holt, Rinehart and Winston, 1970), 298–380. See also Maurice Bowler, "Rosenzweig on Judaism and Christianity: The Two Covenant Approach," *Judaism* 22 (1973): 475–82; Michael B. McGarry, *Christology after Auschwitz* (New York: Paulist Press, 1977), especially 73–93 on dual covenant theory. Note that McGarry's book was published before the pontificate of John Paul II.

34. See *Pilgrimage*, 15.

35. See *Pilgrimage*, 18.

36. *Pilgrimage*, 14.

37. While John Paul II uses a "fraternal" model for the Jewish-Christian relationship, he also tends to depict Christianity as the "daughter" religion of Judaism. He describes the relationship as a "real parentage" (see *Pilgrimage*, 56) and as an "organic" relationship (see 74). In recent years, it has become popular to depict the relationship of Judaism and Christianity as one of siblings, whereas before Christianity was depicted as a "daughter" religion of Judaism. The image one uses has direct implications for interreligious dialogue.

38. See *Pilgrimage*, 174–75. See also *Catechism*, paras. 65, 66, pp. 22–23; para. 840, p. 233; para. 1093, p. 284.

39. See *Threshold*, 100; *Pilgrimage*, 74.

40. See *Pilgrimage*, 15.

41. The removal of collective Jewish responsibility for the death of Jesus is restated by John Paul II and is linked by him to the rejection of any theo-

logical justification for anti-Semitism (see *Pilgrimage,* 63). The *Catechism* (paras. 595–98, pp. 153–54) amplifies further upon this theme and states (para. 598): "Taking into account the fact that our sins affect Christ himself, the Church does not hesitate to impute to Christians the gravest responsibility for the torments inflicted upon Jesus, a responsibility with which they have all too often burdened the Jews alone. We must regard as guilty all those who continue to relapse into their sins.... And it can be seen that our crime in this case is greater in us than in the Jews." Para. 599, p. 155, states further, "Jesus' violent death... is part of the mystery of God's plan."

42. See, e.g., *Pilgrimage,* 62, 128, 139. On his renunciation of the deicide claim, see 124.

43. See John Paul II, "The Sinfulness of Anti-Semitism," *Origins* 23, no. 13, September 5, 1991. See *Pilgrimage,* 140, 158. See also *Threshold,* 97.

44. *Pilgrimage,* 131.

45. *Pilgrimage,* 62. See John Paul II's poetic and moving "lamentation" at Mauthausen Concentration Camp, in *Pilgrimage,* 116–18.

46. See *Pilgrimage,* 151. Note Yisrael Gutman and Shmuel Krakowski, *Unequal Victims: Poles and Jews during World War Two* (New York: Holocaust Library, 1986); Michael C. Steinlauf, *Bondage to the Dead: Poland and the Memory of the Holocaust* (Syracuse, N.Y.: Syracuse University Press, 1997); Antony Polonsky, "Polish-Jewish Relations and the Holocaust," *Polin* 4 (1989): 226–42; Andrej Bryk, "Polish Society Today and the Memory of the Holocaust," *Gal-Ed* (1991): 107–29.

47. *Pilgrimage,* 7.

48. *Pilgrimage,* 131.

49. *Pilgrimage,* 142.

50. *Pilgrimage,* 139.

51. *Pilgrimage,* 120; see also 152.

52. On Pius XII's apparent apathy to the plight of Poles and Jews in Nazi-occupied Poland, see Carlo Falconi, *The Silence of Pius XII* (Boston: Little, Brown and Co., 1965).

53. On Pius XI and Pius XII's alleged pro-Jewish postures, see *Pilgrimage,* 5, 32, 107. For a historically documented study that offers a much different view, one that condemns the often pro-German attitudes and actions of Pius XI and Pius XII, see Guenter Lewy, *The Catholic Church and Nazi Germany* (New York: McGraw Hill, 1964).

54. On the aid given Jews by local churches, see *Pilgrimage,* 14, 62, 107, 203.

55. *Pilgrimage,* 52; see 21.

56. *Pilgrimage,* 91.

57. *Pilgrimage,* 101, 149.

58. *Pilgrimage,* 131–32.

59. *Pilgrimage,* 101.

60. *Pilgrimage*, 209, 150, 123. See Bernstein, 518: "He would fight tooth and nail against 'a new massacre, a true slaughter of the innocents, a new Holocaust.' The Holocaust was precisely the image that came to his mind every time he heard the word *abortion*."

61. See *Pilgrimage*, 127, 180.

62. See Szulc, 7, 22–25, 118, 383. See Waldemar Chrostowski, "The Suffering, Chosenness and Mission of the Polish Nation," *Occasional Papers on Religion in Eastern Europe* 11, no. 4 (August 1991): 1–14.

63. *Pilgrimage*, 98–99.

64. *Pilgrimage*, 99; see also 126–27.

65. *Pilgrimage*, 151. The direct reference here is to the Poles. It could not be lost on his Polish listeners that here the Pope depicts Jews rather than Poles as "the Christ of the nations."

66. *Pilgrimage*, 98.

67. *Threshold*, 99.

68. Harry J. Cargas, *In Conversation with Elie Wiesel* (New York: Paulist Press, 1976), 19.

69. *Pilgrimage*, 95. See also "Advisory Addresses Jewish Concerns about the Canonization of Edith Stein," *Origins* 28, no. 18, October 15, 1998, 301–5.

70. *Pilgrimage*, 93.

71. See Gioia, 407: "The Church is missionary by her very nature." See also *Catechism*, paras. 849–56, pp. 225–26. Note how post–Vatican II documents deal with the claim "Outside the Church there is no salvation" in view of the Church's commitment to interreligious dialogue; see *Catechism*, paras. 846–48, pp. 244–25; and Gioia, 547.

72. Gioia, 577. Here the Curia bluntly states that conversion must be a freely chosen act, but that "[i]n the context of dialogue between believers of various faiths, one cannot avoid reflecting on the spiritual process of conversion."

73. See Szulc, 173. For a more complete account, see Yaffa Eliach, *Hasidic Tales of the Holocaust* (New York: Oxford University Press, 1982), 142–47.

74. Cardinal Edward I. Cassidy, "The Next Issues in Jewish-Catholic Relations," *Origins* 26, no. 41, April 3, 1997, 668 (henceforth: Cassidy).

75. *Pilgrimage*, 19.

76. A few Jewish theologians have attempted to formulate a Jewish theology of Christianity. See David Novak, *Jewish-Christian Dialogue: A Jewish Justification* (New York: Oxford University Press, 1989). For a new Jewish theological understanding of Jesus, see Byron L. Sherwin, " 'Who Do You Say That I Am?' — A New Jewish View of Jesus," *Journal of Ecumenical Studies* 31, no. 3/4 (1994): 255–69.

77. Cassidy, 669.

78. Because of the nature of the Church, it is doubtful that the momentum toward stabilizing and improving Catholic-Jewish relations, as affirmed in

Church documents and as stated during the "magisterium" of John Paul II, would be stifled in the future. His successor would not be anticipated as reversing this momentum; however, whether he would pursue these dialogic relations with the vigor of John Paul II remains to be seen.

79. *Pilgrimage*, 169.

Part Four

MUSLIM RESPONSES

11

Pope John Paul II on Islam

MAHMOUD AYOUB

Historical Overview

Muslim-Christian relations are as old as the Islamic tradition itself. Before his prophetic mission, while still a youth, Muhammad's prophethood is believed to have been recognized and foretold by the Christian monk Bahirah.[1] The truth of Muhammad's mission and the authenticity of the scripture revealed to him were confirmed by the aged Christian savant Waraqah b. Nawfal. Waraqah's testimony to the truth of Muhammad's apostolic mission confirmed him in his resolve to preach his new message of faith in the One God to an idolatrous and stubborn people.[2] When some of the Prophet's followers could no longer endure the persecution by the hostile men of Makkah, he advised them to seek protection with the Christian king of Abyssinia.[3]

Christians are described in the Qur'an as "the nearest in amity" to the Muslims (Q. 5:82). Twice they are numbered among the religious communities whose faith and good works will be richly rewarded by God, "and no fear shall come upon them nor will they grieve."[4] Yet the Christians are sternly reproached for their extremist claims concerning Jesus and even accused of rejection of faith.[5]

Thus the Islamic position toward Christians has from the beginning been an ambivalent one. This ambivalence is characteristic not only of the Islamic view of Christians but of Christian-Muslim relations generally and on both sides. One fundamental reason for this ambivalence is that both faiths are intensely missionary-oriented. Each claims to have exclusively a universal message of truth and salvation for all of human-

169

kind. Each community, moreover, considers the other to be in grave error in its basic understanding of God, his nature, and his relationship to humanity and its history.

While it may be argued that Muslim-Christian relations are now better than they have ever been, in fact little has changed in the basic attitudes of the Church and the *Ummah* toward one another. There has been on both sides a grudging recognition of their common faith in the One God but also a deep mistrust of the aims and intentions of each community toward the other. This mistrust stems from long-held distortions and misrepresentations of the faith and culture by both communities of one another. These distorted images have often been used to justify long and bloody conflicts between Western Christendom and the world of Islam.

On the basis of this common faith in God and commitment to do his will, in 1077 Pope Gregory VII wrote to the sultan al-Nasir, ruler of Bejaya in present-day Algeria, reminding him of this common faith and commitment. The Pope admonished the Muslim ruler, "God approves nothing in us so much as that after loving Him, one should love his fellow." He continued: "You and we owe this charity to ourselves, specially because we believe and confess one God."[6] Less than two decades later, in 1095, Pope Urban II sounded an entirely different note at the Council of Clairmont, which he used to launch the first Crusade against the Muslims. In his famous address the Pontiff contrasted the Franks, "the beloved of God," with the Muslims, whom he called "an accursed race, a race utterly alienated from God."[7]

New Hopes and Old Prejudices

The millennium following these harsh words has seen many positive changes in Muslim-Christian relations. A new era of meaningful and constructive dialogue began with Vatican II, 1962–65. In this essay we are concerned with the position of the Catholic Church toward Islam and Muslims, and more specifically with the pronouncements of John Paul II on Islam. It must be noted at the outset that the following analysis of His Holiness's pronouncements will mirror the same ambivalence that has characterized the relations between the two communities throughout their long history.

In many ways the pronouncements of John Paul II on Islam echo the spirit and letter of Vatican II. In particular, *Nostra Aetate,* one of the Council's major documents expressing the Church's new spirit of openness to dialogue with "non-Christians," has been the primary inspiration for the Pope's approach to Islam. Nevertheless, His Holiness often returns to old and conservative attitudes of the Church toward Islam and Muslims. This is particularly the case, as we shall see, when he addresses Catholic clerics living in Muslim lands. The issue that will concern us in this study is, therefore, the apparent inconsistencies in the Holy Father's pronouncements on Islam and what this means to the commitment of both the Church and the *Ummah* to interfaith dialogue.

John Paul II has been more prolific on Islam than any Pontiff before him. This is undoubtedly due in large part to his numerous pastoral visits to Christian minorities living in Muslim lands.[8] No less important in this regard is the participation of the Pontifical Council for Interreligious Dialogue in international interfaith activities. On such occasions the Pope addressed Muslim participants on behalf of the Catholic Church. Other reasons for the Pope's concern with Muslims and Islam have been international conflicts such as the Lebanese civil strife, the Gulf War, and the tragic interreligious conflict in the former Yugoslavia. Still another reason is the diplomatic relations of the Vatican with many Muslim nations.

We shall selectively examine the statements of John Paul II on Islam chronologically over a fifteen-year period, 1979–94. These statements will be considered under three categories: those addressed to Muslims directly; those addressed to Christians about Islam; and those contained in the Pope's writings, especially his encyclical *Mission of the Redeemer* (1991) and the book *Crossing the Threshold of Hope* (1994). These two recent documents provide the theological framework for the Pope's personal position toward other religions in general and Islam in particular.

The first journey of the Pope to a predominantly Muslim country was to Turkey in November 1979, slightly over a year after his accession to the pontifical office. In a homily delivered at the chapel of the Italian embassy in Ankara, the Pope exhorted the Catholic community to live in peace and amity with fellow Muslim citizens. He praised Turkey's secular system which allows all citizens to practice their own religion without any discrimination. "Although they do not acknowledge Jesus as God," the Pope observed, Muslims "revere him as a prophet, honor the virgin Mary and await the day of Resurrection." He extolled Islamic moral, spiritual, and social values which Christians also hold. The Pope finally called on both Muslims and Christians to collaborate on the basis of their common faith in God in promoting peace and brotherhood "in the free profession of faith proper to each."[9]

It is important to note here that honoring Jesus and his mother is not an Islamic gesture of good will toward Christians. It is rather an essential part of their faith. But to "acknowledge Jesus as God" is for Muslims to associate other gods with God, which is the only unforgivable sin.[10] While we believe such theological issues should not be ignored by Christians and Muslims in their efforts to promote better understanding through honest dialogue, they should be recognized and dealt with patiently and with great sensitivity.

In May 1980, first in Kenya and then in Ghana, the Pope echoed the same sentiments in his addresses to Muslim leaders of the two African countries. He found in the worship of the One God, the creator of heaven and earth, a uniting bond of Christians and Muslims. He affirmed the Church's commitment to dialogue with Islam, but also asked that "her own heritage be fully known specially to those who are spiritually attached to Abraham and who profess monotheism."[11] This somewhat veiled reference to missionary work among the Muslims of Africa is more openly expressed in later speeches, particularly to African bishops and missionaries engaged in medical, educational, and other humanitarian services.

The dual mission of the Church as a "good Samaritan" to the poor and suffering peoples of the world, and also as the maker of disciples for Christ "of all nations,"[12] was emphasized by the Pope during a two-day stop in Pakistan on his way to the Far East. His Holiness exchanged expressions of good will with the late Pakistani President Zia ul Haqq. He observed that, while the primary mission of the Church is a spiritual one, she nonetheless always seeks to promote the dignity of all human beings through schools and other educational, charitable, and social institutions. Then reflecting the spirit of Vatican II, the Holy Father concluded his address with the prayer that mutual understanding between Christians and Muslims grow deeper and that ways of greater cooperation be found "for the good of all."[13]

The attitude of mutual mistrust and hostility which has on the whole characterized relations between the Christian West and the Muslim world had its roots not only in fundamental theological differences, but also in political, economic, and military rivalries. Within less than a century of the Prophet's death, Christendom lost to Muslim domination some of its most central provinces. Asia Minor, Egypt, and North Africa were very early irrevocably lost, and for centuries the Iberian Peninsula and other important parts of Christian Europe were centers of Islamic learning and power.

While, moreover, significant Christian minorities survived in Egypt and other Middle Eastern lands, in North Africa, or the lands of the Arab West (al-Maghrib), the home of Cyprian and Augustine, Christianity disappeared forever. Yet North Africa's pre-Islamic religious heritage left an indelible mark on its popular Sufi piety. This piety in turn provided the basis of spiritual fellowship with mystically inclined Christians such as the well-known Christian marabout Charles de Foucauld. De Foucauld tried and succeeded in sharing his Christlike life with Muslims in Algeria, who saw in him a Sufi saint as well as a saintly Christian hermit. He thus broke the religious barriers that had long separated Muslims and Christians without compromising his own religious convictions.[14]

Another equally significant point of contact with the West has been the deep penetration of French education and culture into most North African societies. Therefore, in spite of the disappearance of indigenous Christianity in North Africa, the Church has enjoyed long and spiritually fruitful relations with the region.

In his address to North African bishops on November 23, 1981, the Pope spoke of the need to strengthen the small Catholic communities in that region in order that they may "bear a genuinely Christian witness among those who receive them." He also observed that this witness may be enriched by Muslim culture and piety. The Pope, however, cautioned that empathy for Islamic spirituality should not obscure the primary responsibility of the Christian, which is to "witness to the faith in Christ and to Christian values." He finally counseled that Catholic women married to Muslim men should always be an object of solicitude by the Church. For, he asserted, their presence in Muslim families allows them to witness directly to their faith.[15]

The approach of John Paul II to Muslims centers on two essential concepts, interfaith dialogue and Christian witness. These appear to be in the Holy Father's mind two closely interrelated terms. Thus the purpose of dialogue is to facilitate Christian witness. But the aim of both is ultimately the conversion of Muslims to Christianity.

This goal was enjoined upon the bishops of Mali during their *ad limina* visit to Rome on November 26, 1981. The Holy Father encouraged the bishops to engage in dialogue with Muslims as well as people of other faiths. "But dialogue itself," he asserted, "would lack an important dimension if it did not foresee the possibility of one freely asking for baptism."[16]

Were this goal to be directed at the followers of African and other nonmonotheistic traditions, an argument could be made that the aim is to lead them to faith in God. But with Muslims, dialogue ought to be a dialogue of faith among the worshipers of the God of Abraham and all the prophets including Muhammad. Otherwise dialogue, whatever form it may take, would be simply a cover for some form of post-colonial proselytization. This is particularly the case when dialogue is conducted in the context of Western Church-related medical, social, and educational missions.

The Pope is, according to Catholic tradition, not only the successor of St. Peter as the head of the universal Church, but also an international political figure. Understandably, therefore, the Pope would have many and at times conflicting agendas, depending on the time, place, and audience that he addresses. This may account, at least in part, for the apparent inconsistencies in his statements.

Speaking to Muslims in Nigeria on February 14, 1982, the Pope called for better understanding and cooperation between Christians and Muslims on the basis of common spiritual and moral values: faith in God and submission to God's holy will, and the commitment to defend human life and dignity. The context of this address was the family and its sanctity as "a precious nucleus of society." On the basis of a common spiritual and moral patrimony, he insisted, we can "in a true sense call one another brothers and sisters in the faith of the one God."[17]

The Holy Father called for safeguarding religious freedom, particularly in the education of children, which is usually taken to mean the freedom to teach the Christian faith. Yet there was no allusion to missionary activities of any kind. Rather, he counseled that religious education be used as a means to "counter the efforts of those who wish to destroy the spiritual aspects of man."[18]

In a highly significant speech addressed to the leaders of the Muslim and Jewish communities in Lisbon on May 14, 1982, the Pope presented a genuinely pluralistic theology of dialogue among the peoples of the Abrahamic traditions. Behind this religious pluralism, he averred, there must exist a unity of faith confirmed by personal conduct. The spiritual life of the faithful of all three communities would, the Pope further argued, help those who are searching for the Transcendent. It may help such sensitive souls to enjoy an inner glimmer of the reality of God in their lives. He continued: "Since, convinced as we are of the good which belief in God constitutes for us, the desire to share this good with others is spontaneous."[19]

The Pope went on to assert that for many people in today's world, God is either unknown or erroneously symbolized by ephemeral human powers. Therefore, interfaith dialogue could foster greater appreciation of the spirituality of every religious tradition. In this way interreligious dialogue could expose the myth of building a new and harmonious world-order without God, one that is solely based on anthropocentric humanism. In doing this, the Pope concluded, we would contribute to the common good of humanity.[20]

This theology of reconciliation and the freedom of faith, spiritual reform, mutual tolerance, and dialogue among peoples of different faith-traditions constituted an essential component of the Pope's message to the world, at least in the early years of his papacy. Concrete expression of this theology of universal faith in the One God was given in the apostolic letter of John Paul II, in celebration of the jubilee year of redemption.[21] One of the themes of this letter is the role of Jerusalem as a symbol of peace and harmony for the followers of the three Abrahamic faiths.

After speaking of the place of the Holy City in the devotional life of the three faith-communities, the Pope declared:

> I think of and long for the day on which we shall be so taught by God, that we shall listen to His message of peace and reconciliation. I think of the day on which Jews, Christians and Muslims will greet each other in the city of Jerusalem with the same greeting of peace with which Christ greeted the disciples after the resurrection, "peace be with you" (John 20:19).

The diversity of expressions of faith and culture in the Holy City should, His Holiness counseled, be "an effective aid to concord and peace."[22]

The theology of the unity of faith among all the believers in God, which the Pope so eloquently presented to the leaders of the three monotheistic religions in Lisbon in May 1982, was again expounded at the Vatican three years later. The occasion was a colloquium on the theme of holiness in Islam and Christianity.[23] The Holy Father began his address to that interfaith, international gathering with the Qur'anic affirmation, "Your God and ours is one and the same, and we are brothers and sisters in the faith of Abraham."[24] He then compared and contrasted the concept of holiness in the three monotheistic traditions and its manifestation as a quality of life in the Christian and Muslim communities. He contrasted the holy life of such virtues as uprightness, righteous living, and goodness, which the two religions enjoin, with such "self-centered tendencies as greed, the lust for power and prestige, competition, revenge, lack of forgiveness and the quest for earthly pleasures." These and similar vices, the Pope observed, turn humankind away from the path to goodness, "which God has intended for all of us." He concluded by observing that there are countless men and women — Muslims, Christians, and others around the world — who "quietly live authentic lives of obedience to God and selfless service to others." Such holy lives "offer humanity a genuine alternative — God's way to a world which otherwise would be destroyed in self-seeking hatred and struggle."[25]

To Muslims and Jews, as we saw, the Pope's message of good will and cooperation in promoting peace and social justice is usually based on a common faith and religious kinship. But when he spoke to Muslim and Hindu representatives in Nairobi, Kenya, on August 18, 1985, he emphasized social action based on general moral and spiritual values common to all the major religions. He thus argued that the communities of these world religions should not remain passive in the face of spiritual and social needs, violations of human rights, wars, and other disasters.

In that gathering the Pope acknowledged religious diversity but also unity in the worship of God. He asserted, "God's will is that those who worship him, even if not united in the same worship, would nevertheless be united in brotherhood and in common service for the good of all." This common quest for spiritual and moral fulfillment, the Pope asserted, should motivate us all to work together in facing the challenge of helping the world to "live in peace and harmony with respect for the human dignity of all."[26]

In a notable address to Moroccan youths delivered on the following day in Casablanca, the Pope added a humanistic dimension to this universal message of good will. Since the Pope referred often to this address in later encounters with Muslims, it must be regarded as an especially significant statement of his position toward Islam and Muslims. The irenic tone of this speech was perhaps determined by its audience. Among other world issues, the Pope addressed the need for more justice in world affairs, the lack of North-South solidarity, and the plight of refugees. The earth, the Pope asserted, is God's gift to all of humankind. All are equally entitled to its resources, and all have the right to live on it in peace and security. Furthermore, since every human being is in a certain sense the image and representative of God, we must love and respect every human being. He added, "Man is the road that leads to God."[27]

For the purpose of this study, however, it must be noted that in this address the Pope spoke unequivocally of the common religious heritage of Muslims and Christians. He said: "I believe that we Christians and Muslims must recognize with joy the religious values that we have in common and give thanks to God for them."[28]

In keeping with his role as a pastor, the Pope presented to Moroccan youths a long list of common beliefs and practices which bind Muslims and Christians. These include prayers, fasting, and almsgiving, as well as hope in God's mercy both in this world and the next. He concluded: "We hope that after the resurrection God will be satisfied with us, and we know that we will be satisfied with him."[29]

His Holiness repeated many of the same ideas in a homily which he preached in the same city and on the same day. But though he was speaking first to Christians, he repeated his call for witness to Christ to Muslims. Again, he couched this call to witness in the pastoral language of Christian love and charity. In their dialogue with Muslims — which the Pope admitted was not always easy — Christians should be ever conscious of the mystery of salvation, which they must communicate to others with love. As the theme of the homily was love, the Holy Father concluded, "If we have no love, our presence here will do nothing. Our witness will remain empty."[30]

On February 26, 1986, in Vatican City, the Pope received in audience Jewish, Christian, and Muslim participants in a colloquium organized under the auspices of the Jerusalem Hope Center for Interfaith Understanding and Reconciliation. The theme of the colloquium was "one God and three religions." The Pope appropriately highlighted the two divine attributes of mercy and justice, which both the Bible and the Qur'an teach. He also expressed the oft-repeated hope of peace and reconciliation among the three faith-communities through the city of peace, Jerusalem, which is a living symbol of God's will for all to live in peace and mutual respect. He continued: "In today's world it is more important than ever that people of faith place at the service of humanity their religious convictions, founded on daily practice of listening to God's message and encountering Him in prayerful worship."[31]

It is noteworthy that when the Holy Father speaks to representatives of the three religions, he places the three faiths on an equal footing as legitimate paths to God. Furthermore, his call for placing religious convictions at the service of humanity gives dialogue its true meaning and purpose. Still another noteworthy point is the absence in such addresses of any missionary motives.

This conciliatory attitude, however, raises an important question. Why does the Holy Father insist on missionary work among Muslims when he talks to Christians, and even to Muslims, but avoids any reference to it when he addresses Jews? One reason, we believe, is that Jewish-Christian dialogue has made far better progress toward achieving a common language among equal participants than has

Muslim-Christian dialogue. Another reason is that most of world Jewry has for centuries shared with the West a common history and culture. Islam, on the other hand, has for long been "the mysterious other" and the Muslim world an archrival to Western Christendom. Be that as it may, at a time when Christians and Muslims live as neighbors in every Western metropolis, the old ambivalence which remains characteristic of some of the Pope's pronouncements on Islam is hardly conducive to constructive dialogue.

Despite the fact that the Holy Father has enthusiastically participated in interfaith gatherings, he nonetheless appears to be uncomfortable with such undertakings. This may be because interfaith activities mean de facto recognition of the equal validity of all religions as paths to the divine or ultimate reality. This admission would of course question the Pope's view of the Church's missionary mandate. The Pope's cautionary attitude may conversely be due to the recognition of the uniqueness and integrity of every religion, which must not be compromised through interfaith activities, particularly those involving interfaith common prayers.

Both the enthusiasm and ambivalence of the Pope toward interreligious common devotions were clearly evinced in his opening address to the World Day of Prayer for Peace, held in Assisi on October 27, 1986. His Holiness began by observing the great value of so many religious leaders coming together for such a noble cause. This shows, he said, "that there exists another dimension of peace and another way of promoting it, which is not the result of negotiations, political compromise or economic bargaining."[32] Through religious diversity, the Pope further asserted, prayers for peace express a common spiritual bond and a relationship with the Power that surpasses all our human capabilities.

As for His Holiness's ambivalence, it may be discerned in the following qualifications that he placed on the aims of the meeting under discussion. He argued that the purpose of the gathering was not to seek religious consensus among the participants or negotiate their faith convictions. Nor did the meeting mean, the Pope said, that "religions could be reconciled at the level of common commitment in an earthly project which would surpass them all." Nor should such a gathering be regarded as a concession to relativism in religious beliefs, "because every human being must sincerely follow his or her upright conscience with the intention of seeking and obeying the truth."[33] But is not the ultimate goal of dialogue to achieve a fellowship of faith, a sort of "religious consensus" that would see in the diversity of expressions of this common faith a divine blessing?

Dialogue or Evangelization?

It was observed above that Vatican II ushered in a new era of Muslim-Catholic relations. However, the Council did not declare acceptance of Islam as a theological belief-system but only an end to hostility toward Muslims and an appreciation of Muslim piety. All that the Council did, therefore, was open the door for Muslim-Catholic dialogue in an atmosphere of mutual respect and tolerance. This new approach, however, still calls for the evangelization of Muslims, as the Pope's attitude toward Islam indicates. But the question remains, Is this openness true dialogue, or could it be simply condescending tolerance aimed at facilitating evangelization?

Since the beginning of his pontificate, John Paul II has been consciously urging African and Asian bishops to engage in friendly dialogue with Muslims, but at the same time to intensify their efforts in "spreading the Good News."[34] Yet in an address to a Christian-Muslim colloquium on religious education in modern society, he went a long way toward espousing a completely free and open approach in dialogue with Muslims and others on the basis of their common humanity. The Pope first admitted that there are basic differences between the two faiths, but he continued: "Christians and Muslims both hold that the true path towards human fulfillment lies in carrying out the divine will in our personal and social lives."[35] A precondition for dialogue is sound religious education, which should inculcate respect for others and openness to them as children of God, regardless of race, religion, economic status, gender, or ethnic identity.[36]

From our limited survey of his pronouncements, it appears that the Holy Father's attitude toward Islam and religious pluralism in general grew more conservative through the years of his papacy. This may perhaps be a reaction to the epochal world events of the last two decades, as well as the increasing secular and liberal challenges within the Church itself. The Pope's attitude toward religious pluralism is expressed in a growing emphasis on evangelization.

In a papal letter addressed to the fifth plenary assembly of the Federation of Asian Bishops, held in Bandung, Indonesia, in July 1990, His Holiness advocated an ever greater commitment to evangelization for the Asian local churches. The praise which he lavished on these churches for their dynamic "witness to the Gospel" is significant in view of the fact that among the most "dynamic local churches" is the Indonesian church. Thus Muslims around the world believe that Indonesia's large Muslim population is a prime target of this evangelization. Whether true or not, this belief helps perpetuate old Muslim suspicions of Christian motives.

The Pope grounded his strong call to evangelization in the document of Vatican II, *Nostra Aetate*, which declares:

> Although the Church gladly acknowledges whatever is true and holy in the religious traditions of Buddhism, Hinduism and Islam as a reflection of the truth which enlightens all men, this does not lessen her duty and resolve to proclaim without fail Jesus Christ who is "the way, the truth and the life" (John 14:6).[37]

Moreover, he acknowledged the validity of the theological idea — based on the classical notion of the seminal divine word (*logos spermatikos*) — that the righteous followers of other religions may be saved by Christ without the ordinary means which God had established for salvation. Yet he still insisted that this "does not cancel the call to faith and baptism which God wills for all people."[38]

Carrying the logic of this argument to its ultimate conclusion, His Holiness repudiated the principle of religious pluralism which is crucial to any meaningful dialogue. He argued that the idea that the Church is only one of many ways to salvation is contrary to the Gospel and to the Church's very nature. He rejected as well the principle of sharing one's faith with another person in the hope of deepening the other's faith within his or her own religious tradition.[39]

John Paul II's position toward other religions is clearly and emphatically argued in an encyclical which he issued shortly after the Gulf War.[40] Although this important document says nothing about Islam in particular, the Pope may have had Muslims, and particularly the Arabs, in mind when he called on people in the latter category everywhere to "open the doors to Christ."[41] In traditional fashion, the Pope divided humanity into two camps, Christians and those who do not know Christ. Since the number of such people in the latter category has doubled since Vatican II, he urged the entire Christian Church to become a missionary Church.

The thrust of the main argument of this encyclical is stated in the opening declaration of the first chapter: "Jesus Christ is the only savior." The Pope elaborated this point thus: "God has established Christ as the one mediator." God also established the Church as the "universal sacrament of salvation." He then concluded, "To this catholic unity of the people of God, therefore, all are called."[42]

To the important question Why mission? the Pope replied that the Church's faith is that true liberation can be attained only through Christ. Only in Christ can humanity be saved from slavery to sin and death. While no one can question the centrality of this doctrine to the Church's faith, it is not one that Islam and Judaism accept, either as part of their own faith or as a common basis for dialogue with Christians. Nor can it serve in today's pluralistic world as a basis for dialogue with any other faith-community. This is because this doctrine leaves no room for a genuine fellowship of faith, which must be the ultimate goal of interreligious dialogue.

On the eve of the twenty-first century, after the development and dissemination of the scientific study of religion and the steady advance of global communication, meaningful dialogue is only possible on the basis of religious and cultural pluralism. This means that Christians and Muslims must accept the fact that God did not only speak Hebrew, Greek, or Arabic, but rather he speaks to every people in their own tongue and to their own cultural and spiritual situation. Furthermore, the universality of divine revelation is attested in both the New Testament and the Qur'an.[43]

While the Pope admits that God mysteriously guides all nations to know him, he insists that true knowledge of God can only be attained through Christ and the Church, "which is the instrument of salvation." He further asserts that "the Holy Spirit offers everyone the possibility of sharing in the Paschal mystery in a manner known to God."[44] But this only means the possibility for everyone to be a Christian, and that should be the Church's universal mission. On this principle of the inner *preparatio evangelica* of every human being, the papal encyclical calls for "mission to the Nations." The objective of this mission is to found Christian communities everywhere and to develop mature and fully functioning churches in areas where Christianity has not taken root.[45]

On the basis of this encyclical and other papal statements of the 1990s, it may be concluded that John Paul II is clearly committed to the old doctrine, "Extra ecclesiam nulla salus." But inasmuch as he advocates interreligious dialogue, he may be considered a neoexclusivist. He is more aware of the diversity and richness of religious traditions than the ancient Church Fathers who first advocated this exclusivist doctrine. But like them, he cannot accept genuine religious pluralism, because it compromises the Church's mission to the nations. He therefore views dialogue as simply an instrument of mission. "Interreligious dialogue," the Pope wrote, "is a part of the Church's evangelizing mission." Dialogue, he further argued, should be based on the conviction that the Church "alone possesses the fullness of the means of salvation."[46]

Conclusion

The theme of the universality of divine guidance to all human beings to the knowledge of God is taken up by His Holiness at some length in his book *Crossing the Threshold of Hope.*[47] Here, however, he does not take seriously such phenomena as animism and ancestor worship as legitimate practices, but wishes to use them as openings for introducing the Christian faith to the followers of these traditions. In the veneration of ancestors the Pope sees some sort of preparation for the Christian concept of the Church as the communion of saints, "in which all believers — whether living or dead — form a single community, a single body."[48] Therefore, missionaries, the Pope observes, find it easier to speak a common language with these people than with the followers of the higher religions.

The Pope's position toward Islam in this book is especially significant, because here he speaks not as the Pope but as a private person. We must therefore conclude that what he says about Islam in this book represents his own convictions. He calls Muslims "believers in Allah,"[49] forgetting that Allah is only the Arabic name for God which was used by Arab Jews and Christians long before Islam. Anyone who knows the Old and New Testaments, the Pope avers, can clearly see how the Qur'an "completely reduces divine revelation." The Qur'an therefore moves away from what God said about himself in the two Testaments, "first . . . through the prophets and then finally . . . through His Son." He concludes: "In Islam all the richness of God's self-revelation, which constitutes the heritage of the Old and New Testaments, has definitely been set aside."[50]

We noted earlier the Pope's Qur'anic affirmation in his address to the colloquium on holiness, "Your God and ours is one and the same, and we are brothers and sisters in the faith of Abraham."[51] In this book he also says that although beautiful names are given to the God of the Qur'an, he remains a God outside the world, a God who is only majesty, never Immanuel, "God with us."[52] Thus we see that the "all-merciful God" of whom His Holiness so often reminded Muslims as the God of us all is absent in his book. The major fault of Islam for His Holiness is ultimately that Islam is not Catholic Christianity.

It was argued above that the ultimate goal of true dialogue is a fellowship of faith. This existential fellowship will not be achieved between institutions, or perhaps even their official representatives. It remains the quest of sincere seekers after the truth, pious men and women of whom Christ said, "You shall know the truth and the truth shall set you free" (John 8:32).

Notes

1. Alfred Guillaume, *Life of Muhammad: A Translation of Ibn Ishaq's Sirat Rasul Allah* (Oxford: Oxford University Press, 1955), 79–82.

2. Waraqah was the cousin of Muhammad's wife Khadijah and may have been a priest (see ibid., 107).

3. According to Islamic hagiographical tradition, the Nagus (*najashi*) of Abyssinia not only received the Muslims hospitably, but is reported to have agreed with the Qur'anic view of Jesus and finally died a Muslim. The personality of al-Najashi represents an interesting example of Muslim-Christian encounter (see ibid., 146–55; see also Montgomery Watt, *Muhammad at Mecca* [Oxford: Clarendon Press, 1953], 109–17).

4. This ecumenical assertion occurs nearly verbatim near the beginning and end of the Prophet's Madinan career (2:62 and 5:69).

5. See, for example, Q. 4:171, 5:17, 72–73, and 77.

6. Quoted by His Holiness Pope John Paul II in his *'id al-fitr* (end of the fasting month of Ramadan) address, April 3, 1991. For the correspondence between the sultan and Pope Gregory VII, see Rev. Thomas Michel, S.J., and Mons. Michael Fitzgerald, M. Afr., eds., *Recognize the Spiritual Bonds Which Unite Us: Sixteen Years of Muslim-Christian Dialogue* (Vatican City: Pontifical Council for Interreligious Dialogue, 1994), 3–4.

7. Edward Peters, ed., *The First Crusade: The Chronicle of Fulcher of Chartres and Other Source Materials* (Philadelphia: University of Pennsylvania Press, 1971), 2; see also 2–5.

8. Between 1978, when he took office, and 1994, Pope John Paul II made sixty trips to 109 countries (see Michel and Fitzgerald, *Spiritual Bonds*, 14).

9. *Origins* 9:26 (December 13, 1979): 420.

10. The Qur'an states: "God will not forgive that associates be ascribed to Him, but other than this, he forgives whomsoever he will" (4:48).

11. *Origins* 10:2 (May 29, 1980): 20.

12. See Luke 10:25–37 and Matthew 28:19.

13. *Origins* 10:37 (February 26, 1981): 592.

14. For a Muslim appreciation of the life and work of this remarkable man, see Zoe Hersov, "A Muslim's View of Charles de Foucauld: Some Lessons for the Christian-Muslim Dialogue," *Muslim World* 85:3/4 (July–October 1995): 295–316.

15. *Bulletin: Secretariatus pro non Christianis* 48 (1981): 182–83.

16. Ibid., 187.

17. *Origins* 11:37 (February 25, 1982): 588.

18. Ibid.

19. *Bulletin: Secretariatus pro non Christianis* 55 (1984): 25–26.

20. Ibid., 26.

21. *Redemptionis Anno, Origins* 14:20 (May 24, 1980): 31–32.

22. Ibid., 32.

23. I had the honor of being one of the participants in that colloquium, which included visits to Assisi and other holy sites in Italy. It was a memorable experience.

24. The Pope here paraphrased part of Q. 29:46 and alluded to Q. 3:64, which invites all the people of the Book to unity of faith in the One God.

25. For the Pope's address and all the proceedings of that colloquium, see *Islamochristiana* 11 (1985): 201–8.

26. Cf. *Bulletin* 60 (1985): 233–37. A few days earlier, on August 12, the Pope delivered the same message to the multireligious society of Cameroon. See Michel and Fitzgerald, *Spiritual Bonds*, 42, 44.

27. Michel and Fitzgerald, *Spiritual Bonds,* 65.

28. Ibid.

29. Ibid.

30. Ibid., 66.

31. *Bulletin* 62 (1986): 147.

32. *Bulletin* 64 (1987): 29.

33. Ibid., 30.

34. This was his message to the bishops of Mali in March 1988, the bicentenary year of mission (see *Bulletin* 70 [1988]: 14–15).

35. The colloquium was organized in Rome jointly by the Pontifical Council for Interreligious Dialogue and the Royal Jordanian Al Al-Bayt Foundation, December 6–8, 1989 (see *Bulletin* 73 [1990]: 14).

36. Ibid., 14–15.

37. Quoted by the Pope in *Bulletin* 75 (1990): 229.

38. Ibid., 230.

39. Ibid., 231.

40. Papal encyclical no. 8, *Redemptoris Missio,* January 1991 (hereafter: *RM).*

41. *RM* 3.

42. *RM* 4.

43. Cf. Acts 14:17; Heb. 1:1; and Q. 35:27.

44. *RM* 21.

45. *RM* 48.

46. *RM* 55.

47. John Paul II, *Crossing the Threshold of Hope* (New York: Alfred A. Knopf, 1994), 77ff.

48. Ibid., 82.

49. Ibid., 91.

50. Ibid., 92.

51. See n. 24 above.

52. John Paul II, *Threshold*, 92.

12

John Paul II and Islam

IBRAHIM M. ABU-RABI

Christians and Muslims in general . . . have badly understood each other,
and sometimes, in the past, have opposed and even exhausted each other
in polemics and in wars. I believe that today, God invites us to change our
old practices. We must respect each other, and also we must stimulate each
other in good works on the path to God.

—John Paul II

This essay offers a critical reading of John Paul II's ideas on Islam as they
have developed from the time he assumed the papacy in 1978. In order
to attain a clear view of his position, I will follow three courses of analysis: (1) I will focus on his understanding of Islam, as both a theological
system and a sociohistorical phenomenon, with all that these two dimensions imply; (2) I will discuss his ideas against the recent engagement
of the Catholic Church in the life of the international Catholic community, especially in the Muslim world; and (3) I will compare his ideas
on Islam to those of a selected number of modern Muslim theologians
and thinkers on Christianity.

At the outset, I should like to state that my choice of terminology
reflects a complex world in transition, one in which such terms as "Muslims" and "Christians" must be understood in the context of the recent
triumph of the Western, that is, capitalist, system both culturally and
economically, and in the Muslim world as well as in the West. In other
words, the reader must not take the "religious terms" employed here
at face value, but must understand them as part of the major intellectual mutations taking place in the world in the wake of the collapse of

the Soviet Union, the triumph of the capitalist system, and the attempt of different contemporary religious movements, including the Islamic ones, to reorganize themselves and revitalize their activism.[1]

As a universal monotheistic religion, Islam is a complex religious phenomenon that has given rise to all sorts of ideas, forces, and conditions over its long history. Regardless of their political motivations and ideological positions, Western scholars, often called "orientalists,"[2] have carried out serious research over the past five hundred years in the field of Islamic studies, including the Arabic language, the Qur'an, *Hadith*, *Fiqh*, Sufism, and various Muslim social and political institutions.[3] Especially since the 1979 Islamic revolution in Iran, the Western scholarly community has preoccupied itself with "Islamic fundamentalism" — its nature, history, and the menace it may pose to Western interests and to the nation-states in the Muslim world. Very often, and even in respected Western intellectual circles, Islam and Muslims are treated as the dangerous "other." It is heartening to realize, as will be amply illustrated below, that the Western religious community, especially the Catholic community under the guidance of its religious leadership, does not share these negative views of Islam and Muslims.

Whether Western scholars consider it an object of fascination, or a pirated copy of either Christianity or Judaism, Islam remains a unique religion, possessing an autonomous *Weltanschauung* that defines its place in the world of ideas and events through dialogue and openness. From this perspective, it should not be surprising that nineteenth-century Muslim thinkers, such as 'Abd al-Rahman al-Jabarti, Hassan al-'Attar, Rifa'a R. Tahtawi, al-Saffar, Jamal al-Din al-Afghani, and Muhammad 'Abduh, accepted, at least in principle, the concept of appropriating the scientific and intellectual spirit of Western civilization, although they were opposed to its political and military agenda, that is, expansion to the Muslim world under the guise of modernity.[4]

Therefore, in dealing with the position of John Paul II on Islam, one must be attentive to both the evolution of the Catholic position on interreligious dialogue, and especially that with Islam, and to the complex manifestations of Islam in the modern Muslim world as well. Furthermore, one must not ignore the nature of coexistence among Muslims and Catholics in different parts of the Muslim world, especially in the Arab Middle East, and in such countries as Indonesia, Nigeria, Sudan, Bangladesh, and the Philippines.

It is clear that the Pope is cognizant of the nature of Islam as a universal tradition, and understands its theological and spiritual dimensions. He appreciates the impact of Western modernity on the Muslim people, the rise of the nation-states in the Muslim world, the intellectual Islamic response to the Western onslaught, and the appropriation of selected Western concepts. In other words, in treating the Pope's position on Islam, I take Islam to mean both theology and history. These two dimensions, multilayered as they are, define the meaning and identity of Islam in the modern world. Furthermore, I think that to appreciate the position of Islam in the modern world and, more specifically, in the Arab Middle East and North Africa, one must note the adaptation of the mainstream Islamic tradition to the modern world, the new relationship forged between Islam and society, and the newly acquired Muslim historical consciousness of the position that Islam must (or must not) take in the new nation-state.

The Catholic Church began to acknowledge the need for understanding the Muslim world and appreciating the religious impact of Islam on modern Muslim lives with the Second Vatican Council (1962–65). It emphasized unequivocally that

> [t]he Church has also a high regard for the Muslims. They worship God, who is one, living and subsistent, merciful and mighty, the Creator of heaven and earth, who has also spoken to humankind.... Over the centuries, many quarrels and dissensions have arisen between Christians and Muslims. The sacred council now pleads with all to forget the past, and urges that a sincere effort be made to achieve mutual understanding; for the benefit of all, let them together preserve and promote peace, liberty, social justice and moral values. (*Nostra Aetate* 3)[5]

With Vatican II, the Church began to stress the common spiritual and moral bonds binding all peoples of faith, including Muslims and Catholics. Religion promotes progress and must be in the business of protecting human rights. According to one observer, the Church is preoccupied with promoting "a doctrine of dialogue."[6] John Paul II, elected in 1978, accelerated the process of dialogue with people of other faiths. He has since encouraged the followers of the Catholic Church to investigate, with both wisdom and intelligence, the spiritual treasures of other faith-traditions, the worship aspects of other religions, and the belief in the one Unseen God. In an address to religious and government leaders in Karachi, Pakistan, in 1981, the Pope stated: "I pray this mutual understanding and respect between Christians and Muslims, and indeed between all religions, will continue and grow deeper, and that we will find still better ways of cooperation and collaboration for the good of all."[7] The Pope's tone is universal, and the spirit of his message is highly reconciliatory.

Both Muslims and Christians constitute the same nation in many countries. The Pope urges both to coexist in peace. In addressing Muslims on a visit to the Philippines in 1981, he stated: "My dear friends, I wish you to be convinced of the fact that your Christian brothers and sisters need you and they need your love. And the whole world, with its longing for greater peace, brotherhood and harmony, *needs to see fraternal coexistence between Christians and Muslims in a modern, believing and peaceful Philippine nation*" (emphasis added).[8] It is interesting to note that the Pope highlights dialogue between Catholics and all believers of other faiths as a method of reconciliation, understanding, safeguarding human dignity, and protecting the rights of the underprivileged — both the poor and minorities. His concept of human rights derives from the inalienable rights given by God to human beings, and this leads me to conclude that the Pope's thinking on the matter of social justice, equality, and human rights is motivated by a new theological understanding of the human being — any human being regardless of his/her social, educational, and religious background and, above all, regardless if s/he is a believer or not. Humans must be protected, respected, and encouraged to do the right thing. The Pope's ethos of universality is to be commended in a world that is getting smaller day by day and in a context that permits the rich to dominate the poor, both intellectually and culturally.

During his visit to Indonesia in 1989, John Paul II stated:

One of the principal challenges facing modern Indonesia is that of building a harmonious society from the many diverse elements which are the source of the nation's present promise and future greatness. Indonesia's Catholics find a deep motivation for their contributions to this enterprise in the vision of universal harmony which the Christian faith offers them. By our belief in one God who is the creator of heaven and earth, of all that is seen and unseen, we who follow Christ are inspired to work for the advancement of peace and harmony among all people.[9]

In a sense, the Pope agrees wholeheartedly with *Pancasila,* the official philosophy or ideology of Suharto's Indonesia. From the perspective of the state, *Pancasila* guarantees the freedom of all religions, namely, Islam, Catholicism, Protestantism, Hinduism, and Buddhism. Although Indonesia has the largest Muslim population in the world, it has stressed the necessity of separating religion from politics while respecting, if not encouraging, the religious wishes of all groups in society. In his response to the Pope's remarks, Dr. H. Munawir Sjadzali, the Minister of Religious Affairs in the Republic of Indonesia (in 1989), stressed that "[i]t is true that the Muslims in Indonesia are a majority. But for us, there is no majority and minority. We are all sons and daughters of Indonesia who have the human right to adhere to a religion according to one's own conviction."[10] In order to clarify the Pope's position on Islam, the following treatment of Muslim-Christian relations, especially Muslim-Catholic relations, in Indonesia is in order.

A main contention of this essay is that both John Paul II and the Catholic Church prefer a secular and democratic system of government in the Muslim world to an Islamist one (that is, a type of government that preaches the slogan, "Islam and politics are one"). It is in this context, one may argue, that the interests of the Christians, as equal citizens of the same state, can be safeguarded. To an objective observer, Indonesia has been a secular country since the proclamation of its independence from the Dutch in 1945.[11] In other words, the political elite governing the country has refused to associate itself with "Islamism" or Islamic revivalism of the type which governs in Iran and the Sudan. In the words of President Suharto, *Pancasila* is based on the rejection of poverty, backwardness, conflicts, exploitation, capitalism, feudalism, dictatorship, colonialism, and imperialism. That is to say, *Pancasila* is based on the conviction that Indonesia must follow an independent foreign policy and a cohesive nationalist policy that preserve the religious, ethnic, and linguistic balance and integrity of the country.

Like any Third World country after independence, Indonesia has faced the "question of religion" (that is, Are religion and politics one?) with an eye to the long legacy of Dutch colonialism and to new, creative ways to imagine the future of the nascent Indonesian nation. Taking into account the different religious, social, economic, and intellectual forces at play after independence, Indonesia opted to create a secular, although theistic, state system while maintaining a clear separation between religion and state. Within this system is a guarantee that all people have the freedom to practice the religion of their choice.

Although Islam has been a potent political and social force in Indonesian society since 1945, various Islamic voices have arisen to express a variety of religious positions and trends. Indeed, one may distinguish four main currents of Muslim thought in contemporary Indonesia: modernism, neomodernism, Islamic social democracy, and internationalism–universalism. Such "neomodernist" Muslim thinkers as

Abdurrahman Wahid,[12] Nurcholish Madjid,[13] Ahmad Wahib, Djohan Effendi, and, to a limited extent, Amien Rais stress the democratization of Indonesian society and reject placing religion at the service of politics, since both deal with different arenas of life. This latter current is very much appreciated by the Indonesian Catholics and the Catholic Church, especially as Catholics voice their concern about the burning of churches in certain regions in Indonesia.[14] Other "internationalist" Islamic voices, although paying lip service to *Pancasila,* would prefer to establish an Islamic state, and warn of the threat of Christian missionaries to the Islamic foundations of Indonesian society.[15]

The way the contemporary Indonesian state is imagined differs somewhat from that of Muslim revivalists within and outside of Indonesia. The Pope seems to support the spirit of *Pancasila,* which is the state's official ideology, and he distances himself from Islamists and their attempt to seize political control. While addressing the Indonesian bishops in 1996, the Pope states that "[w]hen the laity receive a solid Christian formation, they are equipped to play a constructive role in the life of the Nation, with a distinctive motivation and force. . . . This is the attitude which inspires support for *Pancasila,* the body of principles which fosters national unity, religious tolerance and justice among all various communities of your vast country."[16] In one sense, one may argue that the Pope is for the nationalist imagining of the contemporary nation-state in the Muslim world, which is, in the case of Indonesia, based on instilling pride in all Indonesians of their common historical and cultural experience and values, the nationalist fight against Dutch colonialism in the first half of the twentieth century, creating an atmosphere of religious harmony and tolerance within the country, supporting the modernization process, and abhorring all external intervention that is threatening to the political and social fabric of society.[17] The Pope seems to be saying that the rights of the Christian community in Muslim countries can be best served in the context of a democracy and deepening understanding of each other's faith.[18]

In spite of a greater presence of Islamic values and symbols in the contemporary Indonesian public and social space, the Indonesian elite is far more conservative in its Islamic pronouncements than its neighbor, the Malaysian elite. The nationalist imagining of Indonesia stresses the importance of cultural and social integration while shying away from religious tension and disintegration. The message of *Pancasila* as conceived by the writers of the Indonesian constitution is clear: let us keep the multifaith and multicultural composition of society, since pluralism, with its flexible and creative interaction with society, is an important element for the progress and modernization of society.[19] In other words, the vision of those who believe in the nation-state differs substantially from that of the Muslim revivalists. In normative terms, revivalists would like to see the Muslim world linked together by the power of the Muslim doctrine, whereas the nation is linked together by language, common heritage, and past experience. Since this type of nationalist imagining is more suitable to the religious minorities than the revivalist one, religious minorities fear the possibility of the revivalists' ascendance to power in the future Indonesia.

To elaborate John Paul II's understanding of the relationship between Catholics, as a minority in a Muslim society, and Muslims, it is imperative that we take an additional example to that of Indonesia, the Sudan. Since the coming to power of General Omar al-Bashir in 1989, the Sudan has declared itself an Islamic state, meaning that the *Shari'ah* is the supreme law in the land.[20] By and large, the Christian community in the Sudan, be it Protestant or Catholic, has opposed the implementation of the *Shari'ah* since, in their view, it infringes upon their rights to worship and lead a peaceful life. The Sudan is thus a different case from Indonesia. In his visit to the Sudan in 1993, John Paul II was particularly concerned with the unique situation facing the Christian community there. In addressing the President of the Sudan, he maintained that "[t]he inalienable dignity of every human person, irrespective of racial, ethnic, cultural or national origin or religious belief, means that when people coalesce in groups they have a right to enjoy a collective identity. Thus, minorities [that is, Christians] within a country have a right to exist, with their own language, culture and traditions, and *the State is morally obliged to leave room for their identity and self-expression*" (emphasis added).[21] In other words, the Pope believes that the Sudanese state has no right to impose ready-made rules, especially *Shari'ah* rules, on the minority groups in the Sudan. Although the Pope recognizes that especially in the Sudan, religion permeates all society, it is clear that he prefers a secular state to an Islamist one.[22] That is, John Paul II's notion of religious liberty, especially for Catholics in the Muslim context, diverges somewhat from that of the Muslim notion,[23] however variously defined. From a Catholic standpoint, the rule of the *Shari'ah* does not guarantee Christian religious liberty, and old legal formulations do not suffice to protect the rights of the Christians in the Muslim world. Likewise, although not mentioned explicitly by the Pope or any official in the Catholic Church, it is clear that there is a feeling on the side of the Catholic leadership that the application of the *Shari'ah* may lead to religious fanaticism on the Muslim side. The official position of the

Church is that "[r]eligious fanaticism or extremism, which sometimes manifests itself in intolerance and even violence and murder, is a major obstacle to dialogue."[24] The closest John Paul II comes to condemning the type of government ruling in the Sudan or Iran is when he maintains that "[i]n countries where fundamentalist movements come to power, human rights and the principle of religious freedom are unfortunately interpreted in a very one-sided way — religious freedom comes to mean freedom to impose on all citizens the 'true religion.' In these countries the situation of Christians is sometimes terribly disturbing. Fundamentalist attitudes of this nature make reciprocal contacts very difficult."[25] For their part, Muslim revivalists argue that they are the only organized group in Muslim society who take the issue of religious dialogue with Christians seriously and who respect the freedom of the "People of the Book" to worship and to express their ideas.

Likewise, John Paul II takes up another issue that has proven problematic to Palestinians and Israelis: the question of Jerusalem and the rights of the Palestinians. He encourages all, especially Israelis, to preserve the sacred character of Jerusalem as a holy city to Jews, Christians, and Muslims and supports the right of the Palestinians to self-determination by creating their own state.[26]

Besides being preoccupied with the presence of Catholics in Muslim societies, John Paul II is also concerned with the human dignity and social well-being of the Muslim community, especially Muslim workers and their families, in Europe. In addressing the Muslims in France in 1980, he said that "[w]hile the motive which led you to leave your own countries, whether it be work or study, gives your departure a character of undoubted dignity, it is no less true that your condition as immigrants causes serious social, cultural and religious problems both for you and for the country which has received you."[27] It is clear that John Paul II is conscious of the fact that there must be a thorough conversation between Muslims and Europeans about cultural and religious values. He is tireless in his encouragement, not just of Christians, but of Muslims to adhere to their sublime spiritual and cultural values, especially in a Westernized context. Also, one may argue, John Paul II implores the Muslims to reaffirm their authentic values in a secular environment as a way of leading a spiritually fulfilling life. Furthermore, he seems to defend the right of the Muslims to preserve and enhance their cultural values in the face of the encroachment of the atheist values of the secular West.[28] What that means is that John Paul II could be in agreement with a number of leading contemporary Muslim intellectuals, such as Hasan Hanafi,[29] Muhammad 'Abid al-Jabiri,[30] and Mahdi Elmandjara,[31] that the affluent North, that is, Western Europe and North America, refuses to embark upon a thorough conversation on cultural values with the South on the supposition that occidental values are the norm — that is, they are universal values — and that adopting them will mean the solution to the social and economic problems of the Third World.[32] John Paul II believes that cultural diversity protects human dignity and human rights,[33] and that religious and spiritual norms, which are essentially neither occidental nor oriental but human, are the norm.

The Muslim world, like most of the Third World, suffers from the absence of democracy, a crisis in human rights, and a lack of democratic channels that enable people to express their ideas freely. All of this takes place without a major outcry from the West.

Further, another dilemma facing the Muslim world is how to safeguard universal cultural diversity and pluralism in the face of the mounting hegemony of the United States of America! The answer lies in achieving major changes in the thinking of both North and South. The North must recognize cultural diversity, and the South must affirm its cultural independence.[34] Also, the Muslim world suffers from a continuous "intellectual hemorrhage," identified as the "brain drain," which is the exodus of competent people, professionals and intellectuals, from South to North. Many emigrate, not just in search of better economic and social standards, but because the development process in their native countries lacks the appropriate vision to incorporate them productively. Very often, this lack of vision is complicated by blind imitation of the modernized North, leading to transfer of technology with no creative contribution from the South. In other words, the South can purchase technology, but it must create its own forms of modernity and modernization. These forms, however, cannot be created in the context of the continuous exodus of skilled professionals. Therefore, the Muslim world suffers from three major problems: (1) illiteracy; (2) lack of scientific research; and (3) lack of democratic values. In reading the official pronouncements of the Pope, it is clear that these issues have not escaped his attention.

It is possible to argue that John Paul II is for cultural and religious interchange between the Muslim world and the West. In addressing Muslims, he said, "When you are not embarrassed to pray publicly, you thereby give us Christians an example worthy of respect. Live your faith aloud in this foreign land and do not let it be misused for any worldly or political interest."[35] The emigration of Muslim populations to the West can produce positive cultural and religious results. In addition to expanding the cultural horizons of the host country and population, it teaches Christians the viability of piety and prayer in a modern setting.

One perplexing issue that the Pope deals with in various speeches is "political Islam," or Islamic political revival. It seems to me that his concern about this issue stems from the fact that the majority of the Christians in the Muslim world are uncomfortable with an Islamic political system and the application of the *Shari'ah*. John Paul II has stated:

> A particular set of problems arises for the Christian because of the Islamic revival and reform movements in Islam. Catholics who are committed to the new impetus of the spirit which the Second Vatican Council has brought our Christian community can readily understand the desire of Muslim reformers to purify Islamic society.... However, we confess apprehension about the direction which Islamic reform can take and the possible consequences which it might have on our own Christian communities. In particular, we note concern about the status of Christians when Islamic states are created.... Christians cannot limit their contacts to particular segments within the Islamic community. Christians must realize that reformist, traditionalist, mystical, militant, quietist, and still other tendencies are to be found among Muslims. It is not necessary to determine which of these represents "true Islam."[36]

In other words, the Pope maintains correctly that "Islam is a complex religious and historical phenomenon" which has given rise to all sorts of forces and tendencies and which cannot be confined to one particular trend or expression. Furthermore, Islamic revivalism, though a viable tendency on the contemporary Islamic scene, cannot claim the allegiance of all Muslims. In the view of Islamic revivalism, "true Islam" must be practiced only within the confines of an Islamic political system. The Pope seems not to want to challenge Muslim revivalists to implement a societal ethos in which they would be open to treating the Christians as equal citizens within an Islamist state. John Paul II seems, instead, to prefer a modern nation-state to an Islamist state, mainly because he does not want to see the mixing of religion and politics in Islam.

I think that this discussion of John Paul II's treatment of Islam cannot be entirely satisfactory or complete without a discussion of the basic theoretical outlines of the modern Muslim discussion of Christianity. Over the past century, Muslim scholars and religious thinkers have advanced a number of positions on Christianity. The Muslim religious leadership does not enjoy the same hierarchical organization as the Catholic Church. That is to say, Muslims lack a clear-cut "official" position on Christianity, and hence Muslim intellectuals have provided a variety of interesting opinions on Christianity, especially since the nineteenth century. These intellectuals were faced with the dual problem of Muslim stagnation and Western progress, a reality brought about by the Western penetration of the Muslim world during the colonialist era. The Egyptian thinker Muhammad 'Abduh (d. 1905) did not treat Christianity as the antithetic other, but considered Islam, as a monotheistic phenomenon and a divine religion, to be highly intertwined with Christianity; that is, he saw the essence of Islam to be that of Christianity. This is what one also gets from John Paul II's official statements on Islam.

'Abduh analyzes Christianity in response to two major critiques leveled at Islam by Farah Antoun, a Syrian émigré to Egypt and the founder of the secularist journal *al-Jami'ah*.[37] Antoun maintains that Islam, as opposed to Christianity, is intolerant of science and liberalism for two reasons: (1) Islam does not distinguish between "civil regime" (*sultah madaniyah*) and "religious regime" (*sultah diniyah*). According to Antoun, this fusion between the political and religious has had a negative impact on tolerance and civil freedoms in general. Christianity, on the other hand, has known of a distinction between the political and religious, and, as a result, modern Western civilization has come to appreciate freedom and democracy. (2) In the West, science and philosophy have escaped the oppression of the Church. Progress has been but a normal fruit of this. In Islam, however, religious oppression has stifled progress and the freedom of both science and philosophy.[38]

In response to these accusations, 'Abduh decides to tackle the "nature of the Christian religion" (*tabi'at al-din al-masihi*) in order to prove that Islam does not oppose science, philosophy, or the freedom of all religions and minorities to coexist. He argues that Christianity derives its authenticity from the Unseen (the idea of one God), miracles, and the transience of this world. Islam's strong connection to Christianity is based on the strong Muslim belief in Christ as "God's spirit, God's word [or Logos], and His messenger to the people of Israel. Jesus did invite people to follow the correct maxims of the *Tawrah,* and practice a righteous life, and to use reason, as a human faculty, in a righteous fulfillment of life."[39]

In a sense, 'Abduh celebrates the pristine vision of Christianity as a bridge-builder, as an affirming message, not as dividing element or epistemological rupture. He argues that "[r]eligion, [in a generic sense], is God's. It is essentially one religion in past and present. In spirit and fact, religion has never changed: it is the sincere belief in one God and the lending [of] a helpful hand to people in life."[40] This last position is in full agreement with John Paul II's understanding of the rapprochement that has to evolve between Islam and Christianity. One cannot but argue that to both the Pope and 'Abduh, both Christianity and Islam are of the same essence. It is human history which has given rise to theological and doctrinal differences, applications, and results. In the final analysis, 'Abduh argues that Islam's identity is highly intertwined with that of Christianity and the "other" has no theological foundations; it has only social, political, and historical reality.

But a major divergence may exist between 'Abduh's ideas and the Pope's. In his discussion of the relationship between Christianity and "current civilization" (al-madaniyah al-hadirah), 'Abduh argues that

> it is my opinion that there is no connection whatsoever between the Christian religion and the current civilization. Here is the New Testament, before our eyes, and its latent and hidden meanings do not escape us. The New Testament commands the believers to disentangle themselves from this transient life and be oblivious to its transient glory. . . . This civilization, on the other hand, is the civilization of power, glory, luxury, arrogance, and hypocrisy, and its supreme ruler is money and business.[41]

In other words, the material side of this civilization opposes the ideals of Christianity as stipulated in the New Testament. It is clear from the different statements of John Paul II and the official pronouncements of the Catholic Church that modern Christianity is part and parcel of modern civilization and that the evolution in the Church's position on dialogue, from no dialogue to dialogue, is predicated on the complex nature of modern Christianity and its connection to Muslims all over the world.

Some of 'Abduh's ideas were translated into practice by the pioneering work of Hasan al-Banna, the founder of the Ikhwan, or the Muslim Brotherhood Movement, in the Arab world. Al-Banna agrees with some of 'Abduh's basic premises, since his ideas reflect the legacy of the reform school of both 'Abduh and his disciple, Shaykh Rashid Rida.[42] Al-Banna's solution to the question of stagnation and to the problematic of Westernization and direct colonialism was to build a mass-oriented organization in which he translated the ideas of the reform movement into a sociopolitical program that aims, in principle, at altering the social and political state of affairs. In a sense, he was both a thinker and an organizer. It is against this background that one must assess his views of the "other."

Al-Banna builds upon the arguments of 'Abduh, but goes beyond him in two significant areas: first, he does not equate Christianity, as does 'Abduh, with the European "other," since there is an indigenous Egyptian Christian community which, to him, "is indigenous to Egyptian soil and is not part of the Western conquest." Second, unlike Muhammad 'Abduh, who was somewhat soft on colonialism, al-Banna criticizes European Christianity because, in his view, it was used by the secular West to colonize the rest of the world: "Europe retained its Christianity only as an historical heritage, as one factor among others for educating the simple-minded and naive among the masses, and as a means for conquest, colonization, and the suppression of political aspirations."[43]

Therefore, to al-Banna, the strange "other" is to be found in the realm of European education exporting itself to the Muslim world. That is where colonialism and missionary activities coincide. Western powers were able to found educational and scientific schools in the heart of Islam "which cast doubt and heresy into the souls of Muslims and taught them how to demean themselves, disparage their religion and their fatherland, divest themselves of their traditions and beliefs, and to regard as sacred anything Western, in the belief that only that which had a European source could serve as a model to be emulated in this life."[44]

What is even more harmful is that education was a tool used by the colonial powers to create an indigenous mercenary intellectual class made up of "the sons of the upper class alone," and consequently the masses were deprived of basic education in religious and secular sciences. Al-Banna goes on to cite *"mental colonization,"* which was a "well-organized campaign with a tremendous success, since it was rendered most attractive to the mind, and would continue to exert a strong intellectual influence on individuals over a long period of time. For this reason, it was more dangerous than the political and military campaigns so far."[45] The majority of the modern Muslim intelligentsia follow, to varying degrees, the line of argument provided by al-Banna and other Islamic leaders vis-à-vis mental colonization and the role of the Christian mission in effecting such a colonization in the modern Muslim mind. In that sense, it is very important to discuss the Pope's position on the issue of mission, since this has proven to be very controversial from both the Islamic and Christian sides.

The Islamic position is more or less clear that *da'wah*, or mission, is an integral part of Islam and that there are many methods to spread Islamic *da'wah,* one of which is through "kind debate" (*jidal bilati hiya ahsan*).[46] The Catholic Church, under the leadership of John Paul II, considers mission as an integral part in its vision of a better relationship between the Church and the followers of other faith-traditions. The Church sees itself as "the universal sacrament of salvation."[47] In other words, the mission of the Church is totally embedded in the "mystery of Christ," and Christians need to be more aware of this mystery. Love is one of the principal foundations of the mystery of Christ, and, in that sense, the Catholic Church "is a messianic people, a visible assembly and spiritual community, and a pilgrim people who go forward together with all of mankind with whom they share the human experience. . . . The pilgrim Church is therefore 'missionary by its nature.' . . . For every Christian, the missionary duty is the normal expression of his lived faith."[48] Therefore, in its approach toward other traditions, in our case Islam, the Catholic Church is guided by its need to carry out its vision through mission and love. In theological terms, the Church is fully convinced of the validity of its theological pronouncements (God is love, the mystery of Christ, and so on). Thus, preaching the Gospel of Christ to Muslims and non-Muslims alike and building churches as a means of embodying Christian teachings are in line with the theological vision of the Church. Theoretically, building churches and spreading Christian mission emanate from the position of the Church on peaceful coexistence and dialogue between Christians and Muslims. Practically, however, in areas of political tension in the Muslim world, the Catholic understanding of mission might backfire and jeopardize the relationship between the Catholic community and the Muslims.

The issue becomes complicated from a Muslim theological standpoint when the Pope preaches the concept of Christ as the Redeemer: "Man — every man without any exception whatever — has been redeemed by Christ. And with man — with each man without any exception, whatever — Christ is in a way united, even when man is unaware of it. Christ, who died and was raised up for all, provides man, each and every man, with the light and strength to measure up to his supreme calling."[49] Theologically, even the most open-minded Muslims cannot accept the claim that Christ, and not God, is the Redeemer and that Christ, "the Redeemer, is present with grace in every human encounter, to liberate us from our selfishness and to make us love one another as he has loved us."[50] In addition, Muslims cannot accept the claim, however positively made, that "no salvation exists outside of the Catholic Church."[51]

Also, the Pope, as the highest representative of the Catholic Church, does not believe that the Islamic perspective of revelation is as true as that of Christianity. He argues that "[i]n Islam all the richness of God's self-revelation, which constitutes the heritage of the Old and New Testaments, has been definitely set aside."[52] He further says that although the Qur'an addresses God in the most beautiful of names, God "is ultimately ... outside of the world, a God who is only Majesty, never Emmanuel, God-with-us. Islam is not a religion of redemption."[53] What that means in effect is that both Christianity and Islam, according to the Pope, have two clashing religious and theological visions. Whether the preceding statements are the Pope's personal opinion on Islam or represent part of the Catholic teachings on Islam is not the point here. There are many Catholics who believe in these statements, and the Pope seems to sympathize with these views personally.

John Paul II's view that God in Islam is outside the world and distant from humanity does not accurately represent the Qur'anic view of God as being close to man: "It was We Who created man, and We know what dark suggestions his soul makes to him: for We are nearer to him than (his) jugular vein."[54] Also, this position, which is polemical at best, does not reflect the rich history of Islamic spirituality, or *tassawuf,* that has always emphasized the nearness of God to humans.[55]

Finally, it is possible to advance the following conclusions about John Paul II's position on Islam and the Muslim world:

First, one may argue that his position on Islam is politically and socially open, but theologically conservative. Salvation is to be sought inside the Church, and the only true Redeemer is Jesus Christ.

Second, "a doctrine of dialogue," as a reflection of the political openness of the Catholic Church as understood by Pope John Paul II, is far from static. It means engagement, appreciation, sacrifice, patience, spiritual enrichment, and fighting on behalf of the underprivileged in society. Dialogue means a comprehensive and deep reconciliation between Muslims and Catholics in public life. This colossal project of reconciliation entails "a common will [between Christians and Muslims] to build a better world for future generations."[56] In a sense, he encourages both Muslims and Catholics to go beyond dialogue to engagement in the true sense of the word.[57] He sees many common challenges and dangers.

Third, John Paul II does not encounter Islam and the Muslim world, especially in his latest pronouncements, as the estranged other, like the secular press, but as a spiritual community that has deep religious roots and whose fate is highly intertwined with that of the Catholics. This is especially heartening if one deeply examines the great cultural and political mutations taking place in the world in the wake of the New World Order following the defeat of Iraq in the second Gulf War and the collapse of the Soviet system. The Pope does not treat Islam and Muslims as a new universal enemy to the Western civilization. Far from that, he thinks that contemporary Christians have a lot to learn from the Muslim religious experience.

Fourth, the Pope prefers a democratic nation-state to an Islamist state in the Muslim world, the type of state that is committed to treating Christians as equal citizens by protecting their cultural and religious rights as a minority.

Fifth, John Paul II defends human rights — those of the Muslims and the Christians — and in this he challenges the modern Muslim world to come up with its own version of human rights that is congruent with both the lofty principles of Islam and the current situation in the Muslim world. In other words, he is critical of most of the military regimes in the Muslim world that do not promote genuine democracy in civil society. One may also argue that the Pope is implicitly critical of the Western support given to those military regimes that are afraid of democracy.

Sixth, to the Pope's mind, Muslims, especially those who live in Europe, can serve as a religious model for the Christians to emulate. The Pope seems to be concerned about the loss of spiritual and religious values in the contemporary Western world. Although he does not oppose modernity in principle, he would like the modern world to open its arms to basic traditional values, such as worship, transcendence, and belief in the afterlife. The erosion of religious values in modern life is not the answer.

Seventh, although John Paul II has encouraged the Catholic community to be open to Jews and Judaism, he does not support the Zionist attempt at Judaizing Jerusalem. In addition to being a central city in the religious imagination of the Muslims, Jerusalem is sacred to Christians and Jews as well.[58] The Pope emphasizes the uniqueness of Jerusalem as a spiritual treasure to the three monotheistic traditions. He argues for preserving its sacred character and being open to all people.

These ideas summarize Pope John Paul II's religious position on Islam and the Muslim world. At heart, the Pope comes to the conclusion that Islam is a different religion than Christianity and that it has to be treated as such, especially in light of the fact that he does not call openly for the conversion of Muslims to Christianity. Dialogue, and not conversion, is the only true method to reach out to Muslims and peoples of other faiths. Let us hope that both Catholics and Muslims practice the art of dialogue as a way to know about each other and, above all, to know about one's own religious and spiritual treasures and values.

Notes

1. See M. Arkoun, "Emergences et problemes dans le monde musulman contemporain," *Islamochristiana* 12 (1986): 135–61; and M. Watt, "Muslims and Christians after the Gulf War," *Islamochristiana* 17 (1991): 35–51.

2. See Edward Said, *Orientalism* (New York: Vintage Books, 1978).

3. See Albert Hourani, *Islam in European Thought* (New York: Cambridge University Press, 1991).

4. See A. Hourani, *Arabic Thought in the Liberal Age: 1798–1939* (Cambridge: Cambridge University Press, 1970); H. Sharabi, *Arab Intellectuals and the West: The Formative Years* (Baltimore: Johns Hopkins University Press, 1970); and I. Abu-Rabi', *Intellectual Origins of Islamic Resurgence in the Modern Arab World* (Albany: State University of New York Press, 1986).

5. Thomas Michel and Michael Fitzgerald, eds., *Recognize the Spiritual Bonds Which Unite Us: Sixteen Years of Christian-Muslim Dialogue* (Vatican City: Pontifical Council for Interreligious Dialogue, 1994), 3. For an elaboration on the views of Pope Paul VI on Islam, consult M. Borrmans, "Le pape Paul VI et les musulmans," *Islamochristiana* 4 (1978): 1–10.

6. Lucie Provost, "From Tolerance to Spiritual Emulation: An Analysis of Official Texts in Christian-Muslim Dialogue," in R. Rousseau, ed., *Christianity and Islam* (Scranton, Pa.: Ridge Row Press, 1985), 204. For a discussion of the activities of the Vatican in the field of Christian-Muslim relations, consult M. L. Fitzgerald, "Twenty-Five Years of Dialogue: The Pontifical Council for Inter-Religious Dialogue," *Islamochristiana* 15 (1989): 109–20.

7. *Recognize the Spiritual Bonds Which Unite Us*, 21.

8. Ibid., 23.

9. Ibid., 25.

10. Ibid. According to a contemporary Catholic scholar: "Au nom de la philosophie *Pancasila*, les representants de l-Etat estiment du'ils doivent preserver l'harmonie a l'interieur de chaque religion, entre toutes les religions, et entre les religions et le Governement" (F. Raillon, "Chretiens et Musulmans en Indonesie: Les voies de la tolerance," *Islamochristiana* 15 [1989]: 162–63).

11. The official position of the Indonesian government on this matter is as follows: "Indonesia is neither a secular state nor a theistic one" (see H. Tarmizi Taher, *Aspiring for the Middle Path: Religious Harmony in Indonesia* [Jakarta: Center for the Study of Islam and Society, 1997], especially 55).

12. "Abdurrahman [Wahid] and his followers are social democrats and religious liberals" (R. William Liddle, "The Islamic Turn in Indonesia: A Political Explanation." *Journal of Asian Studies* 55 [1996]: 617).

13. Nurcholish Madjid, *Islam, Kemoderna dan Keindonesiaan* (Islam, Modernity, and Indonesianness) (Bandung, Indonesia: Mizan, 1987).

14. To get the view of some people in the Christian community on religious tension in contemporary Indonesia, consult Indonesia Christian Communication Forum, "The Closing, Damage and Burning of 374 Church Buildings in Indonesia from 1945 to 1997," *ICCF Publications* (Surabaya, Indonesia, 1997).

15. See T. Michel, "Militant Islam in Asia," *Pro Dialogo* 88 (1995): 50–53.

16. "Discourse of the Pope to the Bishops of Indonesia on 'Ad Limina' Visit," *Pro Dialogo* 95 (1997): 177.

17. On the differences between the "nationalist imagination" and the "Islamist imagination" in the Muslim world, see Ibrahim M. Abu-Rabi', *Intellectual Origins of Islamic Resurgence in the Modern Arab World* (Albany: State University of New York Press, 1996), especially chapter 3.

18. See F. Machado, "Harmony among Believers of the Living Faiths: Christians and Muslims in Southeast Asia," *Pro Dialogo* 87 (1994): 214–16.

19. See Nurcholish Madjid, "Islamic Roots of Modern Pluralism: [The] Indonesia Experience," *Studia Islamika: Indonesian Journal for Islamic Studies* 1:1 (1994): 57–77.

20. See A. W. El-Affendi, *Turabi's Revolution: Islam and Power in Sudan* (London: Grey Seal Books, 1991).

21. In *Recognize the Spiritual Bonds Which Unite Us*, 136.

22. The Pope does not express this notion quite explicitly. He, however, says that "[r]eligion permeates all aspects of life in [Sudanese] society, and citizens need to accept one another, with all the differences of language, customs, culture and belief, if civic harmony is to be maintained. Religious leaders play an important role in fostering that harmony" (Pope John Paul II in addressing the leaders of the various religions of Sudan in Khartoum, February 10, 1993; in F. Gioia, ed., *Interreligious Dialogue: The Official Teaching of the Catholic Church (1963–1995)* [Boston: Pauline Books, 1997], 509).

23. See M. Talbi, "Religious Liberty: A Muslim Perspective," in L. Swidler, ed., *Religious Liberty and Human Rights in Nations and Religions* (Philadelphia: Ecumenical Press, 1986), 175–87.

24. F. Arinze, "The Engagement of the Catholic Church in Interreligious Dialogue since Assisi 1986," *Pro Dialogo* 95 (1997): 211. See also R. Etchegaray, "Comment assurer le succes des processus de reconciliation et les soustaire aux contrecoups d'extremistes?" *Pro Dialogo* 89 (1995): 140–42.

25. John Paul II, *Crossing the Threshold of Hope* (New York: Alfred A. Knopf, 1994), 94.

26. In *Recognize the Spiritual Bonds Which Unite Us*, 56.

27. Ibid., 29.

28. "Mais la liberation du Sud passe d'abord par une decolonisation culturelles car un des principaux objectifs du post-colonialisme est l'hegemonie culturelle et la propagation des valeurs occidentales. Les conflits a venir seront

des conflits de valeurs et il y a une tres grande urgence a developper une communication culturelle entre le Nord et le Sud" (Mahdi Elmandjara, *La decolonization culturelle: Defi majeur du 21eme siècle* [Marrakech, Morocco: Editions Walili, 1996; and Paris: Futuribles, 1996], 214).

29. Hasan Hanafi is a leading Egyptian philosopher at the University of Cairo. See I. Boullata, "Hasan Hanafi," in *The Oxford Encyclopedia of the Modern Islamic World*, vol. 2, ed. John L. Esposito (New York: Cambridge University Press, 1995), 97–99.

30. Muhammad 'Abid al-Jabiri is the leading Arab philosopher today. See I. Abu-Rabi', *On the Threshold of Modernity: Studies in Post-1967 Arab Thought* (Albany: State University of New York Press, forthcoming).

31. Mahdi Elmandjara is at the University of Muhammad V at Rabat, Morocco.

32. "Le Nord a deploye jusqu'a present tres peu d'efforts pour comprendre et encore moins pour parler le langage du Sud. Il faut accorder une priorite aux systems de valeurs pour se rendre compte que la crise actuelle entre le Nord et le Sud est une crise du systeme total" (Mahdi Elmandjara, *Retrospective des futurs* [Casablanca: Ouyoun, 1992], 164).

33. Not counting its nuclear and military prowess or economic and political influence, "post-colonialism is a weapon that aims at destroying cultural diversity" (ibid., 215).

34. Ibid., 15.

35. In *Recognize the Spiritual Bonds Which Unite Us*, 30.

36. Ibid., 113.

37. See F. Antoun, *Ibn Rushd wa falsafatuhu*, ed. Tayyib Tizine (Beirut: Dar al-Farabi, 1988).

38. M. 'Imarah, ed., *al-'Amal al-Kamilah li'l Shaykh Muhammad 'Abduh*, vol. 3 (Cairo: Dar al-Shuruq, 1993), 263–64.

39. Ibid., 295.

40. Ibid.

41. Ibid., 222–23.

42. See A. al-Abyad, *Rashid Rida: Tarikh wa Sirah* (Tripoli: Gross Press, 1983); E. Shahin, *Through Muslim Eyes: M. Rashid Rida and the West* (Herndon, Va.: International Institute of Islamic Thought, 1993); and A. al-Sharabasi, *Rashid Rida* (Cairo: Matabi' al-Ahram, 1970).

43. H. Banna, *Five Tracts of Hasan al-Banna*, trans. C. Wendell (Berkeley: University of California Press, 1978), 26.

44. Ibid., 28.

45. Ibid., 29.

46. The Qur'an states the following: "Invite (all) to the Way of thy Lord with wisdom and beautiful preaching; and argue with them in ways that are best and most gracious" (16:125).

47. Gioia, ed., *Interreligious Dialogue*, 566.

48. Ibid., 568.

49. Ibid., 573–74.

50. Ibid., 573.

51. See M. Fitzgerald, "Other Religions in the Catechism of the Catholic Church," *Islamochristiana* 19 (1993): 29–41.

52. John Paul II, *Threshold*, 92.

53. Ibid.

54. *The Holy Qur'an,* trans. Abdullah Yusuf Ali (Brentwood, Md.: Amana Corporation, 1989), 50:16.

55. See A. Schimmel, *Mystical Dimensions of Islam* (Chapel Hill: University of North Carolina Press, 1975); and I. M. Abu-Rabi', ed., *The Mystical Teachings of al-Shadhili* (Albany: State University of New York Press, 1993).

56. M. Borrmans, "Les dimensions culturelles et spirituelles du dialogue islamo-chretien," *Islamochristiana* 22 (1996): 1.

57. On the conditions of dialogue, see H. Teissier, "Pour un renouveau du dialogue islamo-chretien," *Islamochristiana* 15 (1989): 95–107. According to the contemporary Algerian thinker Ali Merad, Christian-Muslim amity is eternal: "[L]'amite des Chretiens est une donnee permanente et precieuse pour les musulmans. Elle est inscrite dans leur Livre: V, 83. Et parce qu'ils trouvent son fondement dans la Parole divine, les Musulmans se sentent personnellement responsables de la sauvegarde et de la perennite de cette amitie, comme s'ils s'agissait pour eux de faire en sorte que la realite vivante de l'Histoire reponde comme un echo a la verite–toujours actuelle — de l'Ecriture" (A. Merad, "Dialogue islamo-chretien: Pour la recherche d'un langage commun," *Islamochristiana* 1 [1975]: 9).

58. See G. Irani, *The Papacy and the Middle East: The Role of the Holy See in the Arab-Israeli Conflict 1962–1984* (Notre Dame, Ind.: University of Notre Dame Press, 1986); A. Kreutz, *Vatican Policy on the Palestinian-Israeli Conflict: The Struggle for the Holy Land* (Westport, Conn.: Greenwood Press, 1990); R. Etchegaray, "De Jerusalem aux extremites de la terre, le defi de la paix: Juifs, chretiens, musulmans," *Pro Dialogo* 91 (1996): 33–35; and Roger Friedland and Richard Hecht, *To Rule Jerusalem* (New York: Cambridge University Press, 1996).

Part Five

CATHOLIC REFLECTIONS

13

Pope John Paul II and Interreligious Dialogue

A Catholic Assessment

MICHAEL L. FITZGERALD

Continuity

A few months after his election, Pope John Paul II received in audience the members of the then Secretariat for Non-Christians who were meeting in Plenary Assembly. This office had been instituted, in 1964, by Pope Paul VI, who had always encouraged its activities. John Paul II voiced the question that was in people's minds: Would he give similar attention to other religions? As a reply, John Paul II referred to his first encyclical letter, *Redemptor Hominis*, published the previous month. In that document, he had underscored the way the Second Vatican Council had seen the globe as a map of various religions impinging on the Church's own self-awareness. He spoke of the deep esteem shown in the Council documents for the spiritual values enshrined in other religions. He concluded: "The non-Christian world is indeed constantly before the eyes of the Church and of the Pope. We are truly committed to serve it generously."[1]

The Pope was thus committed to continuity. He would follow in the footsteps of his predecessors, showing the openness of John XXIII, the respect of Paul VI, the smiling welcome of John Paul I. The very name he took as Pope, John Paul II, signaled this continuity.

He had indicated too the foundation for this attitude, namely, the teaching of the Second Vatican Council. He considered the Council to be a providential event, preparing the Church for the third millennium. His task would be to continue implementing the Council, drawing out its teachings for this transitional period.

This essay can therefore be divided into two unequal parts: first, it will treat the actions of the Pope, his initiatives in relation to other believers; second, it will address the doctrinal basis for these actions, with the particular accentuation given in his teaching.

Actions and Initiatives

Apostolic Journeys

John XXIII was the first modern Pope to move out of the Vatican, albeit only to Assisi and Loreto. Paul VI went farther afield, to the Holy Land, India, Uganda, and elsewhere. John Paul II quickly took up the traveler's staff, and has continued to visit far and wide throughout his pontificate.

In almost all of these pastoral journeys, the Pope has made a point of meeting with representatives of other religions. On some occasions, as for instance at Kaduna, Nigeria, in February 1982, his message was delivered even though the meeting itself did not take place.

John Paul's journey across the Tiber to the Rome synagogue has rightly been hailed as historic. I would also emphasize his visits to the two North African countries of Morocco and Tunisia, with an interval of over ten years between them. It was a sure sign of mutual confidence and esteem that King Hassan II should invite the Pope to speak to Muslim youth, in August 1985, within the framework of the international year of youth, and that the Pope should accept the challenge. The speech he gave in the arena in Casablanca has proved to be one of his most important talks to Muslims. The visit to Tunisia in April 1996 did not have such a dramatic scenario, but the address given at the presidential palace was an important plea for Mediterranean cooperation, underlining the role of religious leaders in combating violence.

Prayer in Assisi

Undoubtedly the most important initiative the Pope has taken in the field of interreligious relations has been the Day of Prayer for Peace, held in Assisi, October 27, 1986.

The day was important both for its contents and its style. Prayers were offered, but care was taken to avoid any semblance of syncretism.

The religious leaders gathered around the Pope in a spirit of friend-ship, united both in fasting and in a final fraternal meal. The whole day was like a living icon. As John Paul II said: "Let us see in it an antici-pation of what God would like the developing history of humanity to be: a fraternal journey in which we accompany one another toward the transcendent goal which he sets for us."[2]

In January 1993, the Pope returned to Assisi to pray again for peace, this time specifically for peace in Europe, and especially in the Balkans. It was a Catholic prayer, a vigil on the Saturday evening and a Eu-charist the following morning, but other Christians, Jews, and Muslims were invited to be present. The timing made it well-nigh impossible for Jews to attend, but a good number of Muslim leaders from the differ-ent countries of Europe accepted the invitation. This could be taken as a sign of increased confidence on the part of Muslim leaders to be associated with the Holy See.

Relations at the Vatican

During the present pontificate there has been a noted increase in the number of countries establishing diplomatic relations with the Holy See. This provides a strong network of contacts. It is not some-thing entirely new, since the trend had already started under Paul VI. Nevertheless, the growth has been impressive. The establishment of diplomatic relations with Israel has, of course, its own special sig-nificance. Indeed, official relations also exist with the Organization for the Liberation of Palestine as representative of the Palestinian people.

The annual discourse to the diplomatic corps allows the Pope to make a wide-ranging survey of current events from the point of view of the Holy See. The presentation of credentials by foreign diplo-mats provides the opportunity for comments on specific situations. On these occasions reference is often made to interreligious relations and cooperation.

Many prominent people, political or religious leaders, are received by the Pope in private audience. The Dalai Lama, for instance, has met the present Pope several times. It is not usual on these occasions, except in the case of Church leaders where theological discussions are taking place, for a joint statement to be issued. Questions of common concern are left for discussion at other levels, for instance with the Commission for Religious Relations with Jews or the Pontifical Council for Inter-religious Dialogue, and such discussions can at times lead to common statements.

Special mention can be made of the invitation to representatives of Islamic communities in Lebanon, one Sunni, one Shi'ite, and one Druze, to attend the special assembly for Lebanon of the Synod of Bishops (November–December 1995). The representatives were able to take part in all of the proceedings without any restriction, except the right to vote, and were invited to address the assembly. They were also invited to a meal with the Pope, the first Muslims to be received at his table.

Attitudes to Specific Issues

John Paul II has not been afraid to express himself forcefully regarding certain issues, even if his position may not meet with universal approval. He condemned the Gulf War, and has continued to oppose sanctions against Iraq, as also against Libya. His appeals are based on the rights of populations to their essential dignity and to be spared harsh suffering.

On countless occasions the Pope has spoken out in favor of peace in the Middle East, upholding the rights of the Israeli and Palestinian peoples. He wrote letters to both Mr. Netanyahu and Mr. Arafat encouraging them to adhere to the peace process. About Lebanon, too, he never ceased to raise his voice, and took the unusual step of sending a message to all Muslims (September 7, 1989). He wrote: "The tragedy that the people of Lebanon are suffering prompts me to write to you. I do so with confidence, not in the name of any particular group or school of thought, but *in the name of the same God whom we adore* and whom we seek to serve."[3] Similarly, it is possible to fill a book with the interventions John Paul II made concerning the war in former Yugoslavia.

There are other issues too on which John Paul II has spoken up, such as: international debt, population and development, the role of women in society, the family. It is well known that on such questions he hopes for the backing of people of all religions. As he said on September 23, 1994, to participants in an interreligious colloquium on marriage and the family:

> As members of the one human race, even more conscious of our interdependence, and united as believers, though belonging to different religious traditions, we must work together so that civil society may recognize and safeguard the sacredness of human life at every stage and promote the family as the one way to defend human dignity.[4]

It can be said that the Pope exercises moral leadership in the world. As perhaps no one else, he can voice the concerns of humankind. This was recognized during the opening of the Sixth Assembly of the World Conference on Religion and Peace, a ceremony which took place within the Vatican. Dr. Mohamed Ali, then Secretary General of the World Muslim League, one of four speakers representing different religions, used the time allotted him to express gratitude to John Paul II for the lead he had taken to uphold moral values, especially threatened during the U.N. Cairo conference on population and development. On this occasion the Pope seemed fully at ease in an interreligious context, staying on long beyond the time expected, and telling the participants that they were to feel at home in the Vatican, where they were always welcome.

John Paul II has clearly stated the importance he attaches to interreligious relations. On November 13, 1992, he said to the members of the Plenary Assembly of the Pontifical Council for Interreligious Dialogue:

> Finally, I express my gratitude to you all for your council's generous sharing in my apostolic service to the Church throughout the world. Your work contributes to the fulfillment of what I have always considered a very important part of my ministry: the fostering of more friendly relations with the followers of other religious traditions.[5]

It may not be superfluous to point out that it was during the present pontificate, in 1988 to be precise, that the name of the office of which I am Secretary was changed from the Secretariat for Non-Christians to the Pontifical Council for Interreligious Dialogue. The change may seem slight, but it can be taken as a sign of greater respect for people in their own identity.

The Doctrinal Bases

The foundation for John Paul II's commitment to interreligious relations is his fidelity both to his predecessors — in particular Paul VI — but more especially to the teachings of Vatican II. The way was traced out by the Declaration *Nostra Aetate,* which he quotes at length in his book *Crossing the Threshold of Hope.* It is important that these quotations be borne in mind, and that other passages of his book not be taken in isolation. Though he may express criticism of systems, the Pope's attitude toward people, toward believers, is one of great respect.

Nostra Aetate

It would be interesting to see how much use John Paul II makes of *Nostra Aetate*. He referred to it already in his first encyclical letter, *Redemptoris Hominis*, and again in other letters such as *Sollicitudo Rei Socialis* and *Redemptoris Missio*. Use is made of this text also in occasional discourses, whether speaking to the followers of other religions, such as to representatives of the Shinto religion, in February 1979, or to Catholics, as in Ankara, in November of the same year. On December 3, 1994, he told the bishops of Iran:

> The Second Vatican Council's declaration *Nostra Aetate* gives clear indications that inspire the Church for its interreligious dialogue. They are mainly: respect for one's personal conscience, rejecting all forms of coercion or discrimination with regard to faith, freedom to practice one's religion and give witness to it, as well as appreciation and esteem for all genuine religious traditions.[6]

Other Documents

Nostra Aetate should not be separated from the other documents of the Vatican Council. Of a more practical nature itself, its theological bases are developed elsewhere. John Paul II will refer often to the two great texts on the Church, *Lumen Gentium*, the Dogmatic Constitution, and *Gaudium et Spes*, the Pastoral Constitution on the Church in the Modern World. He will rely too on *Ad Gentes*, the Decree on the Church's Missionary Activity, and *Dignitatis Humanae,* the Declaration on Religious Freedom.

Lumen Gentium. *Lumen Gentium* (*LG*) expresses the new self-consciousness of the Church as sacrament. The term "sacrament" is traditional in theology, but its application to the Church is in some respects new. The Church is held to be "in the nature of sacrament — a sign and instrument, that is, of communion with God and of unity among all men" (*LG* 1). The Church is a sign, and not the complete reality. The Church is *for* all, but not necessarily *of* all. Those who do not belong to the Christian fold are related to the Church, or to the people of God, in a variety of ways. Mention is made of "the people to which the covenants and promises were made"; "those who acknowledge the Creator, in the first place among whom are the Muslims: these profess to hold the faith of Abraham, and together with us they adore the one, merciful God, mankind's judge on the last day"; "those who in shadows and images seek the unknown God"; and "those who, through no fault of their own, do not know the Gospel of Christ or his Church, but who nevertheless seek God with a sincere heart" (*LG* 16). This shows that salvation is possible outside the visible boundaries of the Church. An implication of this is that though the Church is missionary by nature, and "is driven by the Holy Spirit to do her part for the full realization of the plan of God" (*LG* 17), this does not mean that it has to bring all people necessarily into the Church. The Church will invite, not compel; it will propose, not impose. This attitude thus allows for respectful relations with people who follow other religious traditions.

Gaudium et Spes. *Gaudium et Spes* (*GS*) provides a further principle to which John Paul II returns time and time again — the centrality of Christ. "For, by his incarnation, he the Son of God, has in a certain way united himself with each man" (*GS* 22). In this way, no human person can be outside of the concern of a Christian, and *a fortiori* of the Pope. It is the Christian belief that God "has constituted Christ as the source of salvation for the whole world" (*LG* 17). How is this salvation achieved? Through the paschal mystery, that is, through the mystery of Christ's death and resurrection. That this way of salvation is open for all is affirmed explicitly by the Council in a passage often quoted by John Paul II: "Since Christ died for all (cf. Romans 8:32), and since all men are in fact called to one end and the same destiny, which is divine, we must hold that the Holy Spirit offers to all the possibility of being made partners, in a way known to God, in the paschal mystery" (*LG* 22).

This again has implications for interreligious relations. As Muslims would say, *al-hukm li-Llah*, judgment belongs to God. People are not to be condemned because they are not Christians. Recognizing that God, that the Holy Spirit, is at work in them, it is possible to engage in a dialogue which is not mere politeness but is a form of entering together into death to egoism in order to live for others, a true dialogue of salvation.

Understanding of Mission

Does this mean that the Church gives up her mission? Far from it, for, as has been said, "the pilgrim Church is missionary by her very nature" (*Ad Gentes* [*AG*] 2). It is not therefore unexpected that John Paul II should echo the teaching of the missionary decree *Ad Gentes*, and that, as did Paul IV with *Evangelii Nuntiandi*, he should write a special missionary letter, *Redemptoris Missio* (*RM*). What should perhaps be noted is a broader understanding of the concept of mission so as to include interreligious dialogue. The statement "Interreligious dialogue is a part of the Church's evangelizing mission" (*RM* 55) has provoked negative reactions from some people belonging to other religious traditions. It has to be understood correctly. A document of the Roman Curia approved by the Pope presents mission as "a single but complex and articulated reality." Its principal elements are enumerated: presence and witness; liturgical life and prayer; commitment to the service of humankind; interreligious dialogue; proclamation and catechesis.[7] Now these elements are not geared to increasing the number of Catholics. This is not the aim of liturgy, nor of social action; they are not mere means to proclamation, but ways of giving expression to faith and love. Similarly, dialogue with people of other religions is not a means to their conversion, though, as the same document points out, in the course of dialogue "the decision may be made to leave one's previous spiritual or religious situation in order to direct oneself toward another."[8] So John Paul II can state quite clearly: "Dialogue does not originate from tactical concerns or self-interest, but is an activity with its own guiding principles, requirements and dignity" (*RM* 56).

Religious Freedom

Dialogue is characterized by respect for human freedom. The Second Vatican Council, not without travail, gave solemn expression to the teaching of the Church on this matter in its Declaration on Religious Freedom (*Dignitatis Humanae* [*DH*]). This is another document which has been foundational for the teaching and practice of John Paul II. The document states early on that "the right to religious freedom is based in the very dignity of the human person as known through the revealed Word of God and by reason itself" (*DH* 2). It should thus be possible to agree on the principle of religious freedom even with those who do not accept Christian revelation. Yet, not any type of freedom is acceptable, but only responsible freedom. "It is in accordance with their dignity as persons" that human beings "should be at once impelled by nature and also bound by a moral obligation to seek the truth, especially religious truth. They are also bound to adhere to the truth, once it is known, and to order their whole lives in accord with the demands of truth" (*DH* 2). This may explain why the Pope can at the same time uphold so vigorously the right to religious liberty and yet celebrate the force of truth. On October 5, 1995, speaking to the Fiftieth General Assembly of the United Nations, he declared: "How important it is to safeguard *the fundamental right to freedom of religion and freedom of conscience*, as the cornerstones of the structure of human rights and the foundation of every truly free society."[9]

Two years earlier he had written about the "splendor of truth" and had strongly reaffirmed the human capacity to know the truth. John Paul II is thus far from being a pluralist, giving weight only to subjective truth, but he is against forcing people to believe in a particular way: "No one is permitted to suppress those rights by using coercive power to *impose an answer* to the mystery of man."[10]

Particular Emphases

John Paul II's teaching is squarely based on that of the Second Vatican Council. It would be unrealistic to expect him to move outside the parameters fixed by the Council. Nevertheless, there are certain personal accentuations which appear in his writings and discourses which are worth noting. Here I would like to mention three: a humanistic note; the idea of brotherhood; and the role of the Holy Spirit.

Humanism. In his first encyclical, *Redemptor Hominis*, the Pope used a rather cryptic phrase, often repeated but never fully explained: "man . . . is the primary and fundamental way for the Church" (*RH* 14). Perhaps the meaning of this statement could be spelled out as follows: the Son of God, in becoming man, has "united himself in some fashion with every man" (*GS* 22; *RH* 8); this enhances the dignity of the human person created in the image and likeness of God; therefore, the Church has to pay attention to every single person. It should be noted that the human person is worthy of attention quite independently of belonging to the Church.

In relating to persons the Church is to take into account their history and their culture. The Pope has accentuated both these points. Often he comes back to the way history has shaped nations, and he it was who established within the Roman Curia a special office for the study of culture. It was therefore natural that in addressing the U.N. General Assembly (September 17, 1995) the Pope should emphasize respect for culture. He wished to exorcise the fear of "difference":

For different cultures are but different ways of facing the question of the meaning of personal existence. It is precisely here that we find one source of the respect which is due to every culture and nation: every culture is an effort to ponder the mystery of the world and in particular of the human person; it is a way of giving expression to the transcendent dimension of human life.[11]

Since cultures are strongly influenced by religion, respect for culture implies respect for its religious component. So, in his brief visit to Tunisia (April 14, 1996), speaking to a gathering of political, cultural, and religious leaders, the Pope emphasized the importance of cultural exchanges within the Mediterranean basin between peoples strongly marked by either Christianity or Islam.

For John Paul II, as for Paul VI, close attention needs to be paid to the relationship between Gospel and culture. Christianity is often considered to be a Western religion; indeed it is often confused with the West, which has been marked by Christianity (though there are also other strands contributing to Western civilization). Yet, since the incarnation has a universal value, the message of the Gospel is to be integrated into every culture. This, as the Pope said on August 13, 1985, to intellectuals in the Cameroon, requires "an unremitting effort of inculturation." This does not mean that the Gospel is to be domesticated, for it has a prophetic and critical role to fulfill:

Everywhere, in Europe as in Africa, it [the evangelical message] comes to overthrow the criteria of judgment and ways of living.... It must carry out this duty with regard to certain practices which have been brought by strangers along with the Faith, but also with regard to certain customs or institutions which are found among yourselves.[12]

The Polish Pope, so enamored of his own culture, encourages all to develop their cultural identity, while remaining open to the fundamental demands of the Gospel.

Attention to the human person leads also to a stress on human rights. Here is a fruitful field for interreligious collaboration. Speaking on February 5, 1986, to representatives of various religions in India, the Pope made the following appeal:

As followers of different religions we should join together in promoting and defending common ideals in the spheres of religious liberty, human brotherhood, education, culture, social welfare and civil order. Dialogue and collaboration are possible in all these great projects.[13]

The motive for such dialogue and collaboration is truly religious, based on shared values. As John Paul II pointed out to the Assembly of the World Conference on Religion and Peace (November 3, 1994):

These values are not just humanitarian or humanistic — they belong to the realm of the deeper truths affecting man's life in this world and his destiny.... Through interreligious dialogue we are able to bear witness to those truths which are the necessary point of reference for the individual and for society: the dignity of each and every human being, whatever his or her ethnic origin, religious affiliation, or political commitment.[14]

As the Pope had said some years earlier (August 18, 1985) to religious representatives in Kenya: "The close bonds linking our respective religions — our worship of God and the spiritual values we hold in esteem — motivate us to become *fraternal allies in service* to the human family."[15]

Brotherhood. The use of the word *fraternal* in the last quotation can form a link to another feature in John Paul II's relations with people of other religions. He presents himself as a brother. Well known, of course, is his reference in his address in the Rome synagogue to the Jews as "elder brothers." But the brotherhood is wider. In Bangladesh on November 19, 1986, the Pope declared:

I thank the Most High God for enabling me to make this visit as a brother, a brother in our common humanity; a brother in our adoration of the "one God, living and enduring, merciful and all-powerful, who has made heaven and earth, and has spoken to men" (*NA* 3); a brother in human solidarity, listening to the voice of humanity crying out all over the world for dignity, justice and peace.[16]

The clearest expression of this conviction regarding a truly fraternal relationship is to be found in a talk (February 20, 1981) to Muslims in the Philippines:

I deliberately *address you as brothers;* that is certainly what we are, because we are members of the same human family, whose efforts, whether people realize it or not, tend toward God and the truth that comes from him. But we are especially brothers in God, who created us and whom we are trying to reach, in our own ways, through faith, prayer and worship, through the keeping of his law and through submission to his designs.[17]

It may be wondered why this point is being stressed. It seems so obvious that the novelty of the language could be overlooked. The early

Christians, as is witnessed in the writings of St. Augustine, reserved the name *brother* for fellow Christians. Still, within the World Council of Churches there would appear to be a tendency to avoid the term and speak instead of *neighbors* of other faiths. To my mind, speaking of brothers is an indication of the sincerity and intimacy which should characterize interreligious relations.

The Role of the Spirit. The relationship of fraternity is based on the common origin of human beings, but also on the way God's Spirit is at work in human hearts. The large place given to the Holy Spirit has been a feature of John Paul II's teaching, and it has considerable importance for the outlook on other religious traditions.

In *Dominum et Vivificantem* (*DV*), his encyclical letter on the Holy Spirit, the Pope speaks about the action of the Holy Spirit in the world right from the beginning of creation, "especially in the economy of the Old Covenant," but not only there. Indeed this action has been exercised "in every place and in every time, indeed in every individual" (*DV* 53). This is quite a remarkable statement, the implications of which have not yet perhaps been fully understood. The Pope develops it in his missionary encyclical. Here he states again that the Spirit's "presence and activity are universal, limited neither by space nor time." He then adds further: "The Spirit's presence and activity affect not only individuals but also society and history, peoples, cultures and religions. Indeed, the Spirit is at the origin of noble ideals and undertaking which benefit humanity on its journey through history" (*RM* 28).

The Pope makes it clear that this conviction does not remain purely theoretical but has practical consequences for his own ministry:

> I have repeatedly called this fact [the universal action of the Spirit] to mind, and it has guided me in my meetings with a wide variety of peoples. The Church's relationship with other religions is dictated by a two-fold respect: Respect for man in his quest for answers to the deepest questions of his life, and respect for the action of the Spirit in man. (*RM* 29)

John Paul II was acting on this conviction when he invited religious leaders to Assisi to pray for peace. Space was allowed for the prayers of different religious traditions, and in the final moment of the day these prayers were listened to with reverent attention. This could be encouraged since "every authentic prayer is called forth by the Holy Spirit, who is mysteriously present in the heart of every person."[18]

One could perhaps say that, just as the Son of God in becoming incarnate unites himself with every human being, so the Holy Spirit, who prays in the heart with "unutterable groaning," unites himself with suffering humanity (cf. Romans 8:26–27).[19]

Is such language an obstacle to dialogue? People may object to seeing what they consider to be most precious in their religious traditions attributed to the work of the Holy Spirit. It has to be remembered always that the Pope is trying to clarify concepts primarily for the members of the Catholic Church. He is engaged in Christian theological reflection. He is not attempting a universal theology, because he knows full well that people of other religions do not share the most central Christian beliefs. Nevertheless, they may be able to accept that this particular language with a universalistic thrust can provide a sound basis for a respectful and fraternal attitude.

Beyond Categories

John Paul II cannot easily be classified. Is he a conservative? Is he a radical? He is perhaps both at the same time. Or, it may be that these categories are too simple to be applied fairly. Some may consider the Pope to be conservative with regard to questions of sexual ethics, yet his positions are based on a truly radical championing of human dignity. His theological position regarding Christ as the only Savior is uncompromisingly firm, yet he has contributed to expanding the teaching of the Catholic Church regarding the role of religions in the divine plan of salvation. John Paul II has proved himself to be a strong successor in the Chair of Peter, but he has not hesitated to ask for comments and reflections on the way this office is exercised. He shows moreover that he does not consider his role to be confined to the Catholic Church alone.

John Paul II is looked upon as the leading evangelist of our time. He has been tireless in visiting every part of the globe to confirm Christians in their faith and encourage them in their witness. At the same time, no Pope has done so much to foster dialogue with Jews, Muslims, Buddhists, and indeed with people of all religions. A document of the Roman Curia states that interreligious dialogue and proclamation of the Gospel are not interchangeable, since they have their own distinct aims and methods, yet they are intimately related.

> True interreligious dialogue on the part of the Christian supposes the desire to make Jesus Christ better known, recognized and loved; proclaiming Jesus Christ is to be carried out in the Gospel spirit of dialogue. The two activities remain distinct but, as expe-

rience shows, one and the same person, can be diversely engaged in both.[20]

This statement could be applied most appropriately to Pope John Paul II.

Notes

1. Address, April 4, 1979, in Francesco Gioia, ed., *Interreligious Dialogue: The Official Teaching of the Catholic Church (1963–1995)* (Boston: Pauline Books, 1997), 216.

2. Address at Assisi, October 27, 1986, in ibid., 350.

3. In ibid., 416; emphasis in the original.

4. In ibid., 528.

5. In ibid., 501.

6. In ibid., 532.

7. See *The Attitude of the Church toward the Followers of Other Religions* [1984], no. 13, in Gioia, ed., *Interreligious Dialogue,* 569.

8. Ibid., no. 37, p. 577.

9. See Gioia, ed., *Interreligious Dialogue,* 555–56; emphasis in original.

10. Ibid.

11. Ibid., 555.

12. Ibid., 294.

13. Ibid., 327.

14. Ibid., 529.

15. Ibid., 296; emphasis in original.

16. Ibid., 354.

17. Ibid., 235; emphasis in original.

18. "Discourse to the Roman Curia," December 22, 1986, 11; see Gioia, ed., *Interreligious Dialogue,* 366.

19. Ibid.

20. *Dialogue and Proclamation* (1991), no. 77, in Gioia, ed., *Interreligious Dialogue,* 637.

Selected Bibliography

Writings by John Paul II

Crossing the Threshold of Hope. New York: Alfred A. Knopf, 1994.

The Encyclicals in Everyday Language. Ed. Joseph G. Donders. Maryknoll, N.Y.: Orbis Books, 1996.

Interreligious Dialogue: The Official Teaching of the Catholic Church (1963–1995). Ed. Francesco Gioia. Boston: Pauline Books, 1997.

"An Interreligious Exchange [Meeting with Religious Leaders at the Japanese Cultural Center in Los Angeles]." *Origins* 17 (1987): 302–4.

Recognize the Spiritual Bonds Which Unite Us: Sixteen Years of Christian-Muslim Dialogue. Ed. Thomas Michel and Michael Fitzgerald. Vatican City: Pontifical Council for Interreligious Dialogue, 1994.

Redemption and Dialogue: Reading Redemptoris Missio *and* Dialogue and Proclamation. Ed. William R. Burrows. Maryknoll, N.Y.: Orbis Books, 1993.

Spiritual Pilgrimage: Texts on Jews and Judaism 1979–1995: Pope John Paul II. Ed. Eugene J. Fisher and Leon Klenicki. New York: Crossroad, 1995.

The Wisdom of John Paul II: The Pope on Life's Most Vital Questions. Comp. Nick Bakalar and Richard Balkin. New York: HarperCollins, 1995.

Writings about Pope John Paul II

Arinze, Cardinal Francis. "The Urgency of Dialogue with Non-Christians." *Origins* 14 (1985): 641–50.

Bernstein, Carl, and Marco Politi. *His Holiness: John Paul II and the Hidden History of Our Time.* New York: Doubleday, 1996.

Borelli, John. "The Rapid Period of Development in Catholic-Muslim Relations." *Origins* 21 (1991): 535–38.

Carroll, James. "The Silence." *New Yorker*, April 7, 1997, 52–68.

Cassidy, Cardinal Edward I. "The Next Issues in Jewish-Catholic Relations." *Origins* 26 (1997): 665, 667–70.

Federici, Tommaso. "Mission and Witness of the Church." In *Fifteen Years of Catholic-Jewish Dialogue: 1970–1985: Selected Papers.* Vatican City: Library Editrice Vatican, 1988.

Fisher, Eugene J. "Pope John Paul II's Pilgrimage of Reconciliation: A Commentary on the Texts." In *Jewish-Christian Encounters over the Centuries: Symbiosis, Prejudice, Holocaust, Dialogue.* Ed. Marvin Perry and Frederick M. Schweitzer. New York: Peter Lang, 1994.

Gerry, Joseph. "What the Purpose of Catholic-Muslim Dialogue Is and Is Not." *Origins* 21 (1991): 538–39.

Honea, Charla H., ed. *A Reader's Companion to* Crossing the Threshold of Hope. Brewster, Mass.: Paraclete Press, 1996.

Malinski, Mieczyslaw. *Pope John Paul II: The Life of Karol Wojtyla.* Trans. P. S. Falla. New York: Seabury Press, 1979.

Mallon, Elias. "The Challenges in Catholic-Muslim Dialogue." *Origins* 21 (1991): 531–34.

McDermott, John M., ed. *The Thought of Pope John Paul II: A Collection of Essays and Studies.* Rome: Editrice Pontificia Universita Gregoriana, 1993.

Michel, Thomas. "Christianity and Islam: Reflections on Recent Teachings of the Church." *Encounter* 112 (February 1985): 1–22.

———. "Pope John Paul II's Teaching about Islam in His Addresses to Muslims." *Bulletin: Secretariatus pro non Christianis* 21, no. 2 (1986): 182–91.

Miller, John H., ed. *Vatican II: An Interfaith Appraisal: International Theological Conference, University of Notre Dame: March 20–26, 1966.* Notre Dame, Ind.: University of Notre Dame Press, 1966.

O'Brien, Darcy. *The Hidden Pope: The Personal Journey of John Paul II and Jerzy Kluger.* New York: Daybreak Books, 1998.

Pontifical Council for Interreligious Dialogue. *Pro Dialogo: Buddhist-Christian Colloquium, Kaohsiung, Taiwan, 31 July–4 August 1995.* Bulletin 90 (1995), no. 3.

Pope and Buddhism: That New Chapter in Buddhist-Christian Dialogue. Dialogue 22, n.s. (1995).

Rossano, Pietro. "The Basis for Dialogue among Christians, Jews and Moslems." *Origins* 13 (1983): 92–96.

Svidercoschi, Gian Franco. *Letter to a Jewish Friend: The Simple and Extraordinary Story of Pope John Paul II and His Jewish School Friend.* Trans. Gregory Dowling. New York: Crossroad, 1994.

Szulc, Tad. *Pope John Paul II: The Biography.* New York: Scribner, 1995.

Walsh, Michael. *John Paul II.* London: HarperCollins, 1994.

Willebrands, Cardinal Johannes. *Church and Jewish People: New Considerations.* New York: Paulist Press, 1992.

Winer, Mark. "Jewish-Catholic Relations after the Fundamental Agreement." *Origins* 26 (1997): 671–74.

Contributors

Masao Abe has been considered the leading exponent in the West of Zen Buddhism since the death of D. T. Suzuki. He is Professor Emeritus at the Nara University of Education in Japan and has served as a visiting professor at American universities such as Princeton and Columbia. He is the author or editor of many books and articles on Buddhism in Japanese and English, including *Zen and Western Thought* and *Emptying God: A Buddhist-Jewish-Christian Conversation.* A longtime participant in interreligious dialogue, he had an audience in Rome in April 1994 with John Paul II.

Ibrahim M. Abu-Rabi has been described as the "rising star" in Islamic studies in America. He is Professor of Islamic Studies at Hartford Seminary and has authored a number of important studies, including *Islamic Resurgence,* and is coeditor of the journal *Muslim World.*

Robert Aitken retired at the end of 1996 as Roshi of the Honolulu Diamond Sangha. He is heir to the teaching of Yamada Koun Roshi in the Sanbo Kyodan line of Zen Buddhism and is author of *Taking the Path of Zen,* as well as seven other books on Zen Buddhism. He is coauthor with Brother David Steindl-Rast of *The Ground We Share: Everyday Practice, Buddhist and Christian.*

Mahmoud Ayoub is Professor of Islamic Studies at Temple University and Research Fellow at the Middle East Center of the University of Pennsylvania. He is the author of many books and articles, including *Redemptive Suffering in Islam* and *Islam: Faith and Practice.* He is currently writing an interpretation of the entire Qur'an, titled *The Qur'an and Its Interpreters.*

José Ignacio Cabezón is Associate Professor of the Philosophy of Religion at the Iliff School of Theology in Denver. He lived for many years among Tibetans in India and has served as an interpreter for His Holiness the Dalai Lama. He has written several studies of Buddhism, including *A Dose of Emptiness* and *Buddhism and Language*.

Cardinal Edward Idris Cassidy is President of the Holy See's Commission for Religious Relations with the Jews and President of the Pontifical Commission for Promoting Christian Unity. A native of Australia, Cardinal Cassidy served for many years in the Vatican's diplomatic corps.

Michael L. Fitzgerald is a Roman Catholic Bishop who currently serves as the Secretary of the Pontifical Council for Interreligious Dialogue at the Vatican. Born in England, he has taught at Makerere University, Kampala, Uganda, and the Pontifical Institute of Arabic and Islamic Studies in Rome, of which he was director for a number of years.

David M. Gordis, an ordained rabbi and talmudic scholar, serves as President of Hebrew College in Boston and as Director of the Wilstein Institute of Jewish Policy Studies. He serves on the boards of the Academy for Jewish, Christian and Islamic Studies and *Tikkun* magazine. Previously, Dr. Gordis served as the Executive Director of the American Jewish Committee and as Vice-President of the University of Judaism.

Harold Kasimow is the George Drake Professor of Religious Studies at Grinnell College in Iowa, where he teaches courses in Judaism, Islam, and Buddhism. His works on interreligious dialogue have been published in the United States, England, India, China, and Japan. With Byron L. Sherwin, he is coeditor of *No Religion Is an Island: Abraham Joshua Heschel and Interreligious Dialogue,* published in 1991 by Orbis Books.

Byron L. Sherwin, a rabbi, is Vice-President and Distinguished Service Professor of Jewish Philosophy and Mysticism at Spertus Institute of Jewish Studies in Chicago and Director of its Joseph Cardinal Bernardin Center. A veteran in Catholic-Jewish dialogue in America and Poland, he was awarded a Presidential Medal by Lech Walesa for his groundbreaking achievements in Christian-Jewish dialogue in Poland. The author of twenty books and over one hundred monographs, Dr. Sherwin was the protégé of the late Rabbi Abraham Joshua

Heschel. His most recent books are *Crafting the Soul: Creating Your Life as a Work of Art* and *Why Be Good?*

Wayne Teasdale is a Christian *sannyasi* (monk) in the Indian tradition who serves as an adjunct professor at DePaul University and Columbia College, both in Chicago. He is a writer, spiritual director, and retreat master. He is author of *Toward Christian Vedanta* and is coeditor of *The Community of Religions: Voices and Images of the Parliament of the World's Religions.*

Index